OUTLAWS IN BABYLON

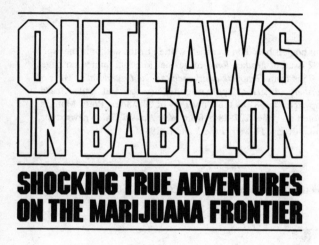

OUTLAWS IN BABYLON

SHOCKING TRUE ADVENTURES ON THE MARIJUANA FRONTIER

STEVE CHAPPLE

LONG SHADOW BOOKS
PUBLISHED BY POCKET BOOKS NEW YORK

To Maxwell, Lisa, Sarah, Fireman,
Lannie, Billie and Carol,
good Americans all, and to Kathryn

This book is based on an article written by the author in the April 1982 issue of *Mother Jones* magazine. Material quoted on pages 73–75 is from *Genocide and Vendetta: The Round Valley Wars of Northern America,* by Lynwood Carranco and Estle Beard. Copyright © 1981 by the University of Oklahoma Press. Material quoted on pages 227–28 is from *West Hawaii Today* newspaper, Kailua-Kona, Hawaii, June 5 and 6, 1981.

Another *Original* publication of LONG SHADOW BOOKS

A Long Shadow Book published by
POCKET BOOKS, a division of Simon & Schuster, Inc.
1230 Avenue of the Americas, New York, N.Y. 10020

ISBN: 0-671-46417-5

First Long Shadow Books printing September, 1984

10 9 8 7 6 5 4 3 2 1

LONG SHADOW BOOKS and colophon are
trademarks of Simon & Schuster, Inc.

Printed in the U.S.A.

Contents

Introduction

If we really must have another Ice Age, this is the right place to sit it out: the Rib Lanai, over the lagoon, Keauhou Beach Hotel, Kailua-Kona, Hawaii. Shouldn't have to sit here long—a few million years at the most. I only hope bar service doesn't deteriorate.

Life is hard here on the Rib Lanai. Someone is playing slide guitar across the lagoon. The palms are shimmering as the trades come up. The mahi mahi was caught two hours before it was cooked. The Kona coffee ice cream has just enough Kahlúa poured over the top. And now the wild orange sun is slipping below the outer reef. If you squint, and squint hard, you can see Kyoto. Clean air. Not too cold, either. A bathing suit will do. You must at least wear a bathing suit. The management insists. Something about these being the Reagan years . . .

Of course, nowhere is completely paradise. We have our problems. The insects. Lots of insects here, Kailua-Kona. Flying cockroaches, cane spiders as big as salad plates. It's not the War on Drugs that concerns us. It's the War on Bugs.

That's where the geckos come in. I like geckos. Lithe little lizards with suction cups on the bottom of their toes and vertical pupils. They can be loud, though, these geckos. They scream. Geckos are the only lizards capable of making sounds. The scream of the gecko can be a terrible thing. Disturbs dessert . . .

Could be worse, I suppose. Could be down in the lagoon, off the balcony, twenty feet below. With the morays. The moray eels. Must watch where you put your toes, down in the lagoon. These moray eels are serious creatures. Spiked fangs that must be four inches long, little gray eyes as cold as frozen yogurt, grins that just don't seem, well . . . sincere.

7

And I like sincere people.

They can be eccentric. They can be dope fiends. Their idea of a good time might be two hours at the bottom of the hot tub with scuba tanks on their backs and nothing else. They can even be mercenary killers, perhaps even narco-raiders, but they must be, well . . . sincere. Life is short in America these days. I mean, with wild Episcopalians a deft lunge away from The Button, we can't afford the usual horse pucky.

This has been a hard book. I suffered a little accident early on in Our Research, although I think that may have turned out for the best. Might have given the work a nice black-and-white quality. Maxwell said this and Sarah said that and Associate Attorney General Rudolpho J. Giuliani replied . . . When you can't use your hands properly, you get quite good at remembering dialogue. But let's save the sordid details for a later chapter. . . .

Everyone in *Outlaws in Babylon* is as real as the morays off the Lanai at the Keauhou Beach Hotel. Those young women and men doing something currently illegal have been disguised, of course. Their names, descriptions, where they live and where they do their business. Those Americans who do what is considered perfectly legal—car dealers who sell Toyotas by the scads to marijuana growers, for instance, or lawyers, sheriffs, district attorneys and those who run the current drug war for the current administration, these people appear exactly as they are, or as close as possible, and with their real names.

Everybody's still out there, too, growing their marijuana and arresting their growers, except for one woman who was beaten to death against her drying room wall.

Marijuana, that elegant, cheap weed, has become as American as computers and apple pie. It started out foreign and illicit, smoked by Mexican farm workers and Negro saxophone players with skins far darker than Nancy Reagan's. Now, in the 1980s, after an amusing media comeback, marijuana, the new marijuana —*sinsemilla*—is as down-home as moonshine, and far bigger business than moonshine ever was. Because marijuana is no longer smuggled contraband. It's home-grown, American-made and better for it, the nation's second-largest crop after corn and soybeans . . . ahead of wheat now, $10 billion plus at the wholesale level. It's farmed mainly in Georgia, Kentucky, California—ten miles from the Santa Barbara White House—and, perhaps the most heated bud of all, within snorkling distance of the Keauhou.

Yes, life is hard here on the Rib Lanai, introducing books.

These strange six-foot morays are not easily satisfied. First you must stand up. Then you must reach across the table to the breadbasket and pluck a roll, perhaps two rolls, one for each hand, if you're a generous sort of person. Then you must wind back and shoot the rolls as far as you can into the sea. The morays do the rest, whipping about and snapping at each other, scaring off the yellow reef fish. It's a horrible sight, all that foam on top of the water, but you get used to it.

O tempora o mores . . .

The sun is down now. In a few minutes the colors will come up. The western sky will run bright with orange and red and lavender like the colors of the bougainvillea that surround the hotel.

In another minute I think I'll have a second dessert. Grasshopper meringue, or perhaps the Kahaluu Delight. I do like macadamia nut pie. After that, maybe a walk along the beach. Full moon tonight. Then perhaps a dip in the Jacuzzi behind the pool. I've made a few friends in the hills. I could call them up. After that, who knows? Scrabble? The Inverted Crow? Frog legs delivered to the room?

It has been all suffering, writing this book, as you'll see. But we Americans must be made to suffer in this world or, surely, we will suffer more in the next.

HARVEST

1

MAXWELL:

Takedown on Rte. 66; Kidnapped Children; Lush Dope for Hard Times . . . Business as Usual . . . The Big Tuna Smile; Black Eyes the Color of a Bad Day; Morphine Screams . . . Keeping Fun on the Front Burner . . . Drug War and the Vodka-drinking Son of an Alcoholic Father . . . Sinsemilla and the Sexuality of Sisters; World-class Dope; Night of the Polyester Sportcoat . . . Yo-Yo Joints; Full Auto; Road Kills; The Grower Who Was Eaten by a Grizzly Bear . . . All Good Things Begin with Water; Guerrilla Growing; The Erotic Farmer

It is harvest season in Mendocino, a rocky green rib of almost-paradise stretching from America's ocean of dreams, the Pacific, on one side, to Highway 101 on the other, a four-lane road that is to California what Route 66 was to the 1950s.

All is not well this October morning at six-thirty, thirty-five minutes before dawn. A takedown is in progress. The thieves are amateurs, although they are armed with a sawed-off shotgun. The property owners are amateurs, too. It is their first year in the trade, yet they are also well armed, each holding a Colt AR-15, a honey of a gun built exactly like the M-16 made famous in

Vietnam, except that a bolt has been inserted at the factory to prevent the AR from being converted into a machine gun. The bolts in these two Colts have been bored out.

The thieves are driving a Land Rover, and their loot fills the bed in back. In fact, the goods are so bulky they push out the windows, the stalks waving in the morning wind like kidnapped children. The thieves are poachers, of course, and they have just finished taking down a crop of good North Coast marijuana. Now the growers are only two hundred feet behind the Land Rover on this twisting, asphalt country road, and they are firing their domesticated machine guns, *rat-a-tat-tat,* like Clyde Barrow and like Bonnie Parker, too, for the grower in the passenger seat of their car is a woman. The thieves are scared shitless, as well they should be. The growers would be frightened, too, if rage had not already chased away their fear.

A lot is at stake here. Properly dried, manicured and packaged, each raggedy green plant in the back of the Land Rover is worth as much as $1,500. The two crazy poachers, neither over twenty years old, have crammed fifty stalks into their vehicle, perhaps sixty. That's enough for some people to kill for. (If you're the sort of American for whom money means anything. . . .) But then, this isn't crumbly Mexican or Colombian grass. This is state-of-the-art ganja: *sinsemilla,* the God-grown connoisseur's dope that has replaced smuggled imports at the parties of lawyers, students and steam-shovel operators across the country. These are the 1980s, I think, and not just anything rolled will get you high anymore. Lush dope for harsh times, you understand. And for some reason everybody's willing to pay.

The poachers are better drivers than the growers. They are taking the curves at 45 mph, twice the speed any sane person would negotiate this road, weaving across the center line again and again, even on the outside curves. The growers know the road. They're biding their time to the straightaway at the bottom of the long hill, trying now to shoot out a back tire and gain the quick advantage. But they can't hit the Land Rover because, if truth be told, they've never fired their weapons at anything besides tin cans, and then only for a few minutes on the day they bought the guns. The growers are peaceful people, really, and they are as out of their element bushwhacking rip-off artists as the thieves are at pulling $90,000 jobs. Everybody is out of their league on this empty mountain road at six-thirty in the morning, doing something they don't want to be doing, but the money's so good that no one can pass it up.

The straightaway now, flowing nicely down a long grade. You can see the start of a new lake created by the Core of Engineers to accommodate power boaters and condo developers and beyond the big blue puddle of the half-filled lake, miles of carefully planted grapes, etched across the dark October ground like rows of thorns. And closer, much closer, two miles away: Highway 101.

The growers step on it. They're driving a ten-year-old Toyota wagon, but their four cylinders are tighter than the Land Rover's six, and the growers are just about desperate. They've got to stop the thieves before the highway because they're in the open now. This is farm country. People get up early. And Ukiah, the county seat, is only five miles south.

The Toyota rips down the wrong side of the road. Fifty, sixty miles an hour. The growers pull alongside the Land Rover. They can smell their hijacked crop now. It smells like a colander of warm asparagus, steaming, beautiful, buttered and skunky, good enough to eat.

"Pull over, fuckers!" screams the woman. She's three feet from the thieves going sixty miles an hour.

"Bitch!" shouts the thief driver.

He inches the Land Rover to the left. He's trying to force the growers off the road, only for a second, though. He's trying to gain time, too, trying to make the freeway.

There's only one thing for the woman to do now. Waste the fuckers.

She starts to aim the AR-15. She starts to cry. This woman is thirty years old. She is an arts graduate of Sarah Lawrence College in Bronxville, New York, a place where nice girls from good homes are rarely taught how to waste rude fuckers on country roads at dawn.

She pulls the muzzle inside the car.

"We'll catch them," says the driver, who has also gone to Sarah Lawrence on an exchange program with Yale.

The poachers make the freeway, and then they get scared. Seventy-five is top speed for them, and they're doing eighty now. The Rover is vibrating.

They're almost in the suburbs of Ukiah. Parducci Wineries on the right, Cresta Blanca on the left, the big billboard of the John Birch Society: GET US OUT OF THE UNITED NATIONS! and then the first exit, North State Street. The thieves take it too fast. The high-centered Land Rover goes up on two wheels and comes down again with a slam that rocks the poachers in their seats. Still moving. A boulevard of trees, Monterey pines, Pete's 24-Hour Henny Penny Coffee Shop across from the Yokayo Bowl, Fjord's Smorg-Ette and the Lu-Ann Motel, whose sign board reads: PATIENCE IS THE COMPANION OF WISDOM.

Last chance. The poachers aim to ditch the growers in the streets. The kids live in town. They grew up in Ukiah. They're almost home free.

The Sarah Lawrence woman, who's only been in California eighteen months, pushes her weapon out the speeding car and lets rip a clip despite her tears. *Tchu!Tchu!Tchu!Tchu!Tchu! Tchu!Tchu!Tchu!Tchu!Tchu!* Ten bullets, half the clip. They all miss. A stupid thing to do. The punk in the passenger seat of the Land Rover fires his sawed-off shotgun over their heads. An even stupider thing to do. The shotgun goes off like a bomb. This kid goes to bartending school in Santa Rosa, and his brother, the driver, told him they wouldn't have to fire their gun.

Somebody in the Henny Penny must have gotten up from the counter and phoned the Mendocino Sheriff's office.

Outside, at the four-way light, the growers finally caught up with the rip-off artists. They cut them off three-quarters across the bow. Jammed the Toyota right in front of the Land Rover. The high-school thieves panicked. For no good reason the two dip-shit punks jumped out of their vehicle. They left their shotgun inside. The two growers piled out of their Toyota. The woman was still crying. She and her partner left their weapons on the seat, too. The male grower, the Yalie, stepped up to the poacher driver, a boy six inches shorter than he was, but perhaps thirty pounds heavier and clean-shaven, and smashed him full in the face with his fist. This grower (if it is fair to call him that after so short a time in the trade) had not hit anybody full in the face since he was a child.

None of the four stopped to consider their position: duking it out fist to chin in the middle of a four-lane highway, the Land Rover screaming with bud, combat weapons loaded on the seat, the early morning traffic to the Masonite Mill honking at the tie-up, a town of 10,000 waking up all around them, the sheriffs on the way. No, growers and poachers alike had lost proper . . . perspective.

The male grower was put in the same cell with the two poachers.

The poachers were charged with felony possession of marijuana. The two growers were charged with illegal possession of automatic weapons.

Maxwell and I are at the top of the fire road. From this granite lookout you can see as far north as Ukiah, where poachers and growers may have lost sight of the true business at hand.

"Love it!" says Maxwell.

Max smiles at me. He loves a good story and the one about the novice poachers and growers is a good one in these parts. It's six years old now, since it took place in 1977, but still three-quarters true, remembered in different ways by different people, though always remembered fondly, whether by veteran growers like Maxwell or by deputy sheriffs.

"I don't think there was a woman involved," says Maxwell. "No, just four dumb guys. Yahoo-spudinks. That's the way I heard it."

Max smiles straight at me—full and friendly. He smiles under a tanned mountain of a forehead. Short, jagged, unthinkingly wild blond hair in back, no hair at all in front. Aviator glasses, thick and prescription, yet tasteful and expensive. A web of tiny drops rims the cheeks where the lenses end. Maxwell is sweating under his eyes and today is not a hot day.

"Oh, yeah," says Maxwell as he climbs back in the big pickup, still sorting out how the story came down.

End of the Sonoma County blacktop. End of our break. It's been Forest Service land for the last five miles. Now, suddenly, as if we are entering a sanctuary, which we are not, the land becomes private and the road turns to coarse dirt, a narrow, winding fire road with sloppy, Cat-tractored turns and badly shaved grades.

Maxwell reaches under the seat. The pickup lurches. The truck is already in four-wheel drive but the road has turned so ragged that the steering wheel twists back and forth. Maxwell comes up quick with his eyes on the road and his right hand as steady as a hand can be.

Maxwell is gripping a pistol in his fingers: a fat, fancy Colt Auto. Eyes still on the crazy snake of a fire road, he lays the gun on the seat. Hammer back, safety on, a round in the chamber.

No big deal, you understand. Business as usual. Professionalism. No expected danger. We're heading in-country, off the road, and it's that time of the year, early October, start of the harvest, and, well, things aren't as gentle as they once were on top of this big, dry whalebone of a mountain at the tip of Sonoma County, somewhere in northern California.

"Wish I'd had one of those," says I. I'm talking about the pistol.

"Betch you do," says Maxwell. He flashes me a real Maxwell smile, the Big Tuna Smile, patented by Maxwell, all teeth and eye wrinkles and spontaneous ambiguity.

His tongue parts his lips but his eyes keep to the road. His eyes always keep to the road, black eyes the color of a bad day with no trace of brown or green. Maxwell's eyes scan to the left. They scan to the right. They stake a moving perimeter as the big papa pickup pushes through the dirt to Maxwell's hideaway.

I remember almost two months ago to the day. I'm lying in the hospital bed with both my arms in plaster casts from fingers to shoulders and so much morphine in my body that I can't feel the pain. I can see it. It curls around the casts like clear fog and covers the sutured knife cuts underneath. I'm lying back in the big motorized bed wondering what I'm supposed to do if the pain decides to toss the morphine aside and run up my arms to my face. How loud do they let you scream in the hospital when all their morphine has quit working?

And then the phone starts to ring. It rings like a ship's bell way off in San Francisco Bay. I let the sound swim into my ears.

A nurse holds the receiver to the side of my head.

It's Maxwell.

"I hear they got you." I can tell he's chewing on something at the other end. Chow mein? A rib? "You all right?" he asks. I can hear him laughing. He's laughing at me in my hospital bed and why not? It's a ridiculous situation.

"Nothing I could have done, really," I answer and I'm surprised how clear I sound through the morphine. "Two fucking . . . two fucking dickhead junkies jumped through the window almost on top of us. We were in bed. Only way for clear victory would have been if I'd been sleeping with a loaded revolver beside the pillow."

This almost makes me laugh in the stupid hospital cradle of a bed, if I could laugh, my stomach empty these past twenty hours since the start of surgery. What kind of American sleeps with a loaded .45 beside his pillow?

"Hey," comes the bear's bellow of Maxwell's voice through the long-distance wires, "I *always* sleep with a loaded .45 beside the bed!"

The laugh again, then a cough.

"You eating something?" I think I asked.

"Oh. Oh, yeah. A rib."

Courtesy call to the author on his bed of pain, you understand. Max wasn't kidding about the .45. Naturally, he's toned down the act since Da Nang. "Oh, Jesus! You walk around with an M-16 and the Vietnamese wouldn't bat an eye. But when I carried a twelve-gauge Ithica pump, they'd dive into the bushes. That shotgun made a hole like a brick going through your chest."

The Old Days. When paranoia was fun. Now it's a business. In the old days, not so long ago, when little Maxwell, six feet four of him, came marching home from Saigon, he slept with the shotgun against the wall, the Colt to the right of the pillow, a holstered .38 slung over the bedpost at his feet, a loaded 30.30 leaning behind the door. But that was silly. That was show. That was the act. Who wants to keep checking into Holiday Inns with a forty-pound duffel bag full of guns? *Fun,* you understand, but it's essentially a ritual to cover the embarrassment of being Stateside, something to recreate the feeling, that lovely adrenocorticotropic rush, the eyes clear and the tip of the tongue dry, just the beginning of *ooze,* sweet sweat starting to pucker the underarms . . . nothing else like it. No substitute for Nam, except sex (and how long does that last?) and maybe dope. Marijuana. Growing *sinsemilla.* Growing dope kept Maxwell's campfires burning when he came home from the war. It kept the good organic speed slithering hither and thither in the old veins. Kept *fun* on the front burner. Yes! Keeps you laughing. Yes. Well, keeps you from yawning at least. ("Shit, I'd get so bored in a normal job.")

The Big Tuna Laugh flies out of Maxwell's face.

"This road is so bad. It hurts to drive it, doesn't it?"

He means me. It does hurt. I hold my wounded arm away from the window frame, the right arm with the little leather gimp brace that resembles a falconer's glove and helps to rebuild the main nerve. These freshly spliced ulnar nerves do tend to jangle so. . . .

Actually, the pickup rides the road as smooth as a salmon in a trough. Maxwell had it factory-fitted with every heavy-duty option available. The twin gas tanks hold enough so Max can drive between San Francisco and Denver, a distance of 1,200 miles, and only have to stop once for fuel.

The cab is immaculate. Washed out with a hose, scrubbed and uncluttered. On the seat there is only the Colt, under that a down vest and across the dash a newspaper at least three days old. The gang at the hideaway doesn't get to see the paper every day, but that's not the only reason why Maxwell is bringing in the San

Francisco *Chronicle,* a paper he considers "the most amusing daily rag in America." (He also enjoys the New York *Post.*) The *Chronicle* holds a front-page story of immediate professional interest to Maxwell.

NEW U.S. WAR
ON POT GROWERS

WASHINGTON: The Reagan administration plans to use military helicopters and "hard-hitting" special strike forces against marijuana growers who use isolated federal lands in California and other states to produce their multibillion-dollar crop, a Justice Department official said yesterday.

Frank V. Monastero, assistant administrator for operations of the Drug Enforcement Administration, testified at a hearing on illegal marijuana cultivation before a Senate agricultural subcommittee headed by S. I. Hayakawa, R-Calif.

Another witness, George L. Farnham, national director of the National Organization for Reform of Marijuana Laws, said $10 billion worth of marijuana would be grown in the United States this year, making it the nation's number-three cash crop behind corn and soybeans.

Monastero, the drug official, testified that the new paramilitary operations would combine "an aggressive search effort with highly mobile eradication teams."

He said this effort was necessary because local law enforcement officials lacked the equipment and the staff needed to deal with heavily armed marijuana growers. . . .

In addition to obtaining helicopters from the Defense Department, he said, the drug agency will ask governors to "mobilize elements of the National Guard to support the effort." National Guardsmen have already been used in the fight against marijuana in Hawaii and Arkansas, Monastero said.

In California, state and local authorities have carried out paramilitary anti-marijuana operations with some federal assistance. The new operations apparently will be the first conducted with federal equipment and personnel. . . .

He said the Reagan administration's crackdown on

drug imports was causing an expansion of the domestic marijuana crop. . . .

Robert Buford, director of the Bureau of Land Management, estimated that illegal marijuana production on the 340 million acres controlled by his agency probably exceeded $5 billion last year. He said the annual marijuana crop on federal land in California was believed to exceed $1.2 billion a year. . . .

"Domestic marijuana producers have really developed what can be termed one of the most aggressive, progressive processes of agriculture known to man," he said. . . .

Buford also said the value of the marijuana and the increasing number of plantations around the country had caused a sharp increase in the number of dangerous confrontations between growers and federal employees and visitors to public lands. More than 800 such incidents were reported last year, he said.

"Employees have not only been threatened with rifles but have actually been shot at. In addition, booby traps constructed with pipe bombs, hand grenades, land mines, shotguns and punji sticks have been discovered, as have other traps such as fishhooks suspended at eye level."

Farnham, the NORML representative, said that instead of focusing on wiping out the marijuana crop, the government should legalize the weed. Regulation and taxation of both domestic and imported marijuana could raise several billion dollars for the U.S. Treasury each year, he said.

"It is futile to spend billions of additional dollars to control what can no longer be controlled within the confines of the criminal justice system," he said.

At the same time, on television, President Ronald Reagan, vodka- and wine-drinking son of an alcoholic father, is personally running up the narco flag against other people's poisons, the reefer madness of at least 30 million adult Americans: "The momentum is with us. We're making no excuses for drugs, hard, soft or otherwise. Drugs are bad and we're going after them. As I've said before, we've taken down the surrender flag and run up the battle flag. We're going to win the war on drugs."

The president smiles when he says this because, as Maxwell points out, the president is always smiling. Smiling sincerely, the way a cheeseburger would smile. The president is smiling when he

names one of the most destructive missiles ever built, "The
Peacemaker." He's smiling when he resuscitates that charming
maxim, "Better dead than Red." ("'I would rather see my little
girls die now, still believing in God,'" Mr. Reagan quotes an
anonymous young father, "'than have them grow up under
communism and one day die no longer believing in God.'")
Maxwell is a strange student of President Reagan's maxims. He
memorizes them like lines of blank verse. He assumes Ronald
Reagan is probably smiling as he stares at the ceiling of the White
House bedroom through tanned eyelids and a custom sleep mask
blottoed on two Valiums. (Does Ronald Reagan use a sleep mask,
a nice black leather one like the Lone Ranger's? I don't know.
Does he use Valium, the most prescribed drug in America, a
sleep-inducing prescription tranquilizer that accounts for more
emergency-room admissions than any other drug, "hard, soft or
otherwise," including heroin? Golly, who knows that either? No
spokesperson at the White House or the Department of Justice
will tell me.)

Ronald Reagan is calling the new drug war Operation Hot
Pursuit.

"This is *it!*" Maxwell has said more than once on the long ride
out of the hideaway. Each time he's taken the carefully folded
paper off the dash and slapped it smartly back. This is really it.
DRUG WAR! Run up the battle flag! Mobile eradication teams!
He can't believe it and yet he can, because he's always figured it
would happen someday. Someday they'd come for him. In fact,
truth be told, in his paranoid, action-freak heart of hearts,
Maxwell has secretly looked forward to this wild moment of
personal drug war Armageddon. Ronnie's Raiders. Rocketing out
of the dawn sky on red-white-and-blue helicopters, gripping
M-16s, wearing flak jackets. Just like . . . just like in . . . it's too
fucking much! These guys, these narcos, the troops in the copters
—they're bound to be vets just like him. Maxwell laughs like a man
puking when he says this: If Ronnie's Raiders land on top of him,
how many will he recognize from I Corps?

Maxwell loves to talk about the vet growers he knows.

"They turned us on to dope over there," he says. "That's where
I learned to smoke it. We came back and we moved up here, some
of us. The country was our escape hatch. We didn't like the army
and we didn't like the cities, either. You know what badgers are
like, don't you? They'll run and run and dig and dig and they'll
avoid confrontation for as long as they possibly can, and then when

their backs are against the wall, they become the most vicious animal on earth and fight to the death. That's what these guys are like. I've talked to them. The government is going to try to confiscate their land, and some of them'll come out firing." Maxwell easily switches from the "other" vets to himself. "I've always told my mom I'm going to go out with a gun in my hand. She says, 'Oh, Maxwell, don't say that.' But I'm serious."

Max still can't believe the news of the Drug War. His voice rises and his head shakes from side to side.

"With all the crime! With all the unemployment! With all the heroin, man, they're coming after marijuana growers!"

("I have trouble separating out marijuana at one end from heroin at the other," Rudolpho J. Giuliani, associate attorney general and the Italian field marshal in Ronald Reagan's Protestant army, will tell me four months later.)

The road winds and winds, climbs and twists along the bony brown ridge. We pass homesteads every quarter-mile or so. Odd-shaped cabins sit here and there in clumps of eucalyptus and pine. Some are standard frame-and-shingle affairs. Others are more eccentric. An elaborate three-story tower built of raw-milled redwood sits next to one house.

"I asked Roscoe what he *did* at the top of that thing," explains Maxwell as we drive by, "and he said, 'Man, that's my money-counting, dope-packing tower. I sit up at the top and I can see anybody coming from miles around.'"

The Big Tuna Laugh: "Fuck, when I'm counting *my* money, I like to have a real clear view, too."

We pass a locked metal gate, which is so elaborate it looks as if it should be guarding a mansion in Bel Air or Terrytown. A sign is wired to the center of the gate: TRESPASSERS WILL BE SHOT.

Most folks here 'bouts seem to pursue Max's line of work.

Another couple of miles and the thick scrub forest of manzanita, chaparral and black oak gives way suddenly on the right to a naked slope of grass, still long and brown from the summer. Maxwell points down the gulley to the bottom of the hill where it is rocky and dry. The hideaway.

"Welcome to Tobacco Road," says Maxwell.

Max doesn't bother to open the cyclone gate. He maneuvers around it. The driveway is only two tracks in the grass, and the angle of the hill is so steep we both must brace ourselves for the descent.

"I really should get myself some belts," says Maxwell, "and belt us down. We could get thrown out."

Yes. The pickup is bouncing now. Maxwell's smiling. He loves this. Max is an off-the-road man. He's taking the descent at twice the speed a sane man would and he's doing it not to impress me but because it's fun.

We slide to a bare spot at the bottom and Maxwell honks three times. Nobody comes out.

"I really should get a couple of Dobies for this operation," says Max. "Don't you think?"

"Keep a low profile, Max," I say, "like the tiger farm."

"Yes," says Maxwell. He slams the GMC into park and waits.

The Tiger Farm. Now that was an operation. We've talked about it, too, on the way out. The tiger farm was not particularly low-profile. Some 500 plants, worth perhaps one million dollars wholesale, had been visible from the spotter plane of the California Bureau of Narcotics Enforcement (BNE). The spanking-new five-bedroom house where the growers lived was in plain sight of the busy highway that winds from San Jose to the beach, not 200 miles from where we are. And then there were the tigers. Three of them. Full-grown Bengals, the size of imported pickup trucks. Not to mention the leopard, two German shepherds and a brace of Dobermans, one of which quickly lunched on the leg of a narcotics officer. Luckily for the state's raiders, when the bust began the big cats were locked away, growling and pacing in enormous wire cages, each one larger than a fenced-in tennis court.

"It would have been hard to sneak up on the tigers," Mitchel Brown, the BNE agent in charge, had said. "They sure make good watchcats."

"Tigers!" Max howls from the cab of the truck. "Can you imagine what it cost to feed three tigers and a leopard? They would have had to butcher a steer a day. Talk about drawing attention to yourself!"

What Maxwell had done for guards was hire guys who used to work steel in Pittsburgh. He paid them $350 a week with a $40 food allowance. This was cheaper than tigers any day, and tigers can't hold a shotgun.

Maxwell has no trouble sympathizing with a bunch of lunatics who guarded their crop with wild tigers. He was considered overly militaristic himself in the mid-seventies. He established defense perimeters and used land-line field phones around this operation at the bottom of the hill. He was one of the first to rent a plane and

fly over the land to make sure "L.E.," Law Enforcement, the
bogies, the narcos, couldn't see what was going on.

Maxwell has always considered himself a creative entrepreneur.
His marijuana plantations were run on the principles of vanguard
capitalism. "We even sold futures at two-thirds to three-quarters
of market value. This way I got my working capital up front. We
would divide the spoils along a line of ownership, as you would a
private corporation. The value of your input determined your
profit. Input might be your four-wheel-drive vehicles or your land
or your investment money. The system worked great because it
enabled us to avoid personality hassles. The concept of The
Company served as a scapegoat."

Corporate thinking comes easily to Maxwell. He's descended
from a long line of big-time ranchers in southern Colorado.

But all this is the old days. For the middle eighties Max has
scaled down his expectations and gone discreet, unlike the tiger
farmers south of San Francisco. "Small is beautiful," says Maxwell.

He smiles. He honks again. It's been three minutes.

"Hope they're not fucking," he says.

A figure starts out of the clump of black oaks across the gulley.
It is a woman. I'm surprised. Max hasn't mentioned that one of his
partners on this operation is a woman. And she's dressed in blue
rayon short-shorts, a clean white T-shirt with "Avenue of the
Giants Marathon" across the front over a logo of a redwood tree,
and aqua-blue Nikes. I've got on long red underwear and insulated
boots myself. Maxwell's wearing the down vest over a Pendleton
shirt over a T-shirt. It's fall. It's cold. This woman doesn't seem to
care. She's got a big smile on her small mouth, and her enormous
breasts—yes, they are—can't help but jiggle. Except for them,
there isn't an ounce of fat on her body because she gets up at six
every morning at the hideaway and runs seven miles along the fire
road. Carol, which is our name for her here, is in training for this
year's Avenue of the Giants Marathon, north two counties, in
Humboldt. Growing marijuana is her business. Running mara-
thons is her life. I'm not prepared for this. She gives Maxwell a kiss
that makes me sigh and Maxwell wriggle.

"Where's Billie?" Maxwell asks.

"Trimming."

We walk down into the trees. Even though it's only three
o'clock, the hideaway cabin is in shade. Maxwell's land is part of a
long-abandoned pig farm. The hideaway is an old clapboard

cottage, the white paint almost all gone across the lapstraked cedar, a shake-shingled roof covered with green moss. The old pig farmer and the pig farmer's wife are long gone, too. Now the cottage is a drying shed, hardly airtight, without insulation. There's a new prefab window cut into the wall above a prefab sink with no source of running water. The old well has fallen in. The crew hauls dishwater in a five-gallon plastic jug. Dirty dishes with unfinished spaghetti are junked in the sink. In back is a sleeping loft rigged of used plywood.

As soon as we get close a dog rushes out. This dog is enormous, a tan-and-black German shepherd, perhaps 140 pounds. The dog seems all mouth. The mouth is happy to see Max. The dog whines and strains to touch him. The dog's tongue must be a foot long and its teeth are moray teeth. This is Ginger. Ginger is all sloppy kisses to Max. I start to pet her and she suddenly rolls back her lips and lunges for me.

"Only me, Carol or Billie can touch Ginger," says Max. He's kissing her on the top of her hairy head. "After her mouth, there's no more room in her head for a brain. She knows her job, though."

Good Ginger . . . nice Ginger.

Ginger is kept on a wire cable, which is strung ten feet high among three trees. Ginger can guard three sides of the hideaway and then some on her leash.

On the left side of the cabin is a yellow nylon rope stretched taut between two black oaks. Thirty marijuana plants hang upside down from the rope, splayed out like Christmas trees, green as emeralds and as fluffy as fresh-washed sheep. It's a sight that brings the Tuna Smile right out of old Maxwell. Oh, yes.

Billie stepped under the clothesline.

Billie is about five feet ten, young, very good looking with a slight overbite that raises his lip across his upper teeth. His hair is short, curly and blond. He's wearing a black snap-button cowboy shirt and tight blue jeans. A cigarette dangles unlit out of the corner of his mouth. He reminds me of a young cowboy, assistant foreman on a ranch outside of Durango, maybe, close to the San Juans. That's not too far from what he is.

First thing Mr. Max does is whip out the *Chronicle* and stab the headline with his finger.

Billie reads the drug war article in his cool, ranch-hand manner. At times his lips move as he reads. He takes the unlit cigarette out of his mouth and smiles across the expanse of white teeth. "Well, guess that'll raise the price some."

This reaction is not strong enough for Maxwell.

"That's not all it'll do, Billie. They want to picture you and me as Charlie Mansons. They want everybody to think we're fiends. Isn't that something? Isn't that something?"

Carol reads the article, too.

"Jeez," she says. She raises her eyebrows a little. Several years ago there was a fly-over above the hideaway. A fly-over, in which a Bureau of Narcotics Enforcement plane dips low to do a final check on the search warrants, is almost a sure sign of a bust. Carol refused to leave. No hassle, she said. There was a marathon coming up and she wanted to stay and train. She was also trying to grow broccoli in the garden for the first time. Maxwell picked her up and carried her to the truck. That's what Maxwell says.

Billie and Carol are not reacting to the article.

"Sooner or later," Max runs on, "they'll be coming down the canyon with copters and M-16s—only we'll be the Viet Cong."

Billie is twenty-two years old. Carol has never served in the new women's army. Such nostalgia is lost on them.

Max snaps back to the task at hand. He introduces me. Then, after a couple questions about how the crop is doing, he puts a smile behind his black eyes and asks something else of Billie.

"Plums still dropping?"

"Yeah," says Billie.

Billie's got a machete hooked to his belt, with no scabbard.

"Gonna cut that plum tree down if it's okay with you, Max."

"Cut it down, Billie. I mean, cut down the top. It's not a bad tree."

A plum tree stands beside the cabin. Maxwell planted it years ago. This was a nice idea but it had disturbing results. The plum tree bears plums the same time the marijuana is ready to harvest. At night ripe plums fall off the tree and some of them hit the roof of the cabin. Billie sleeps on a framed waterbed in the loft. Every time a plum smacks the roof, Billie reaches for his machete. It takes him a couple of seconds to realize nobody's outside prowling. It's only the plum tree.

Max understands the problem, but he doesn't see any point in rectifying it. He likes the plum tree and he figures when Billie goes over the edge from harvest paranoia he'll crawl out of the cabin naked and chop down the tree. Maxwell wonders whether Billie will be considerate and only lop off the offending branches or whether he'll flip out and destroy the entire tree.

"Got the first thirty in," says Billie soon enough.

"Good," says Max.

Thirty plants out of the ground drying in early October is a good lot. Good enough but not as good as Billie, Carol and Maxwell thought they'd have six months ago. Six months ago they had a fourth partner. The fourth partner functioned as maintenance man. He camped out in the cabin during the winter. He was supposed to have the grounds in shipshape come spring planting when Maxwell was to bring down the starts from Salmon Creek Road in Humboldt. When Max arrived with the starts, little four-inch seedlings, he discovered a pile of beer cans, breakfast food boxes and miscellaneous trash in front of the cabin. Maxwell started shouting. What was this filth? The maintenance man shouted back. Max told him to get fucked. He did not temper himself. The partner backed off. Max could see the man had probably been up a night or two doing cocaine. He decided to leave and come back the next day. But the partner thought Maxwell was going to the truck to get the Colt. He ran for the trees. Now Maxwell got paranoid. He couldn't remember whether the partner had a rifle stashed up the canyon. Next day Maxwell made a deal. The maintenance man could have a quarter of the starts and 10 percent of the harvest if he left then and there. That was a good deal. The fourth partner split. Maxwell understood he would have to give the man an investment in the harvest, even though the partner would do none of the work, so that he would not be tempted to poach or, worse, rat them all off. Carol and Billie were not happy with the deal but the deal had been made. The reality was that Maxwell called the shots. He bankrolled the operation. And that Maxwell had his tempers.

There is a plank deck in front of the old house. On the deck are two braided-plastic lawn chairs. Beside the chairs are plastic buckets. Billie doesn't talk a whole lot. He lifts a plant off the drying line, walks over to the porch, sits down and starts to trim. This plant is mature but it's not large, four feet at the most. Billie's trimming wet, which means the plants are still damp and green like limp celery. First he cuts off the crown cola, the topmost part of the plant. The crown cola is almost all bud and it is as long as his forearm. Then he cuts off the branches and hangs them all on a piece of string tacked to the wall. He takes a branch and snips off the big leaves, using a pair of dime-store scissors. The leaves fall into the bucket. He clips the smaller leaves around the buds. The little leaves are called *especiale,* but they get tossed out, too. The manicured buds look like furry cobs of green corn. When he has a sheaf of them, he takes them inside and hangs them on a fishline for further curing.

Maxwell lifts a branch off the outside line and sits down at the second chair where Carol must have been and starts to trim, too. Carol goes inside and comes out with a 2.5-gallon soybean can, the kind you can get in San Francisco's Chinatown on garbage night, plunks it down and gets back to the trimming.

I'm not much of a trimmer with my bum hand.

"Well, shit," says Maxwell after a few minutes of this. We're all the same, I can trim dope just like anybody else shuck and jive (and he is a pretty mean trimmer). "You want to do a number, Billie?"

"Sure."

Max pulls a joint out of his shirt pocket and fires it up with a Zippo. There is a certain amount of interest in this cigarette because it comes from another of Maxwell's operations, a place where neither Carol nor Billie have been but a place that has seeded several of the plants here.

"Yeah," says Billie after a drag.

"Like it," says Carol. She shrugs her shoulders.

"It's really not bad, is it?" says Maxwell. He's pleased.

He hands the joint to me.

Yes, I must agree. The smoke is very, very smooth, a million miles away from the Mexican and Colombian marijuana popular in this country fifteen years ago. This is state-of-the-art vegetable smoke. You feel nothing, yet everything changes. What we have here is a reality shift. The light on the October oaks is a shade more golden. The clear air is a trifle fuller. You've poured a feathered rainbow down your throat and your socks are now a little looser. Two tokes, suggests Maxwell, and you can see the strands of your own DNA. Why not?

The amount of tetrahydrocannabinol (THC), the active ingredient in good sinsemilla, is five to ten times greater than in most Colombian grass. A year ago I asked Steve Helsley, chief of the state Bureau of Narcotics Enforcement, if the extreme potency of California sinsemilla didn't make it far safer to smoke since you only had to inhale a very small amount of burning vegetable and paper matter into your lungs.

"I chuckle when you say that," Helsley had answered.

Maxwell spends his life chuckling. Each day from wake-up puff to sleepy-time joint, he smokes eight cigarettes or so. Dope relaxes Maxwell. He calls this particular strain "polio." "Want another hit of polio?" Because it's so strong it cripples. . . .

Sinsemilla is stronger than plain marijuana because it consists only of the female plants. The word means "without seeds" in Spanish. Sinsemilla is not a strain but a growing technique. Normally, a female plant will channel some 40 percent of its energy to the task of making seeds. However, if all the male plants are culled out by heartless growers, the female cannot usually be pollinated. She throws all her energy into the task of producing more gummy resin in hopes of trapping male pollen. This resin sparkles and gleams like ice crystals in the sun as it sticks to the hairs of the plant, and it is this resin that holds the highest concentration of THC.

"Sinsemilla is come," a San Francisco dealer once told me. "Juice. Fucking. The female puts out resin and puts out, and there is no male pollen to fertilize it. Sinsemilla is the sexuality of sisters."

Maxwell got in on sinsemilla at the ground floor, blown by accident, fate and boredom, perhaps the three wild harpies that have whispered his life along. He and Carol were enrolled in a junior college south of San Francisco, taught by draft-dodging professors hardly older than they were. Driving home from classes one afternoon, they picked up a hitchhiker who had just returned from Mexico. Maxwell offered the hitchhiker a J, and the hitchhiker started chattering about sinsemilla technique. Maxwell was all ears. Marijuana was already the greatest thing to him since three-way sex. By the time they dropped off the hitchhiker half an hour later, Maxwell was already scheming. He and Carol dropped out of school and bought land in the North Country, forty acres for $10,000 with a thousand down. Big dreams, cheap price. They never looked back.

All of a sudden, I notice things have grown quiet here at the hideaway. The sun's still high, three o'clock, but the three spooks, Maxwell, Billie and Carol, have quit talking. Something's always going on here that hasn't been spoken for. After a bit of clipping, Carol looks over her scissors and laughs with her tongue pushing out her lower lip, the laugh coming deep and sly from within her chest.

Maxwell asks without another cue, "You find out where I got the coat?"

"No."

Billie looks up and clears his throat and smiles.

"That was a night," says Billie.

Nobody says anything more, and this is all that is said about the matter during our visit. What happened is this: Max and Carol got extremely drunk two weeks ago in town. They were so shitfaced they couldn't make it all the way up the road. They spent the night on a neighbor's land, miles closer to 101, the main road. Maxwell had lost his leather coat; in its place he was wearing a tacky blue cross-hatched polyester sports jacket. In the breast pocket was another man's wallet. There was some money in the wallet but Max didn't take it. It wasn't much money and he was scared and he wouldn't steal from another man anyway. Where had the sports jacket come from? They picked through the wallet and looked at the man's pictures and came to the incredible conclusion that Maxwell must have killed the man, taken it off him in a fight and rolled him for sport. This seems like an exaggeration of one's powers to me, but I don't know Maxwell well enough yet to fathom the story. Max was genuinely worried that something awful transpired. The next day, Sunday, he and Carol took the coat and wallet, drove up 101 a few miles and stuffed them into a mailbox.

The conversation on the porch becomes basic and the basic topics of discussion among nonfamily growers of the North Country are four: Drugs, Guns, Sex and Travel to Exotic Lands.

Drugs: an appraisal that this year's crop at the hideaway can, once again, safely be considered world-class dope. No arguments here. More drugs: Max mentions a friend who used to fix "yo-yo" joints. (Basic weed mixed with little lumps of coke, spotted intermittently with paregoric. This was in the old days. Yo-yo joints pulled you first one way, then the other, a push-me-pull-you smoke Dr. Doolittle missed.

Guns: Billie tells how he was awakened the week before by automatic weapons fire. The burst was not aimed at poachers but rather at deer. A neighbor had lost some $6,000 in bud to coastal blacktails and would brook no more losses. "Pretty effective predator control," opines Maxwell. "Yep," says Billie. "Billie," asks Maxwell, "how long does it take to switch a legal Uzi over to full auto?" "'Bout a second," says Billie, who's handy with a screwdriver.

Sex: Maxwell recounts a story about a bar from his youth located in the Mexican state of Michoacan where you could get a B&B, beer and blowjob, at the same time, and where the girls sometimes walked around with lit cigarettes protruding from their vaginas. Carol and I enter into a discussion of whether or not women these days are more reluctant to suck men's cocks than men are to eat women out. Everyone has a heartfelt opinion on this important controversy with the sides dividing neatly: The men on the porch feel that men get short-shafted while Carol insists that women end up performing the bulk of oral duty in our modern society.

Exotic lands: "Ever seen Oakies cook up salmon in Alaska whole, guts and all and uncleaned, by wrapping the fish in newspaper and sticking it into a wood stove?" asks Billie. Carol recounts a story about a friend of hers who went out to check his patch in Alaska (where cultivation of marijuana for personal use is legal) and was killed and *eaten* by a silver-tipped grizzly. This discussion of food reminds Billie of how when they had nothing left in the refrigerator in Alaska they would drive down the railroad tracks in the jeep until they found a moose that had been freshly killed by a locomotive. Such meals were called road kills, and a road-kill moose could provide food for weeks. Which reminds Maxwell of a breakfast of duck embryos in a mountain village in Peru. Which reminds Carol of a time in Louisiana when they ran out of food and ate the tropical fish out of the tank in the living room.

Max watches Billie walk inside the old cottage several times without really needing to. When Billie brings out a gram or so of cocaine and lines it out on the side of a Cream of Wheat box, Maxwell wants to know if Billie and Carol are doing all-night lines. "No way," says Billie.

"Just something to start the day," says Carol.

Maxwell does not like cocaine. He has done more cocaine than most people in America, which is a lot, and he thinks it is a vastly overrated drug. Maxwell believes that coke changes people. He says that it is an evil drug that fastens on the character flaws of abusers and twists that imperfection until it dominates them. If you're a little egotistical, he says, coke will transform you into an arrogant maniac. If you're naturally suspicious, coke will have you jumping at every shadow. Maxwell feels coke has a nasty tendency to suck the honesty out of land partners who do too much of it. He even quotes a Pulitzer-Prize-winning author too famous and litigious to mention by name: "Cocaine is the only drug that makes me enjoy beating up women."

No mention of who I am. I may be a dealer. I may be an investor. I may be a partner of Maxwell's in another venture along for the fun. My hair is unkempt and uncut. My beard is six months long. (I have spent two months in French Polynesia and two months recovering from the injury to my hands.) I am wearing a duck-billed black cap with the letters "ARCTIC CAT" printed across the front, a strange and authentic snow-mobile cap that only a serious person seriously engaged in this serious line of work could seriously wear. (I like this cap.) I may also be a writer. That possibility has probably occurred to Carol and Billie. They are both smart people. They never ask.

Maxwell stands up. This is a lazy inspection tour in which everything gets done and decisions are made as we go along. Time now to check the crop.

Maxwell's lower ten are not easy to walk. The plants are sheltered by madrones, hidden along ditches, scattered about a hillside goats would not enjoy. The plants receive less sunlight than they would if they were growing in the open like Iowa corn. Less light makes them smaller. Maxwell does not care.

"I've had my fourteen-foot plants. I've had my immense ego stroked. I'm not into ego now. I'm into not getting caught."

Such attention to aerial surveillance is called *guerrilla growing,* and Maxwell has been a master at it for years. He buries his water lines and stashes shovels and fertilizer bags in the bushes. He instructs his people to take different paths to the plants each day so that the trails won't be visible from the air.

The plants are not put into the ground at all. They live in grow bags, green garbage bags with drainage holes in the bottom. Grow bags can be shifted at will, and they are filled with good mulch. The ground in these mountains is too dry and unfertile to raise perfect marijuana, and Maxwell enjoys perfection in these matters.

The plants are watered with a sophisticated drip system. Plastic piping runs out of an enormous plastic bag known as a collapsy tank. (Thousands of collapsy tanks are bought by marijuana growers in California and elsewhere. The company is headquartered in the Midwest, and for no reason at all Maxwell is convinced that it must be owned by either Baptists or Mormons.) The piping is two inches thick at the tank. It quickly forks and runs down both sides of the little hill, then forks again and again until the lines empty into the grow bags. Valves regulate the flow, and battery-operated timers regulate the valves. The emitters at the end dribble water onto the roots instead of wastefully spraying the plants like sprinklers. Once the timers are set, the system doesn't need attention for two weeks.

The only thing Max doesn't have is water itself. All good things in California begin with water. Unlike the honest moguls of the early twentieth century in southern California, Maxwell has not found it necessary to divert aqueducts, hire thugs to beat up farmers and con thousands of voters with phony drought hysteria. Max leased the use of the spring at the top of the mountain. The land at the top belongs to a retired pig farmer. He gave the pig farmer $2,000 in June, exactly when the typical family grower, former pig farmer or not, is most broke.

Oh, in the glory days before aerial surveillance became *de rigueur* by law enforcement, Maxwell had his fun. He cultivated outrageous patches that stood out like elephants in Central Park. Once he grew 900 plants in one field many miles from here. "God, you grew 900 plants?" people ask him when he tells the story. "How come you're still growing?" The answer is that Maxwell was young and dumb. He sold cheap: $450 a pound, a quarter of what he gets now. His wholesaler lived in Oakland. An hour after Maxwell was gone, the wholesaler took the pot to Sausalito and sold it for $1,000 a pound. This was a crushing revelation to Maxwell, but 900 times $450 is still twice what the president of the United States makes. "I had my fun," says Maxwell.

As we slip and slide around the jagged slope, examining the plants, Maxwell strokes the cola, or crowning bud cluster, with his thumb, index and middle fingers. He draws his fingers across his nose and alternately sighs and snorts. I do the same. To me the smell is vegetable: wonderful, magical vegetables, fat cooked asparagus shoots with hollandaise sauce crystallized as resin. To Maxwell the smell is sexual. Sliding his fingers across deep dark pussies. God, he loves it!

Maxwell is the erotic farmer, walking along with a bemused smile on his randy mug, a watering can full of Hi-Bloom in one hand, the stink of good sinsemilla smeared across the other. Each lady, each strain, variety and phenotype has a smell he can pick out from the rest. Maxwell touches and talks to his plants. He has a fond name for each one: Ms. Virginia, Sally Go Round the Roses, Roscoe X, Possum Weed.

But they're not friends.

"More like business associates. I see producers and I see consumers. I don't like consumers. I like producers."

"Which is your favorite?"

"Possum Weed."

"Why?"

"Size, shape, smell, smoke, stone."

There you have it.

At the bottom of the ravine, we stumble across a fairly unsheltered patch of plants. They all look different from each other and something looks wrong with each one. Too leggy, too little bud, too squat; mutant, misshapen, miscolored.

This is the freak ward.

Maxwell pouts.

"Look at this one," he says, reluctant even to touch it. "What a nasty little cunt. Look at her. She just wouldn't put out."

That's how Max talks.

Time to climb back toward the cabin. The sun is setting.

"Money grows on trees," I say.

"Only problem," says Maxwell, "takes money to grow the trees."

The stars have come out on this gentleman farmer and on me. Now the night is beginning because, huffing and puffing up the hill, Maxwell has decided to run the first twenty pounds out of the hideaway to San Francisco.

This task presents a certain risk.

2

LISA:

> The Salamanders Slog It Out with the Indians in a Gene Kelly Monsoon While Ducks Chew the Upholstery; Lisa Turns Up in a Pair of Gold High-heels and Flashes Her Deep-water Eyes; Sexual Trends in Reporting; The Naked Cleaning Ladies; Seduction in (Long) Red Underwear; and More (Always More)

Two nights later.

We're still in America.

I know it's America because there's a football game being played. The South Fork Bear Cubs vs. the Hoopa Warriors. Biggest game of the season, too. Homecoming.

Not much school spirit tonight, however. Only 200 people in the stands. That's because of the rain. The rain here in Miranda, Humboldt County, California, is serious rain: as much as 200 inches a year in nearby Honeydew. Most of it occurs in four winter months. This year is already the worst year for rain in the entire twentieth century. And as the harvest proceeds, this will become the wettest season in California history.

Here, 150 miles north of Maxwell's hideaway, the countryside is broken into soft, steep hills bunched together like mounds on a green dragon's back, topped by fog and redwoods and cleaved by steep fern canyons. This terrain is as rugged as the land around

Maxwell's, but it is less jagged, less chaotic. The hills have a rolling logic. The vegetation is lusher, with more redwoods than ponderosas, more good Douglas fir than scrub oak and chaparral. The reason is water. Three-hundred-foot redwoods do not grow in the desert.

The Hoopa Warriors on the football field are for the most part real Indians, descendants of one of the angrier tribes in the western United States. The Hoopas repelled and slaughtered early Anglo settlers for years. Now, more often than not, they grow marijuana. The Cubs are more than symbolic, too. Black bears still amble down the South Fork of the Eel River. Still, the names of the teams should be changed. Tonight it should be the Hoopa Newts vs. the South Fork Salamanders because the rain here is like the phony rain in those old Gene Kelly movies where the key grips toss washtubs of water down on the actors through screens. Everybody in the stands is covered with garbage bags and sheets of Saran wrap over their yellow and green rain suits.

Out on the field the boys are slogging it out like male mud wrestlers. I recognize South Fork's quarterback, Jessie. Jessie is Sarah's son, and so far in the game he's South Fork's star. He's scored their only touchdown. The score is 26–7 in favor of the visiting Warriors.

It's not a happy night in mudville. Sarah is a friend of mine, an old friend, but I'm not really searching for Sarah. I'm looking for her younger sister, Lisa. Ah, Lisa. Lisa and I have spent only one night together. I'm looking forward to the next. The first night I met Lisa in Bolinas, a village that juts out on the West Coast of these United States, twenty miles north of San Francisco. Lisa had temporarily abandoned the grave responsibilities of dope growing in Humboldt County. The crop was sold. The new plants had not been started. I'd never met Lisa although I came recommended as a man of integrity by her sister. Lisa and I spent two hours talking in a bar (Smiley's), two hours talking in my car (I kept the motor running and the heat on because it was December and I get cold easily), two hours kissing and shivering on a park bench on top of Little Mesa, which overlooks the neck of the Bolinas Estuary. You can see Sutro Tower and the lights of San Francisco from Little Mesa. I only saw, for the most part, Lisa's closed eyelids. (The human species may be divided into two groups: those who kiss with their eyes open and those who kiss with their eyes closed. I like to see what's going on.)

But Lisa was not to be found. I located Sarah at the top of the stands. It was already the third quarter and she was deciding whether to leave now or to wait and see if Jessie would score another touchdown. A mother's place is with her boy on the gridiron, but she and Wyatt, her current boyfriend, were planning on staying at Lisa's tonight to help with all the cleaning. Lisa, it turned out, lived at the top of one of the worst roads in all of Humboldt County.

Sarah is forty and Lisa is twenty-six. Sarah is the oldest of four daughters raised on Upper Broadway near Columbia University in New York City. Lisa is the youngest. Sarah and Lisa are considered the black sheep of their family. They enjoy the label. They call the two New York sisters "two-fers" because they have two of everything: two children, two cars, and in the case of one, two husbands (one is an ex, of course) and in the case of the other, two psychiatrists. "What do you say to two psychiatrists?" Sarah asks when the family is discussed.

Sarah gave up a master's degree in education at Santa Cruz and moved to the North Country to do Shiatsu massage. Lisa visited her on July Fourth weekend, three years ago, and decided to stay. There was fun of all sorts to be had in Humboldt County.

Sarah and Wyatt abandoned the submarine wars at the beginning of the fourth quarter. I wondered whether Lisa had drowned. To shake the rain off, I cheered on Jessie. It was amusing to note that while seventeen-year-old Jessie does not do dope, his mother grows it for a living and his aunt is rather prominent in the trade. Jessie is a young junkie, however. He is a Coca-Cola addict. I've seen him knock down six or eight cans in a day. This should make certain heavy dealers in our society happy, but it displeases his mother Sarah. "God, those chemicals! I tell him if you can't pronounce the ingredients on the label, you shouldn't drink it. But does he listen?"

Lisa did not arrive until the last two or three minutes of the game. By now the players looked like Tootsie Rolls with legs; they were so filthy in mud. Lisa was wearing a green felt hat—it looked like a home-dyed Stetson, the 3X Beaver model—jeans, a sleeveless T-shirt and gold high heels. This during a monsoon. I was wearing L. L. Bean hightop Maine hunting boots (rubber bottoms, leather uppers), wool kneesocks, wool sweater, blue Sierra Designs down parka, two-piece army raincoat from a local surplus establishment called Picky Picky Picky and, underneath it all, my red flannel union suit. Union suits have buttons from neck to crotch and a (sexy) little flap at the back so that you don't have to disrobe in the crapper. This, to my mind, is proper gear for the harvest season in Humboldt County. Not sleeveless T-shirts. Certainly not gold high heels.

Lisa has tricked me. She's said it would be easy to get to her house. In fact, the barely paved road off 101 is as slick as owl shit. The clay fire trail after the secondary is fudge, covered with salad oil. And we're not driving Maxwell's sure-thing four-wheel-drive pickup. We're driving the Incognito Mobile, a tricked-out 1973 Chevy Impala. This is the last great car America ever produced, and I am proud to own one—mag wheels, four on the floor, fuel injection. It's called the Incognito Mobile because it's anything but. I have an even better machine, a 1953 Buick Roadmaster, painted lung red like the Chevy. (Chevy, by the way, as in "chopped." Hard "CH." This is California, you understand.) The Buick is safely back in San Francisco in the garage. If you owned Secretariat would you race him on a muddy field?

The Incognito Mobile screams up the hills, slapping mud against the wheel wells like a paddle steamer, but she's a heavy beast and we're sliding sideways down the steeper grades. Lisa's laughing every time we skid, and I can understand that. Lisa's ripped to the gills. So am I. But unlike Lisa, I'm worried. We don't have a competent driver at the wheel. We have me.

This is only the third time I've driven a car in three months, since my hands were slashed. The first time was for maybe two minutes when a screenwriter I know in Venice, a militaristic young man named Rick Natkin ("Boys in Company C"), had just spray-painted his brand-new Volkswagen Rabbit convertible camo green and brown. Mr. Natkin insisted I drive this ridiculous car around the block so that he could take Polaroids of it. The second time was in Montana, two weeks ago, on top of the Bozeman Pass. Freak snowstorm, a blizzard really. James Rado Jovanovich, one of my oldest friends and a petroleum engineer who would never consider smoking marijuana, is so drunk on bourbon that he must pull over and let me drive. No snow plow, no chains. Jim passes out, and I'm driving with the thumb, middle and ring fingers of my left hand. Finally, a Consolidated Freightways truck comes along and we follow in its tracks for twelve miles.

So I'm scared most of the way up to Lisa's house, which sits on top of a small mountain overlooking the south fork of the Eel River. Lisa likes views.

We abandoned the Incognito Mobile a quarter-mile below the

house. As long as ducks don't chew upholstery, I knew the car would be safe. Lisa put on a pair of Converse tennis shoes she had brought in a pack.

The house was a converted barn. We were sopping wet when we reached the door. There was no lock. We stepped inside and Lisa reached for the kerosene lamp. In the dark the place smelled as if pots of chicken soup had been cooking for days. I stepped forward a foot or so and my head hit on something that felt like a Christmas tree or a strand of kelp. The lamp glowed on. The entire old barn, which was divided into an enormous kitchen and living room on the first floor and into several loft bedrooms above, was hung with drying marijuana. The next day I counted ninety plants.

"Um," says Lisa, "do you feel comfortable in here?"

"Sure. It's warm. It's dry." That was close to what I answered.

"There's the trailer."

"Lisa?" says a sleepy voice. It's Sarah.

"Trailer's just out the door, in the trees," says Lisa.

"Whatever you want to do."

Lisa wants to sleep in the trailer.

Perhaps I make too much noise at the moment of completion. I don't know.

The trailer was a little twelve-foot job with a Formica table at one end and a tiny bed at the other. I saw the German movie *Das Boot*, but I'd never slept in a submarine before. This trailer sub had the torpedo locks open. Outside, it was raining swimming pools from Miami. Inside, fog would have drowned in the humidity. We were on a journey to the deep with Jacques Cousteau.

Lisa took off her clothes.

Let's linger here. Lisa has brown hair that turns blond about ten inches out. I don't know why. She doesn't dye it. It must be the sun. (When the sun happens to shine in Humboldt County.) Her feet are rather nice. The heels and ankles are narrow. The flat of the foot broadens like her hips. The toenails are usually freshly painted with satin red polish. She has a great number of freckles on her body, as many freckles as there are lakes in Minnesota (or almost as many). Her thighs have a blond swelling on the insides that just about makes me faint. I've spent hours of my time on earth licking those thighs. Her ass is kind of funny, especially from the back. It is small and pert for a young woman of her height (five ten), like a little pear held close to a narrow tree trunk. Her breasts are not the breasts of a sixteen-year-old. They hang wondrously until they light up in yellow nipples the color of farm-fresh eggs. Even when I was sixteen and spent Montana nights with real farm girls I longed for the mature, hanging breasts of an American like Lisa. Her neck has wondrous muscles also. There is a depression in the center above the collarbone that my tongue has come to know. Her face is very sure of itself. She used to model toddlers' clothes for department stores in New York. Her eyes: I have been lost twice in my life—once about twelve miles off the Kona coast and once at the top of the Beartooth Mountains in Montana. Both times I was afraid. When I look into Lisa's eyes after we are done, I am always lost, yet never afraid. Lisa's eyes are light blue, the color of island water before it drops off the reef. I don't know what her eyes will look like when she is eighty-five. I'd like to look up from her fucking oozing vulva and see. I don't think they'll be any different.*

As for me—it took me two seconds to strip off my clothes. My dick was thick against my stomach, warm and thick, and I like that feeling.

But the trailer was so wet!

At six in the morning, we wake up. The sheets are sopping. The quilt is wet. Our hair, the hair under our arms, our pubic hair, is thick with Humboldt ooze. I'm wide awake. Lisa is more awake. Her jeans are damp on the chair. My wonderful long underwear is streaked from condensation that has dripped from the ceiling. The trailer smells like rain and like us.

Lisa needs to make a phone call. Dealing. The nearest phone is twenty minutes away at Marty's homestead.

This is news.

"Okay," I say, "why don't I meet you back at the barn?"

Sarah and Wyatt are still asleep.

The dryest place is in front of the Fisher wood stove, and there is a tattered red couch beside the Fisher that pulls out to a bed. I put my damp long johns back on for extra protection. Under a dry quilt in front of a live stove I'm dreaming of drinking New Zealand beer butt-naked on the Ka'ū Desert. No more rain, please.

Lisa comes back in an hour. Those turquoise eyes of hers could light up the dark now. She's tooted a little coke over at Marty's, but that's not why she's chattering so.

---

*A note on sexual trends in reporting. I believe it is still permissible for a heterosexual to have a good time in America. Besides, I'm just a Montana boy and we were all raised with the hogs.

Marty's is a scene from Camarillo State Mental Hospital. *Camarillo Brillo*. The wigs are off the lunatics and everybody's flipped out.

The cleaning ladies can't take any more. That's what's happened.

This has been a better year for Marty than he had ever imagined, just as it has been for Lisa. For two weeks he's employed three women to cut and manicure his plants. He pays them $100 a pound and he walks around all day with jars of coffee and bottles of Kahlúa to keep them happy. But this morning at dawn, the three women OD'ed on snipping bud.

Two of them punched in with a snort of coke, picked up their Weiss brand thread-cutting scissors—and just started giggling. Anything one said made the others fall into hysterics. They wrapped wreathes of crown bud worth hundreds of dollars around each other's heads like laurel branches, and they stripped off their clothes and threw them at each other, and water poured out of their eyes, they were laughing so hard. They couldn't take this piecework any longer. They jumped up and down and watched their breasts bob in the big floor mirrors that Marty has, and they snapped towels at each other like cheerleaders in the locker room after the homecoming game. They tweaked each other on the ass and they threw quarter-pound plastic bags of sinsemilla at each other, and they just, well, lost it.

When Lisa opened the door, one of the women, who, as described by Lisa, has this curly red hair from top to bottom, said, "Hey, I've got to get out of here. I've got to get back to my husband." She pulled on her jeans and T-shirt and coat and walked out to her truck barefoot. This woman, explains Lisa, is a Jesus freak. She doesn't smoke dope. She used to. Lots of it. Then she gave birth to an autistic child and something snapped in her and she changed.

The Naked Cleaning Ladies!

Kind of turns me on, lying here on top of the pull-out couch in my long johns like a big red baby hearing all about them. I'm glad I didn't break sleep to go over and visit, yet Lisa has described the scene so sensuously. . . . Lisa starts to massage my neck. She has that faraway look in her eyes and she pops her fingers into that cute flap in the back I was telling you about.

"You want to go back to sleep?" she asks.

"I could nap later," I say.

"You could be seduced?"

"I might lie still for it."

Lisa trips her tongue along the outside of my ears. Her hands disappear to the elbow inside my long johns. She starts to cup my balls and after I pull off her pants I can feel that she's as wet as the muddy Eel itself. She puts her coke-dried tongue in close communication with mine and then she sits up as stiff as a poker.

"Oh, shit, I forgot my jelly. It's down in the trailer."

This is a disappointing twist of fate for your author.

"There's other options," says she.

"What would be the most civilized, Lisa?"

"I would say oral."

It is a dark, lonely job being an investigative reporter, but someone must do the hard work in our society.

Lisa is not as good a sleeper as I am.

A half-hour later she's up and searching the barn for something. Finally, she doesn't care if she wakes us all up.

"Sarah! Sarah! Have you seen my old blue raincoat?"

Sleepy voice from the top loft. Sarah's.

"Why?"

"It's got $16,000 in it."

This gets me up.

It turns out Sarah has hung the coat over an upstairs window to deflect a leak along the window molding.

Lisa takes the soggy money out of the pockets. Stacked up on the kitchen table, all in $100 bills, the pile is about as tall as five slices of white bread.

On each and every $100 bill someone has stamped in red letters with a rubber stamp: NO NUKES!

3

RETURN TO MAXWELL'S HIDEAWAY:

Maxwell Turns a Catholic Mass into a Shocking and Is Knocked Flat on his Back by a Sledgehammer; The Horse People Writhe on their Beds at the Colorado State Mental Hospital; SAVAK Takes Off Another Grower; The First Shipment of the Season Meets an Unexpected Roadblock

Back down the big road, 101, at Maxwell's hideaway cabin, Carol and Billie were packing the cleaned quarter-pounds in Seal-a-Meal as Maxwell and I came over the hill. One thing has gone unsaid this day at the hideaway ranch. *Maxwell does not sleep with the plants.* Maxwell sleeps in motels. You may see this as hierarchy. If you are one of Maxwell's partners, you may resent this nightly defection. Maxwell would not care what you think. He used to sleep with the plants. He slept beside the fields for years. In the morning he chewed Alka-Seltzers before breakfast. At lunch he dissolved Alka-Seltzers in his Coca-Cola. At night he ate Alka-Seltzers for dinner. His stomach hurt. It hurt a lot. Bravado, you recall, is for vets who sleep with four guns. Maxwell only sleeps with one now, and he prefers to sleep in motels. The plan tonight is to eat dinner and leave with the first twenty pounds of the season. These twenty pounds of sinsemilla are worth from $1,700 to $3,000 a pound depending on the deals Maxwell makes, so Carol and Billie do not complain that they will be sleeping with the rest of the plants tonight. They don't have the connections to move

44

this kind of weight and Maxwell does. That's another reason why Maxwell gets to sleep in motels.

But Maxwell is more than a businessman. Maxwell is Maxwell.

In a second he can see that the cleaning, sorting, weighing and packing is proceeding to perfection.

And so he starts goofing.

"Drink up. Drink up," he says, "your Maxwell needs those bottles. I *require* those bottles!"

Maxwell wants us to finish our Heinekens, and as we guzzle at record pace, he sticks a candle down their green muzzles and plants them like glowing flowerpots in every nook and cranny, shelf and stove surface in the old cottage. Soon there are six, a dozen, twenty candles flickering in the little cabin.

"Catholic mass!" shouts Max, who is anything but Catholic. "Catholic mass!"

It is a boyish thing to do and Maxwell is a boy. The cabin, which was dark twenty minutes ago, now glows like the shrine of Our Lady of Guadalupe. We can all smell the wax. No longer are we hunkered down in a crummy drying room during harvest season, the ceiling festooned with hanging marijuana like mistletoe, automatic weapons fire sounding across the ravine, and the narcos only waiting until first light before the final fly-over and the landing of the helicopters.

Maxwell takes the edge off the paranoia, and that's another reason why he's the boss. He controls reality even when we all know reality has a way of escaping control.

The little cottage is lit now like an old-time Colorado carny show. Not Denver, not Colorado Springs. Talking weird now— talking Durango, the San Juans, Telluride, miners, Silverton, talking turn-of-the-century because Maxwell's people go way back.

Maxwell cracks open one of the large, expensive ice chests that holds the Heinekens. He's cooled the beers in dry ice. He pries out a chunk of dry ice and juggles it from palm to palm. Whoah! It's hot. He tries to pretend it's not.

"Here, Carol," says Max.

Carol won't touch it.

He drops it in Billie's hands. Billie lets out a howl. At first dry ice is cold like regular ice and then so quickly you don't have time to drop it, it turns as hot as fire.

Maxwell laughs. He gingerly takes back the ice, with his fingernails, and drops it into the cooler.

"Reminds me of the shocking," says Max. He raises his eyebrows, little smiles all over his face. Story coming . . .

"Last time I did a shocking," says Maxwell, "it was my fourteenth birthday. All these kids were downstairs at my house. Someone took a lamp, cut off the cord and stripped the wire back four inches or so. Then everybody held hands, maybe ten people in a circle holding on to the bare wire. You put the plug in the socket. Now the electricity is making a circuit, but with ten kids we felt only a pleasant buzz. The charge became stronger and stronger as kids dropped off. Ten, nine, eight, seven, you know, until there was just me and this other guy, and we were both receiving a hell of a surge. I could hardly take it. My jaw is actually clamping. I can see the muscles knotting across his face. The other kid finally lets go. I thought I'd won. Then the kid looks at me. He's smiling. He reaches out with his index finger and touches me right square between the eyes."

"What happened?" Billie asks.

"I fucking fell over backwards like I'd been struck by a sledgehammer."

"What happened to the other kid?"

"He just smiled. He was cool."

"No, I mean what happened to him later?"

"You mean, whatever happened to him?"

"Yeah."

"He died in Thailand. They did an autopsy and they said they found cocaine in his asshole. Can you believe that? Who ever died from coke?"

"The guy who shocked you?"

"His name was Scooter Rydell," says Maxwell. A gentle smile comes across his mouth. It lasts only a second. "I loved that guy," says Maxwell. And then the soft smile breaks open. "You know where I was the morning of that fourteenth birthday, before the party? I was in the Colorado State Mental Hospital. No, shit. My father was the state attorney general."

The mental hospital was old and enormous. Maxwell was at the end of the tour. He was a little afraid to be along in the first place. He forgot what he was doing, and all of a sudden, his worst fear came true. He was lost.

"I'm, like, opening door after door, trying to get back to the tour, and this place is fucking cavernous, and suddenly I throw open a door and there are all these naked fucking girls, maybe two dozen of them. I'm in the girls' shower room or something. I look at them and they're all gleeful and giggling and touching each other, and their tits are jiggling up and down and their bushes are waving and, oh, *God,* I can hardly stand it. I'm only just fourteen, and then I sense there's something wrong. These girls had the bodies of eighteen-year-old women but they had the minds of three-year-olds. I was just blown over."

Maxwell stood watching for more than a minute. Then he noticed he was getting wet. He ran through the shower room, and through the lockers beyond, and he kept going, and then somehow he opened another wrong door, and there before him, strapped to beds, were humans whose heads looked like horses' heads. But they were real people, retarded and deformed. Their legs looked like his legs and their torsos looked like his torso, and their arms were his arms, but their heads were the heads of horses, long and fleshy, all mouth and exaggerated eyes, covered with coarse hair, the tongues as thick as cardboard.

Maxwell panicked and ran and when he finally rejoined his father, he couldn't stop crying.

Everybody's quiet. The clapboard cabin with all the flickering candles no longer looks like a cathedral. It looks like a mortuary.

"I don't think too many people have seen sights like those," says Maxwell.

Carol's looking at the floor. She's a little scared. Max has overdone it. We've gone from candles to death, from sweet, flickering light to too much intensity. Humans with the heads of horses. Maxwell started out covering up everyone's paranoia and he ended up feeding it.

It's almost time to leave.

Max and Billie continue to weigh out the bud into quarter-pound bags and wrap the bags in Seal-a-Meal. Max uses an expensive scale because he is religious about getting the weight right. Some of the pot is still wet, not completely cured. Maxwell adds an extra quarter-ounce or so to these bags since they may dry out and shrink a bit during shipping. Maxwell offers a money-back guarantee. If you don't like the dope, return it and he'll refund your money. Not many growers anywhere in the world offer a money-back guarantee, and wherever Maxwell does business he is treated with respect. Only once did someone break trust. Maxwell was accused of packing thirteen-ounce pounds. Maxwell whipped out the refund on the spot. Next year this customer wanted to do business again. "You had your chance, fucker, and you blew it,"

Maxwell told him. But this stuff is being sent to a Preferred Customer in New York City. A Preferred Customer is one who pays in advance. There are about as many Preferred Customers in the marijuana trade as there are money-back guarantees. This shipment is being sold for $700 a quarter-pound. The first big lot of the season. The partners need the money.

Maxwell sells quarter-pounds for $450 to $700 depending on the variables. The variables are: How much do you want? When do you want it? How much are you willing to pay? Transportation costs must also be figured in. Driving the pickup from San Francisco to Denver, say, extracts a certain value-added tax: two days of paranoia. These twenty pounds are going east with Emory Air Freight. You've seen the ads on television. The harried junior exec must get the contracts to big boss overnight. Not everything sent by air courier belongs to IBM and Exxon.

Maxwell tapes the packages with a specially lined tape and crisscrosses the brown paper in a subtle pattern. If someone opens the shipment, takes out a few pounds, and tries to repackage it, Maxwell has a chance at tracing down the source of the rip-off.

The pot is put into the coolers which carried the Heineken. Nobody's talking much. Everybody is both tense and giddy at the same time. A lot of watering, and fertilizing, and sexing, a lot of hours scanning the sky for spotter planes went into this first shipment. It is not at all a given that these twenty pounds will make it to New York. First they must ride down the road to town, which means nobody who could create a problem can know that Maxwell is transporting tonight. Nobody must pay a midnight visit to Max in his San Francisco motel room, either, where he will sleep with the coolers beside the bed. Nobody must tamper with the stuff en route. (While Maxwell does not particularly trust Emory Air Freight, he trusts the Post Office and United Parcel even less.) The Preferred Customer must retain his reputation for the honest count, and, lastly, nobody must stick a gun in the customer's face and take off the shipment at the New York end, although that is not the worst calamity in the long chain of risks. If the Preferred Customer gets ripped off, well, that's his problem, or so it will be argued.

The greatest concern centers around poachers. Last week three men hit the parcel closest to 101, many miles east. The grower was watching TV with his youngest child held in his arms. A small, dark man rang the bell. The grower's wife answered the door. The man stepped inside and explained that he was lost. When he saw that the grower had a baby in his arms, he put a German Walther PPK, a very expensive automatic pistol, indeed, to the woman's head and told them both not to move. The man's two partners then ransacked the greenhouse and cut the crown tops off the plants. The man spoke with a Middle Eastern accent, which is not, to say the least, typical of people hereabouts. Some speculated the raiders were Israeli Mafia.

Maxwell thinks the poachers were Iranians and says the grower was very lucky because, "SAVAK *lived* to torture people and now they're all over here."

But the shipment could also be taken off by the county sheriff. In terms of interdicting marijuana, California sheriffs are highly sophisticated. Maxwell does not want to run into someone like Bill Stewart, for instance. Bill Stewart may be the most hated narcotics agent in America, not so much because he is famous, although he is not unknown, but because he excites, well, a certain intensity of feeling among the 30,000 dope farmers of northern California.

For years Stewart was the deputy sheriff in charge of narcotics enforcement in Mendocino County. Stewart's raiders lead the state in cultivation busts and pounds seized.

Bill Stewart once almost busted Maxwell. Maxwell was helping to guard a friend's crop up in Mendocino when the grower's girlfriend ran into the big green surplus tent they were using to dry the plants and shouted, "Oh, Lord, it's the fucking feds!" The woman's eyes were sympaku. You could see white all around her pupils. And she yelled "fucking feds" in such a goofy, stereotyped, right out of Elliott Ness, late-night-TV sort of way that Maxwell had started to laugh before he and everybody else had jammed out of the tent.

Maxwell kept running for hours, too, even though he knew the terrain. Bill Stewart had sent runners, particularly fit cops in shorts and athletic shoes, to run them down. The chase went on for three hours, according to Maxwell. More than once he and the runners were so bushed they sat down and panted in each other's faces, less than a hundred yards separating them. Maxwell finally shook the runners and doubled back to the scene of the bust. Stewart and his raiders were still there. Maxwell managed to slip a deer rifle out of the truck and sighted down the scope until he had the top of Bill Stewart's skull in the cross hairs.

"Could have wasted that sucker then and there," Maxwell recalls wistfully, "but I don't happen to think revenge is worth the price of incarceration."

(I will interview Bill Stewart and the first thing he will say to me is: "I have no liking for press people. Half the fucking reporters smoke dope.")

No, we don't want to run into Bill Stewart tonight, with twenty pounds of Maxwell's world-class dope packed into the coolers.

Ready to go. The coolers are packed. The wild, skunky odor is gone, which is the point of all the packing. Maxwell snaps the clasp but I notice just the slightest smile.

"You hear something, Billie?"

Billie's pouring himself a cup of rum. He stops. I freeze. Carol moves to the window.

Far away, there is a buzz, a plane high in the sky.

"It's the . . . it's the . . . don't you hear the planes?"

"Oh, shit," says Billie. Now he knows Maxwell is joking. "Ain't been no planes in weeks. That one's commercial."

"God, I love those planes!" says Maxwell.

And now I can see what he's doing. Maxwell is changing the mood once again.

He tucks his arms behind his back and charges around the cabin, circling us, circling the cooler, making wild *whooshing!* sounds as if he were a five-year-old boy imitating a jet.

"Wish a plane *would* come down tonight," says Max. "Oh, fuck! Would I like to start this run out with a plane blasting down the canyon. Now that would be good luck."

The planes. F-15s or even "XPs" for "Experimental Proto-type." They come screaming down the canyon like banshees on fire so low to the ground—a hundred feet, sometimes fifty—that you can read the faces of the pilots under their oxygen masks. The after-burners are enormous holes, ten feet wide and twenty feet long, as big as the hideaway itself.

"Imagine the amount of air they suck in!" shouts Maxwell.

One morning a few minutes after dawn, Maxwell heard an XP at the entrance to their canyon, still twenty miles away, and he rushed outside stark naked from his sleeping bag and the jet came straight—*straight*—at him. These monster planes cause hysterical complaints from ranchers and retirees but Maxwell loves them. He's jumping up and down and screaming, cheering the pilot on. This is the way to greet the dawn! The pilot is clearing the madrones at a mere Mach 1, but the far side of the canyon looms up three seconds away and Maxwell just *knows* the pilot is going to wipe out the way pilots did week after week in Nam, so often that Max and selected buddies would stretch out on the bunkers near the air base, light up a number and watch the U. S. Air Force crash into Vietnamese mountains. But this pilot is better than those in Nam, and he crams that joystick into his crotch and the jet tips straight up like a cobra striking and the after-burners go off with rocket thrust and the machine climbs 10,000 feet in seconds and the valley reverberates—*shakes*—as if an earthquake has hit, and Maxwell looks down at himself and he sees that he has pissed his pants. Except that he is not wearing pants.

Unfortunately, the XPs are not out tonight. Too dark.

As we load the coolers and climb back into the cab, I happen to knock over my Heineken on the floormat.

"Take a cup of water," commands Maxwell in a soft voice. "Wash out the smell good."

No joke. We're moving now. California's drunk-driving law is one of the toughest in the country. It's not worth a California cop's time to bust you for a joint, but he gets a gold star for a DUI (Driving Under the Influence). We cannot risk being searched. Maxwell says everything now in a strange, soft voice. Maxwell is zoned. This is serious. This is business.

"Head 'em up. Move 'em out." Billie waves from the trees.

The big pickup starts up the hill in four-wheel drive. Top of the long ridge. You can see Highway 101 from the crest where Maxwell first pulled out the Colt. The line of headlights far below is like a line of phosphorescence along the night ocean's shore.

I don't think anything's going to stop us before we get to town.

Two more miles and a kid appears in the headlights.

Maxwell stops and rolls down the window.

"What's the matter?"

The kid is about thirteen, army jacket, short blond hair. He's got a big green duffel bag beside him. Kid's hysterical.

"You've got to help me," he almost cries. "A man just threatened to kill me."

Maxwell swivels his head and looks first off the shoulder of the road to the right, then to the left, then he searches in back of the truck. The Colt is on the seat, hammer back, safety on.

"Who threatened to kill you?"

"Right here," says the kid. "I'm trying to poach his crop. He says I'm trying to poach his crop! He says he's going back to get his gun and then he's going to kill me!"

The kid is serious.

Maxwell looks at him.

"You're 'X's' kid, aren't you?"

"Yeah, man, you've given me rides."

"What do you have in the bag?" I ask in a very neutral tone.

"Nothing, man, nothing. My clothes from the laundry."

He looks over his shoulder because time is wasting and then he opens the top of the bag and starts pulling out skivvies, T-shirts, dropping them in the road.

Maxwell looks at the kid again.

"Well, hey, what I think you ought to do, kid, is keep off the road here. Keep to the hill. You only live a mile farther in. If he comes back he'll follow the road and you'll be able to see his flashlight and crouch down."

No way Maxwell is going to get mixed up in this mess with the first twenty pounds of the harvest riding in the back of the truck.

The kid hustles off to the side of the road with his laundry bag.

"Ah, the bane of growing up in marijuana country." There's more sly cruelty than warmth in Maxwell's smile this time. "Hey, if the kid was so afraid, why didn't he jump in back of the truck and let us take him to town?"

4

SARAH, FIREMAN, THE FAMILY FARMERS:
>Outlaws in Babylon; The Garbage Society; Seven Plants; Country Feminists; Firemen Are Abandoning Boston Firehouses for Northern California; The Wrong Attitude; Blooded Scythes and the Literary Way; A Dark Afghani Squares Off Against a Blond Spaniard; When You Cannot Make a Human Decision, Trust an Inanimate Object; Luther Burbank

Sarah's trailer is about three miles below her little sister's mountain-top barn. When it's raining, the network of roads between the two camps is as slick as a salamander run, but today the sky is clear. So clear you imagine you can see San Francisco to the south and Portland to the north. The rain that night at Lisa's was the first really big one of the winter season. The rains begin in fits and starts in September and often don't stop till June. Living in northern California in the winter is like living inside a carwash.

Sarah's trailer is also located on top of a ridge. This is a land of views. A muddy green bend of the Eel ambles far below the front window of Sarah's vintage Airstream trailer, and out the side window, thirty miles east, is Bear Butte, the talisman peak for southern Humboldt. For years Sarah dreamed of living where she could wake up and see the strange bald top of Bear Butte. Sarah is a woman whose dreams usually come true.

The trailer was built in 1957, but like a classic automobile it has been restored with love. New windows have been cut into the walls to bring in the sun. Tacky Formica has been replaced with redwood burl. A little wood stove is built into the corner. Sarah wants to put up a cabin on this ridge someday but she is in no hurry. All things in their time. Impatience is the daughter of greed. That's how Sarah thinks.

Sarah is whipping up a tasty grilled cheese sandwich for me from good Gruyère cheese and whole wheat bread. She doesn't want anything for herself. It's Yom Kippur, the Jewish Day of Atonement.

"God, every time I pass the blender," she says, "my lips pucker."

Sarah has nice lips. They're round and they smile more ingenuously than Maxwell's do, although Sarah's eyes are as wise as his. The difference is that Max is cynical and a lustoholic and Sarah is an optimist and always in love. Or always looking for it.

Sarah moved to Humboldt seven years ago. A long time yet not long enough to make her part of the original back-to-the-land movement. Still, she shares the old values. Essentially, Sarah is an unreconstructed hippie, although a resilient and savvy one. Sarah is not interested in making big money from marijuana like Maxwell. She's not even interested in pocketing fistfuls of play money the way her little sister Lisa is. Sarah just wants to live in the country and do right and get by. She does not want to end up like her parents: spending the first half of her life hustling for the American dollar, and the last half still worrying when there is no longer any reason to.

Sarah feels America is a garbage society. To Sarah this is a nation of scatophagites: eaters of shit. The country produces shit and loves it. Pintos and Vegas, throwaway razors, Twinkies and lite wines, MX missiles, television. Television means roughly the same thing to Sarah as marijuana does to Nancy Reagan. It is an object of pure horror. There are probably fewer television sets in the hills of Humboldt than there are Republicans who free-base cocaine.

When Sarah gets theoretical, which isn't too often, she talks about the patriarchy and quotes Helen Caldicott, the anti-nuclear doctor whose Oscar-winning film biography the Reagan administration once tried to censor.

Sarah is a country feminist, and there are a lot of them in the woods these days—as many, I would bet, in western Massachusetts, Georgia and Arkansas, as there are in California.

And like most country women, discounting the religious zombies (and not all of them), she likes to fool around.

"Briefly, this summer, I was in love with this Jewish cowboy. You should have seen him. He was covered with tattoos."

After that, in July, she met a greenhouse mechanic. The greenhouse was set up to trick marijuana plants the way a chicken coop is set up to trick chickens. Black plastic came up and down on rollers so that two twenty-four-hour days were made into three sixteen-hour days. The idea was to finish the crop long before the first BNE fly-overs in the fall. This young agronomist's bed was laid out in the middle of his plants. The plants brushed Sarah's back as they made love.

"I think it was the smell I liked most."

Unfortunately, Sarah's pregnant now, and not by one of these two, but by a man she doesn't much like any longer. She tried to tell him what had happened. He told her he couldn't have her up to his house for a week or so. His daughter was visiting from Tennessee. She waited. Then he told her his old lady was visiting. Maybe one more week. Fuck you, said Sarah. Too bad, though, says Sarah now. This kid was cute and he had been on spirulina, the algae supplement, for the entire year, just as she was, so the child would have been born healthy. Also, this botanist had lots of money. He could have bought the forty acres next to Sarah's. They might have launched a dynasty. So went the fantasy and Sarah is good at fantasies.

Well, abortions are not the worst thing in the world. Although, says Sarah, reflecting, "They do rank near the bottom of life's pleasures. . . ."

At least she had made the move out of Phillipsburg this year. Phillipsburg was a little hectic, since it already had two restaurants and was thinking of putting in a stoplight. Living in a little house in metropolitan Phillipsburg was not the same as living on The Land, certainly not land she could call her own.

Sarah had always wanted a home of her own, but she could not afford to buy a house, even in Phillipsburg. Sarah has never made more than $10,000 a year in her entire life.

Sarah has only seven marijuana plants on The Land.

"How many plants do you have in the ground?" a friend in town might ask.

"Seven."

"How many do you think you'll grow this year?"

"Seven."

"Seven?"

"Seven."

Seven is not a lot of plants, but seven is manageable. Seven plants can be grown without thinking too hard, without obsessing, without bending one's life out of shape in any way. If Dr. Helen Caldicott were not an activist pediatrician and she grew marijuana for a living, how many plants would she grow? Probably seven. Seven plants, handled right, yields from $5,000 to $10,000.

Even if you have yourself and three boys, you can get by on seven plants if you keep your wits about you. Let's say you grow most of your own food, tomatoes, squash, apples, carrots, corn and broccoli. You buy brown rice and tofu turkeys. (Yes, there is such a thing as a tofu turkey.) For a family of four, Sarah's food costs are only $75 a month. Her car is a fifteen-year-old Dodge van that is rarely driven. Her medical costs are covered by the state of California and a health center where she knows every doctor, nurse and lab-tech by their first names. The Airstream sets her back another $75 a month. These are the payments. Total home price: a whopping $2,500. The five- and ten-year-old sleep on one side of the bedroom in the back. The seventeen-year-old sleeps across from them. (He doesn't like it.) Sarah sleeps in the next room, alongside the kitchen. Payments on The Land cost $125 a month. If that was your lifestyle, seven illegal marijuana plants might be plenty for you, too.

Sarah is playing a reggae tape on the little AM–FM cassette deck at the front of the trailer. It's Hugh Mandell, the sweet Michael Jackson of reggae:

> *Once I was a worrier*
> *Now my faith is in Jah*
> *Today you have no money*
> *Tomorrow, money and love*
> *Because in Zion there is milk and honey.*

Outlaws in Babylon . . . America is the new Babylon. Sarah finds herself the new outlaw.

A correction: all is not milk and honey, even in Sarah's Zion. Sarah tends a few plants for a hidden partner, a nameless city

friend who kicks in on land payments, and she also shares this
forty acres with a couple whose lifestyle is in many ways the
opposite of hers. If Sarah is the wily old hippie who never burned
out and kept her faith in Jah, the Jamaican God of ganja, night
love, fate and everything else, Fireman and Lannie are the new
traditionalists.

Back in 1981 Fireman drove a hook-and-ladder truck in Boston.
He got tired of the winters, the endless turfing and killing between
blacks and whites, the polluted fishing, the grandstand full of bozo
hunters who turned out on the opening day of deer season like so
many zombie inmates from Mass Mental. The taxes sickened him.
His sons came home from school crying. Little gangs of little jerks
had stolen their lunch money.

How did an American like Fireman wind up in Humboldt
County, California? The same way anybody winds up in the
beautiful wasteland of northern California, Humboldt, Mendocino, Sonoma, Lake, Del Norte, Trinity and Butte counties, land of
monsoon, redwoods, salamanders and ganja.

He wandered out with a U-Haul trailer behind a Chevrolet.

Fireman had this cousin who had this friend who built retainer
walls for concrete office buildings. A new shopping center in
Eureka, county seat to Humboldt, was sinking its retainer wall.
Fireman was nothing if not a hard worker.

The job was really there. Afterward, however, Fireman couldn't
find work. The lumber industry had laid off nearly 90 percent in
California and Oregon. Livestock prices had been bad for years.

On the other hand, Humboldt was the most beautiful place
Fireman had ever laid eyes on. There were more deer within
dirt-bike distance of his forty than in all of Massachusetts, and the
fish that swam up the Eel were—salmon! Have you ever tasted
salmon roasted half an hour after it's been caught?

And, of course, nobody who worked a firehouse in Dorchester
and did what nobody who lived in Uppie's Corner had ever done
before—driven out to California with no money, the wife, two
kids, two more by the wife's previous marriage—no Boston
Irishman who lays it all out like this wants to come home with his
tail between his legs. Especially when the foreman of the retainer
wall crew, in the year after they were all laid off, had made $37,000
in pot. That's money.

And so Fireman cast about for land. He quickly discovered that
land in northern California cost at least a $1,000 an acre, owing to
pot. He knew he couldn't afford forty acres by himself and forty

acres was the minimum parcel of land not governed by the state's careful subdivision laws.

Fireman's wife Lannie suggested a friend of hers who had a boy in the Bear Butte Day Care Center with their girls.

Sarah wanted land of her own, too, and for reasons of her own she did not want to borrow from her little sister Lisa who had barely arrived in Humboldt and was already pulling down enough marijuana money to buy gold heels and vacations in Bora Bora.

But Fireman and Lannie did not live like cool old hippies. They worked like dogs, up at dawn to tie up the branches on their plants when the night wind had broken them off, evenings spent trimming bud and reading cultivation manuals. Fireman and Lannie harvested their first marijuana plant on the anniversary of their wedding. That way, said Lannie, "We'll be sure to remember both dates."

They do not view Sarah's seven plants as seven plants, but simply as $10,000. The plants could be soybeans. They worry when Sarah brings tattooed cowboys home from the Branding Iron in Garberville because tattooed cowboys, Jewish or not, may have done time in prison, and losers don't respect other people's pot patches.

Sarah moved onto The Land to make life even simpler. Worrying about this and worrying about that does not make life simpler.

Besides, Fireman and Lannie use chemicals on their plants. *Chemicals.* To Sarah, pouring inorganic ferts on the roots of her seven marijuana plants is like Helen Caldicott going to work for United Nuclear. (Fertilizer is a hot issue in the North Country. Sarah has not made her mind up about the richest organic fertilizer, blood meal. Blood meal comes from rendered animals, not just dissolved cows from the slaughterhouse but, according to certain skeptics up here, from dogs and cats melted down at the ASPCA. Now, would you enjoy smoking pot fertilized with rendered cats and dogs, that is, would you want to *smoke* cats and dogs? I'm not sure the average soybean farmer in Illinois weighs these questions as carefully as Sarah does. But then, soybean plants are worth one-quarter of a penny. Sarah expects to reap at least $1,500 a plant from her marijuana.)

Fireman told her that she had the wrong attitude. All he wanted to do was make some money. Sarah said that's all she wanted to do, too, but, of course, they meant different things.

"All my life people have said I have the wrong attitude," says Sarah as she cleans up the tiny kitchen and puts the bread in the ice-cooled cold box. "All attitude means is that other people think you're different than they are and they want you to conform to their way of doing things."

The harvest moon will be out tonight.
Sarah smiles. It is a slow smile I can swim with.
Okay, we'll strip off our clothes, rub our bodies with linseed oil and clove and chop down the plants with blooded scythes. That would be the literary way.
Unfortunately, Sarah must pick up Jacob, the five-year-old, at the child care center.
A daytime harvest will have to do.
Sarah points out pottable herbs, arrowroot and mint, as we step out to her plants. Even though she has only seven plants, they are scattered in three plots and hidden well. Like Maxwell, Sarah believes discreet is the way to go. The plants are tucked behind thick stands of young Douglas fir, and also surrounded by nine feet of chicken wire to discourage the deer. Sarah's been lucky this year because no wood rats have gnawed through. But then, Sarah is always lucky. Her life smoothes along on what most people would call luck, although she considers it fate, and those few times when luck, fate and the goddess do not prevail, there is always that nifty chalk eraser of the species: human denial. What happened didn't happen. The man who used her was only being used by her. Her partners don't like her because her wild lifestyle frightens them, not because she brings dangerous characters around.
Small is beautiful is an ideology that takes the stink out of new-age poverty.
No matter. Sister Marijuana believes Sarah. Her plants have come out perfect.
Sarah grows marijuana differently than Fireman—or Maxwell. She does not keep track of strains, let alone phenotypes. Her seven plants are basic *Sativa–Indica* crosses. Now, generally speaking, *Sativa* comes from the New World, especially Colombia and Mexico. The garden variety hemp that grows wild throughout the Midwest is *Sativa*. *Sativa* is taller, rangier, more spread out than *Indica*. *Sativa* looks like, if you will, a tall, blond Spaniard. *Indica* looks like a short, dark Afghani. If they square off on a barroom floor, the Spaniard tries to talk his way out (and he's very good at it) while the Afghani plants both feet and pulls out a thick, twisted knife. *Indica* gives a body stone. *Sativa* is more of an intellectual high. Connoisseurs like to discuss Hegel on *Sativa* and

tongue kiss with *Indica* . . . assuming you are the sort of good American who likes to do either.

Sarah's plants are long and leggy—the *Sativa* influence—and bushy along the bud line—the *Indica*. Such a combination is not a bad way to go. From the purely commercial standpoint, the advantage of *Indica* is that it is heavy in bud or flower clusters, and pure bud commands the best prices. Perhaps the main advantage of *Sativa* (again, discounting taste and high) is that *Sativa* molds less. Plant mold can destroy a harvest, and Humboldt's monsoons bring mold. As Sarah says, planting, fertilizing, watering, guarding and growing a marijuana plant from seed to maturity only to lose it to mold is like raising a boy to age eighteen only to have him commit suicide.

In practice, most marijuana plants grown commercially in America are *Sativa–Indica* crosses, although purists like Maxwell (and Lisa) keep an array of breeders in their seed stable so that their patches range in appearance from tight, furry Christmas trees such as Murangi *Indica* to Javanese *Sativa*, which resembles a wispy three-year-old willow tree out of a Robert Frost poem.

Some of the lower branches on Sarah's plants have been broken by the early storms. She has not bothered to tie them up with string the way Fireman does. This makes no difference. Marijuana is a tough weed and the broken branches are growing along the ground like vines.

Sarah's plants have an airy look not attributable to the *Sativa* genes. When the big stem leaves yellow, she pulls them off and uses them for mulch. This allows more light to reach the buds and makes harvest cleaning far quicker. Removing dead leaves sounds like nothing, but such boldness is almost as controversial as using chemical fertilizers. Many growers believe that pinching off leaves traumatizes the plant. Sarah does not grow marijuana to reinforce obsessive personality traits. She tries to do what comes naturally, and this often drives her male grower friends bananas.

Like most old-style growers, Sarah does not own a gun. A gun would destroy the reason she moved to the country. It would shoot out the windows of her fantasies. It's not that she believes seven plants are not worth firing over some punk's head for. It's that she believes that if one acts as if nothing will go wrong, then nothing *will* go wrong.

(It is a month before I realize that Sarah's sister Lisa owns a pistol, an efficient little .25-caliber automatic, and that she will use it under environmentally correct conditions.)

Sarah feels that people grow marijuana according to the precepts of their own personalities. This is a basic bit of gardener's wisdom. But which works better—cataloging and agonizing, or loving looseness?

Sarah surprises me. She is without prejudice.

"Plants react to sun, water and nutrients. You can have a baby or a gun on your hip; it makes no difference."

In fact, Sarah, like Maxwell, believes that seeds are 90 percent of the story. A shoddy pot farmer with excellent seed will grow better dope than an ace agronomist with lousy seeds.

Sarah looks closely at her plants. They are not quite ready to be harvested. The little blond hairs on the buds are not dark enough yet. The plants could use another week in the ground. Still, the rains are upon her. She doesn't want to lose everything to mold. It's time for scientific decision-making.

Sarah leans down and pulls her necklace over her thick bowl of curly black hair. This necklace is fashioned of blue cut-glass beads. At the bottom of the first circle of beads is a smaller second loop which holds a Capricorn pendant. The lower loop with the golden goat has independent motion. Sarah holds the necklace close to the marijuana plant, which is seven feet taller than she is.

"Clockwise means I should cut it down."

After a second the little goat spins counterclockwise.

"All right, we leave it standing," says Sarah. "Now for the test."

"Will it rain again in the next two days?" she asks the necklace.

Again, the pendant moves counterclockwise.

"All right, if it rains," says Sarah, "we know the pendant isn't any good. If you can't make a human decision, trust an inanimate object."

I thought it was a nice touch for the daughter of a geophysicist at Columbia University to include a control.

On the way out of The Land from Sarah's is a house that has already made me curious. It is a scene from suburbia in the middle of the redwood bramble. A large prefab house cantilevered off a gently sloping hill. Fuchsia and flowered trellises cover one side. A porch patio runs off the other to a corral with a Shetland pony, a gaggle of geese, and two pet lambs. A long string of Pacific Gas & Electric poles bring in electricity and telephone, wild luxuries not present for miles. I wondered who the urban settlers were. I imagined they would be a retired couple who had fallen in love with the rash beauty of the mountains above the Eel.

Except that at the bottom of the parcel was an outrageous greenhouse, perhaps sixty feet long, sixteen feet tall, and snaking into the Lucite building were coils of black pipe. This soft PVC pipe is called growline in the trade, but I couldn't imagine anyone growing pot so brazenly. Anyone farming dope would bury the lines, and who would set up a marijuana greenhouse in a region where legitimate greenhouses were few and far between? I decided the structure housed melon hybrids, superstrains of rutabaga, perhaps.

I knocked on the door and waited for Luther Burbank to appear. An old couple with no pot on their land might be free to tell some good stories.

But nobody was home, and I didn't have time this trip to wait. Maxwell was expecting me in Ukiah, 150 miles to the south, and Maxwell doesn't wait long for anybody. I wanted to find out what happened to the first shipment.

5

THE RETURN OF SISTER MARIJUANA:
Land, Home-grown and the Significance of America's Newest Last Frontier; The Family Farm Finds a Savior While the Truth Is Better Left Unsaid; Hippies Pipe Willie Nelson into the Greenhouses While Rednecks Grow their Hair; Paraquat Panics the Youth of America, and the U. S. Government Can't Win for Losing . . . also, Menstruating by the Full Moon and the Proper Way to Treat a Lawyer

The 1970s was the decade that reversed, or at least slowed, the population shift of the last two hundred years. By the millions, Americans moved out of the cities and back to the country. It was a strange migration, motivated more by emotion than economics, because, by and large, there were few jobs to be had in the boondocks. Lumber was on the decline. Commercial farming had gone large-scale and corporate, and farming or ranching in the mountains, whether northern California or northern New Hampshire, had not been particularly profitable for a hundred years. The retired newcomers managed to live on social security and their savings. The youngsters at first filed for welfare or relived frontier dreams of self-sufficiency.

Land in Humboldt and Mendocino counties, an area about twice the size of Connecticut, 180 by 50 miles, was truly cheap in the early 1970s, especially by California standards. Sixty acres of land could be bought for $20,000, $5,000 down, if that. To hippies abandoning the hard drugs, crime and ambivalent vibes in San Francisco, Los Angeles and New York, such prices sounded like the Garden of Eden without a mortgage. Drifting Nam vets and assorted short-haired back-to-the-landers agreed. The new settlers bought old logging shacks or threw up tepees, tents, domes, cabins, anything to get through the awful winter rains. Come spring they planted a garden of organic vegetables. Since most newcomers had turned on to marijuana in college, the streets or Nam, it was only logical to till a little home-grown, too, and since many of the more serious gardeners had green thumbs in a fertile land and a yen for experimentation as well, they began to toy with the sinsemilla technique.

In the 1950s Mexico had been the home of vanguard marijuana agriculture. In the 1960s it was Hawaii. As more and more old hands settled into the North Coast along with a disproportionate number of experienced farmer's daughters and sons from the Midwest, the green baton passed to Humboldt and Mendocino. At the least, marijuana was a way to pay off the mortgage without a lifetime of work—in a corner of America where work had rarely been easy to come by.

If many of these earnest settlers could have been called hippies, throwing the *I Ching* to decide which way to turn their VW buses, east to Garberville or west to Honeydew, the values of the territory soon changed and toughened them as they had toughened and changed earlier waves of immigrants. Inside of five years, half the old hippies were shooting deer out of season with double-ought buckshot just like the rednecks who had sneered their arrival.

And the rednecks were starting to resemble hippies. Turn down the sound while you watch the Country Music Awards on television. There's Willie Nelson, his burnt-red hair held in a ponytail by rubberbands. The Charlie Daniels Band, Hank Williams, Jr., Waylon Jennings, even the Oak Ridge Boys—their hair and beards are longer than Jerry Garcia's of the Grateful Dead. . . . "Hey, mama, while you're up, grab the can of Copenhagen on the tube and boot the J my way, wouldja?"

In the 1970s the broad mass of rural hippies and the broad mass of indigenous rednecks melded together. (In Hawaii a similar miscegenation occurred as hip white-skinned *haoles* taught the local Hawaiians that more Mainland dollars could be made growing *pakalolo* in the lava jungles than waiting tables for Conrad Hilton.)

Few old-style hippies were left in America, perhaps a handful in the cities, mostly diehards with bald foreheads, burned out and disoriented, so the media arbitrators decided with relief. By 1980 "hippie" had become a trashbag term, something historical like wobblies, suffragettes, commies and beatniks.

And yet, what were these people *doing* in northern California, New Mexico, Hawaii, Idaho, Arkansas, Vermont, northern Michigan, rural Georgia, Upstate New York and among the cornfields of Iowa? Thousands of Americans, sleeping in schoolbuses and homemade cabins, harvesting and menstruating on the full moon, marking time on Druid calendars, trotting off to the rodeo and betting on the quarter horses, wearing sawed-off jean vests slung across their naked backs, rainbow patches plastered everywhere, scads of misfits just generally living their calm, wild lives as if New Wave music, New York–L.A. fashions, Tom Wolfe's "Me Generation," Baptist presidents, the Moral Majority and Ronald Reagan did not exist.

The funny thing is that without really trying, these gentle rejectionists, be they short-haired hippies or long-haired rednecks, had become the major producers of an essential leisure-time commodity.

Naturally, it was the U. S. government that brought this awful result to pass. Perhaps all governments are the same. Perhaps ours has a special affection for irony. But just as our government introduced millions of plowboys and ghetto dishwashers to the certain pleasures of marijuana (and the uncertain pleasures of heroin) after it shipped them to Southeast Asia, it has brought home the war on drugs in a way it surely never intended.

Marijuana had been a foreign treat for decades, like Spanish fly or contraband copies of *Ulysses,* smuggled across southern borders in ever larger shipments.

In 1978 the Puritan intellectuals of the Carter administration had a clever idea. Ninety percent of the marijuana smoked by troubled American youth came from Mexico. Why not persuade our southern sister to spray her crop with paraquat, a herbicide that, it turned out, could cause permanent lung damage and surely stop Americans from wanting to smoke dope at all? For reasons that can only be explained in terms of obtaining increased foreign aid, Mexico agreed.

American consumers panicked. They telegrammed their congresspeople. Radio stations in Los Angeles received thousands of calls a day and one news anchorman renamed himself Paraquat Kelly.

But the desire for boo did not go up in smoke. Americans turned to Colombian weed and to domestic sinsemilla, which had until then been considered a rare connoisseur's pot.

Again, the U. S. government caused an increase in domestic production, this time by interdicting the traffic from Colombia.

"With the continued pressure on foreign sources by [the Reagan administration]," said Frank Monastero of the Drug Enforcement Agency, "the temptation to the trafficker to seek other sources of supply, especially domestic, is becoming irresistible."

Aptly if dryly put, Mr. Monastero. In other words, a lot of people had discovered it was easier to drive down from Mendocino with a load in the trunk than to fly out of the Guajira Peninsula in Colombia with Uzi-armed, double agents on their tail and Fat Albert, the DEA's sophisticated stratospheric spy balloon, sending microwaves over their shoulders.

Testifying before Senator Hayakawa's hearings on the cultivation of marijuana on public lands in 1982, Mr. Monastero claimed that marijuana from Colombia comprised three-quarters of the U.S. market. "Illicit domestic production" accounted for only 7 percent.

Reporters and the observers in the gallery laughed at the assistant administrator for operations of the Drug Enforcement Agency. Most marijuana experts wondered if the DEA's mandate to operate outside the country for the most part and the agency's thirst for surveillance hardware, including mini-AWACs, hadn't led it to overlook an obvious domestic growth industry, much as J. Edgar Hoover used to turn a blind eye toward organized crime because it was omnipresent and hard to combat successfully.

("Heck," Terrence Burke, head of DEA's Cannabis Desk will tell me, "two years ago I didn't even know what the word 'sinsemilla' meant, let alone how to pronounce it.")

By the end of the year the DEA report on "Eradication/Suppression" stated, a little incredulously, that 38 percent more domestic marijuana was eradicated in 1982 than was "previously *believed to exist.*"

The National Organization for the Reform of Marijuana Laws (NORML) believes with considerable evidence, that marijuana is now as basic to the American way of life as Wheaties, although not so loved yet as cornflakes. NORML estimated in 1983 that pot was worth over $10 billion at the farm level, placing it third behind corn and soybeans, just ahead of wheat. And in early 1984, the Congressional Select Committee on Narcotics Abuse and Control estimated that marijuana was the nation's second most profitable cash crop, edging out corn and gaining on soybeans

California, Hawaii and Kentucky are the leading grower states followed by Oregon, North Carolina, Oklahoma, Tennessee, Arkansas, Florida, Georgia, Missouri, Kansas, South Carolina and every one of the rest of these United States. In the last year, for the first time, more marijuana was grown in the South than in the West.

NORML pegs marijuana at $1.8 billion in California, making it the state's leading agricultural product. NORML's estimate is far below the combined estimate of California's sheriffs. The sheriffs figure they are grabbing only 2–10 percent of the crop. Since over $600 million is expected to be seized this year in the forty-three counties (of California's fifty-eight) that report arrests for cultivation, this leaves an incredible $5 billion worth to be harvested. The figures include a spectacular $2 million bust not ten miles away from President Reagan's ranch in Santa Barbara.

Back in 1979 Mendocino County Agricultural Commissioner Ted Erikson, twenty-eight years into the job, got himself into big trouble by slipping an extra line into the ever-dull yearly report of crop estimates. After surveying farm equipment companies, nurseries, car lots and his own sources, he estimated that marijuana had edged out grapes to become the county's biggest crop, worth $90 million (a year later $100 million, and now, much more).

"It became obvious that marijuana was a significant part of our economy," he said. "So I thought I just better include that as a realistic fact of life and I didn't really think it would create the amount of concern and comment that it has."

The county supervisors voted 4–1 to force him to tear out the marijuana page from each and every copy of the annual crop report.

"It's best left unsaid," said Doug Bosco, the state assemblyman who would soon become a congressman in part because of the anti-nuclear, pro-pot vote in northern California. "But what do you do when 6,000 people in Mendocino are growing marijuana? What do you do when so many people decide to disobey the law?"

Purse your lips, perhaps? That's what Richard Rominger,

director of food and agriculture for the state of California, did when I asked him. He acted as if he had just bitten into a medfly-infested apricot.

"The tendency is to exaggerate," he said.

In this he's right. NORML and the sheriffs have their respective axes to grind. NORML supports legalization. The sheriffs want more money.

The middle truth, however, still seems awesome. Reefer madness is here to stay, just like Lawrence Welk.

"When I started," said Lieutenant Louis Stiles of Kentucky's state police, "I found it difficult to believe marijuana could be Kentucky's biggest cash crop, but I don't find it too hard to believe anymore."

"People aren't stupid," explained Tom Dial, director of the Mississippi Bureau of Narcotics. "The economy gets rough and people are trying to make ends meet."

"If you put out one acre of marijuana, you can make more than on your entire farm operation. Think about that." This from Sheriff Yale Jarvis of Washington County, Iowa.

"It was a way to raise a little money," explained Melvin Shaw when he was caught with 3,000 pounds of bud at his Steeleville, Illinois, farm. In times of higher sorghum prices, Melvin Shaw had processed molasses.

Marijuana, not too often, but often enough, had become the savior of the family farm.

By 1983 perhaps 100,000 to 200,000 Americans grew marijuana as their primary source of income. NORML's educated guess is that domestic production now supplies 50 percent of the country's marijuana craving, and that the domestic share has been growing at 25 percent a year for several years. The DEA has finally admitted that the domestic share is at least 25 percent.

Washington can't win for losing.

And from now on Ronnie's Raiders, and the raiders of successive administrations, will be duking it out not with a mess of mercenary foreigners and smugglers producing a crumbly, stem-ridden crop of inferior pesticided weed, but with red-blooded American agronomists who *believe*, brothers and sisters, in what they are doing: Patriots of Pot! Yes. And there will be car dealers, bankers, and real estate salesmen, sheriffs, DAs and members of Congress who support the trade or at least sit nimbly astraddle the fence, and then articles will appear on the op-ed page of the New York *Times*, as they already have in the Washington *Post*, likening marijuana to beer and Scotch, and then millions of pot smokers and non-pot-smokers alike will compare the current inquisition to Prohibition, and the government will crack down even harder because how can any Sane Person compare a Dangerous Narcotic to something as beneficial to the human spirit as grain alcohol, and the crackdown will incite an uproar among marijuana consumers who thought the entire issue was won long ago, and the expanded raids will only jack-up prices and lead more rural farmers and urban greenhouse mechanics to plant more seeds and take up the trade—and what will be the awful result? Why, America will GO DOWN SLOWLY like the paunchy, dick-sucking, brain-poisoned Romans who swilled their contaminated drinking water from solid lead pipes!

Yes.

It's a whole new ball game with home-grown, you see. The mystique is no longer South of the Border, Top of the Khyber Pass. It's Harlan County, Kentucky; Steeleville, Illinois; Santa Barbara, California. Marijuana is no longer the drug of Lenny Bruce, black saxophone players and those oversexed hippies. Now it is smoked by country and western stars, for God's sakes, spritzed in growbags by make-a-buck Manhattan loft dwellers and southern rednecks wearing bib overalls. And no matter what the feds do, it won't go away. Good times increase demand. Times of recession create more growers.

All of this has been lost on the media. To media trendies, the gentle psychedelic marijuana had been part and parcel of a gritty rebellion that had (thank God) failed.

It never occurred to anyone who mattered that marijuana, a drug like any other, might have become by 1980 as American as Jamaican rum in the eighteenth century, German beer and French bourbon in the nineteenth, and Scotch whiskey in the twentieth.

By the 1980s some 30 million Americans smoked marijuana, according to the National Institute on Drug Abuse. Ninety percent were adults. Most of these deviates worked as secretaries, steam-shovel operators, lawyers, receptionists, legislative aides, computer analysts, butchers, bakers and candlestick-makers. If we are to believe the various grand juries and investigative committees in Washington, a goodly number of congresspeople were also partaking along with more than a handful of senators.

Still, the media spotlight had shifted. It dazzled another drug—cocaine—hardly newer than marijuana, really. Sigmund Freud had written his Ph.D. on this hoary class I narcotic and later snorted down himself while Cole Porter sang its charms. Sir Arthur Conan Doyle got hooked and Sherlock Holmes, his creation, kicked in a popular movie, *The 7 Percent Solution.* Julia Phillips, producer of *Close Encounters of the Third Kind* estimated she had spent more than one million dollars on her cocaine habit. In some ways cocaine is the perfect American drug because it stops you from thinking. You rush ahead pell-mell, chattering and feeling good about yourself, and you never—until your nose won't stop running and your septum rots out in a most unsightly way—quit working. And isn't that (I can hear Maxwell asking this question with his twisted smile), isn't that what America is all about? Producing Academy Award-winning films and stamping out the next K car?

Sister Marijuana didn't mind the lack of attention. All the while she was perfecting herself, soaking up sun and putting out resin, acquiring desired genes from the Hindu-Kush and St. Ann's Bay. Growers were busy spreading bat guano on the roots, culling out males with the fervor of futuristic lesbians, playing flutes in the fields and piping Charlie Mingus or Willie Nelson into the greenhouses.

The pot of the 1980s had become a new tiger entirely: American-bred and as powerful as a California puma running down a Colombian tree sloth.

Who would ever have thought? All this while James Watt was praying for Armageddon, and Caspar Weinberger and Ronald Reagan asserted on national television that the Soviet Union seemed to be arming for imminent nuclear war?

Well, perhaps the comeback made sense after all. At least here was an added explanation. Once again the government was encouraging drug use, this time by scaring the bejesus out of the populace, forcing the weak-willed and the sybaritic to reach for short-term relief. When humans are asked to step into showers with bars of stone soap and gas jets, they have a strange, animalistic tendency, if they're not with the ones they love, why, to strip off their clothes and love the ones they're with. Faced with the prospect of our flesh dropping out in chunks from nuclear radiation, many of us have made a serious decision to party. . . .

In 1982 the theme of the New Orleans Mardi Gras, America's biggest formal party, was Apocalypse Now, and what could be better for pure partying than thick, resinous *ganja,* more powerful than anything anyone has ever lit up before?

Why, nothing, except, perhaps, for beer and cocaine. Two American party drugs not usually linked, either to themselves or to the new marijuana, at least in the minds of the media.

But it occurs to me, looking back on several months of all-night drunks and all-day stones, bareback canters across mountain ridges under the full moon and dirty motel carousing, that to whom we may call America's new frontiersmen, the three drugs are pretty much inseparable. There are growers who use marijuana but will not touch cocaine, dealers who do coke but feel uneasy tasting state-of-the-art bud, as well as sixty-five-year-old sheep ranchers who swig down a fifth of Old Crow while they watch their grandsons and hired hands clean pound after pound of marijuana that they refuse—ever—to sample. But such purists are rare. To most of the travelers on our highway, different drugs are different tastes at a meal that never ends. Good *ganja* sets the wayward course, if you will. Beer pulls in the sails where needed, lays the keel, you understand, while cocaine calls out the winds wherever necessary to keep the ship moving.

Not the safest way to live one's life, perhaps, but we're talking a pretty intense crew here. I bring up the linkage because, again, I think the media in its coward's stance of always playing voyeur, while never taking off its pants and jumping into bed, sees drugs the way it sees fashions in clothing: as trends fitted to one sort of people at one time, a different set a few years later, here today, gone tomorrow. But drugs in America, at least from now on, are not going to be here today, gone tomorrow. This is a nation of extreme substance abusers.

It could be argued that we are the only species of substance abusers, since as far as I know, lemurs and orangutans, goats and woodchucks just do not seem to like to get either high or down for the pure hell or pleasure or forgetfulness of it.

But enough of these remarks on the sad state of American debauchery. We must return to history and economics for a few necessary pages. And then it's back to the fun. . . .

If the original growers were a mottled American bunch of hardy hippies, bikers and Nam vets mixed with a goodly number of heavy-partying, indigenous rednecks and a few green-thumbed lawyers and professors who managed the obvious contradiction in their positions without too much discomfort, they were all soon joined by a rather large and even more heterogeneous group: the unemployed of rural America, at least those with a certain amount of courage and not a whole lot of respect for the law. The unemployed came on board in the late 1970s when the post-Vietnam recession became the worst downturn since the 1930s, a time, some may recall, when a large number of similarly rural unemployed found work distilling sour mash and smuggling in liquor from less puritanical countries.

It is no accident that the leading marijuana-growing regions in America today are, with the natural exception of Hawaii, among the areas of the country that set up stills by the thousands during the Great Depression.

In several of the counties north of San Francisco, especially Sonoma, Mendocino and Napa, wine grapes were grown during Prohibition as they are now. The big wineries did not simply close shop to please midwestern and southern Methodists who had successfully lobbied for a dry America. Many establishments continued to do what they had always done, only now it was called bootlegging instead of winemaking and it required pay-offs to county, state and federal officials instead of *pro forma* taxes.

California is said to be a state where the past is left at the border and the future begins at breakfast, and this is certainly true. But in California north of San Francisco, plenty of old-timers recalled Prohibition as they watched the new outlaws begin to seed the rugged land with the new contraband—marijuana. When the recession of the late 1970s killed the housing market, tens of thousands of free cutters, timbermen, and millworkers also noticed that many of the grotty newcomers weren't doing too badly.

Sheep and cattle ranchers were the last to turn over. Like the lumbermen they got their incentive in the 1970s when stock prices were depressed at the farm level, and more than any other group they had the perfect cover. Who would suspect that on the back forty of Dave Molinari's thousand acres, two hundred marijuana plants were taking in south slope sun? After all, the Molinaris had been ranching since 1860 and they still ran four hundred sheep, although, truth be told, the Molinaris, like every other sheep rancher, haven't been pulling down too good a price for lamb and wool as of late, and Dave's grandson Bobby spent several years after that tragic conflict in Southeast Asia just lolling about, real despondent. . . .

In fact, the settling of the American West has rarely conformed to the righteous principles of most historians. The gentle Christian virtues of "The Little House on the Prairie" didn't count for much during the Johnston County land wars, the Oklahoma settlers' rush or the armed rebellion of Colorado's gold and silver miners. The basic imperative was land and money . . . and everywhere the first order of business was Indian removal.

In northern California this meant the Wiyots, Lassiks, Yukis and Hoopas, somewhat imperfect names for tribes and bands that formed and regrouped as the whites moved in. These tribes fought back with a success and savagery rare in the history of this country's Indian wars. In 1863 the governor of California finally sent enough troops to wipe them out, and the end is worth a paragraph, since the most feared marauders were incinerated in what is now the center of the primo dope-growing area of the world, Ft. Seward, twenty-one miles from Garberville, the most prosperous little town in Humboldt County and all of northern California. Local mystics even claim the Indians laid a serious curse on this land. . . .

At last I come home [recollected Lucy Young, first cousin to Chief Lassik]. Before I get there [Ft. Seward], I see big fire in lotsa down timber and tree-tops. Same time awful funny smell. I think: somebody get lotsa wood.

I go on to house. Everybody crying. Mother tell me: "All our men killed now." She say white men there, others come from Round Valley, Humboldt County too, kill our old uncle, Chief Lassik, and all our men.

Stood up about forty Inyan in a row with rope around neck. "What this for?" Chief Lassik askum. "To hang you, dirty dogs," white men tell it.

"Hanging, that's dog's death," Chief Lassik say. "We done nothing, be hung for. Must we die, shoot us."

So they shoot. All our men. Then they build fire with wood and brush Inyan men been cut for days, never know their own funeral fire they fix. Build big fire. Burn all them bodies. That's funny smell I smell before I get to house. Make hair raise on back of my neck. Make sick stomach, too.

In nine years the white settlers murdered and starved 10,000 of the 11,000 Indians in the region.

The man who perhaps gained most from the torching of the aborigines was one George E. White, a sheep and cattle baron who became known as the King of Round Valley.

White was a hard-working southerner who developed a mania in the post-Civil War period for controlling what is now marijuana country. The county physician described him as a "tall, handsome man, uneducated, spelling cat with a 'k,' but shrewd and able who had a retinue of retainers who were as loyal to him as highlanders to their chief, and who did his bidding without question, hypnotized by his remarkable personality."

George White acquired over 35,000 acres by creative means: arson, poison, murder of legitimate homesteaders and stock rustling. His "faithful headman" was a dapper rider nicknamed Wylackie John "who did not smoke or chew tobacco, dressed well for the mountain country, and was suave and polite to the local people, always touching his hat and inquiring about their health." But if homesteaders moved near the open range used by George White, Wylackie John hired men to kill them and provided alibis in the already corrupted courts of the region.

> When [Wylackie John] invaded the surrounding country to steal another rancher's sheep or cattle, he would station herds of other sheep or cattle at different points along the trail and cross the area with their tracks to confuse pursuit. If he contracted large debts, the creditors died. When one of White's buckeroos grew restless and showed signs of talking, he died, and the danger of speaking out was soon understood. In one well-known incident, [he] shot a man from ambush. In another he pled guilty to a killing he had nothing to do with, except to plan it, and on the plea of self-defense he went free as he knew he would. He assembled a gang of perjurers who blasted the good name of White's first wife, thereby getting the divorce White wanted. Wylackie John was preparing to do the same to White's second wife when the good lady fortunately died, and he was actively engaged in performing the same service in the case of White's third wife when her brother, Clarence White, put a bullet through his scheming brain.

"Scheming brain!" Yes!

America is always amusing. Travel to marijuana country and the history of the region before anyone has ever heard of marijuana turns out to be stranger than it is now. (This, according to the fascinating and detailed history of the Round Valley Indian Wars by Lynwood Carranco and Estle Beard.)

Rightly or wrongly, little has changed, except perhaps that the new outlaws are nicer.

Historians Carranco and Beard show that more than fifty murders took place in Mendocino County between 1850 and 1880 for which no suspects were ever arrested. (An agent for the California Bureau of Narcotics Enforcement will tell me later, after we have each consumed five beers—his Budweiser, mine Heineken—in the elaborate back bar of the Palace Hotel in Ukiah, county seat to Mendocino, that one reason the Reagan administration should bring in the helicopters is that homicides are occurring at will in marijuana territory.)

Back in the nineteenth century, the mountains were a rough green paradise for outlaws including Black Bart, who robbed twenty-eight stagecoaches along what is now Highway 101. "The only law was the .44-40 model 1873 Winchester administered from behind a tree," according to Carranco and Beard.

Strong stuff. About strong men.

What about the strong women of the north woods? Surely there were strong women? Yes, there were.

One such was Kate Robertson Asbill. Kate married George White's friend Pierce Asbill when Pierce was forty-five and she was eighteen. Pierce gave her three children before he was swindled out of most of his money by certain flim-flam sheep merchants and lost the rest through strong drink and weak gambling. Kate divorced him and married a lonely friend named Basley Manley Cox, who was dying and wanted to leave her his money. B.M. (as he was called) had a lawyer who realized the executor of the will would lose a bushel basket full of money if B.M. acquired a wife. The lawyer-executor "spread vicious rumors" about Kate. He refused to sit with her at breakfast at a leading Eureka hotel, the Vance. So Kate bought a rawhide riding whip at a saddle shop and met the lawyer on Second Street:

> Kate, who was small but strong and quick, lashed at his face and neck again and again while darting from one side to the next as [the lawyer] desperately tried to stop her. He finally fell on his knees bleeding from the many cuts on his face. Kate finally threw the whip at him, yelling: "You dirty cur, the next time a lady sits at your table you treat her with respect."

This is the way to treat a lawyer, then or now or any other time! Or consider, if you will, the common-law wife of a friend of

Pierce Asbill's, William Woods. William and Pierce were out murdering Indians one day* on Island Mountain when they came across two women stragglers. The women charged out of the chamise bush rough, "their breasts bouncing and their breech-cloths flapping," and Woods shouted after the younger one, "She's mine if I can ketch 'er." He lassoed her and "as the noose settled over the girl's shoulders, she jumped up, scratching, biting and spitting."

The honeymooners spent the next sixty-odd years "extremely devoted to one another."

There have been outlaw regions in America. Belle Starr's Oklahoma Indian territory, Sheriff Plummer's Virginia City in Montana, Butch Cassidy's San Juan Mountains, the Seminole Swamp, the mountains of Humboldt, Mendocino and Trinity counties from 1850 to 1870. (Some might argue that the South Bronx qualifies today, and that the Nixon White House did a few years ago.)

Outlaw territory is a place where the law is afraid to go. The new marijuana regions are not really outlaw sanctuaries. After all, deputy sheriffs tool around from time to time in marked cars. District attorneys are elected. Prosecuters try growers in court and once in a while send them to jail. Still, more than most places I can think of, the citizenry have their own opinions on just what does and does not constitute a criminal offense, and enforcement is often left to the parties involved, all of whom have their reasons for not bringing in the law.

What we really have in the marijuana counties of northern California and in perhaps a few other spots around the country today, is an honest-to-God new frontier. The feeling is more like Alaska during the Klondike or North Slope explorations. Losers, winners, square pegs, the sexually raw. Only the adventuresome like frontiers.

Actually, what makes an American frontier is very basic. The chance, not necessarily the probability, that the average sucker can get his hands on good green cash, fistfuls of it. More than he's ever seen. This has a way of bringing out the fun-lovers. . . .

---

*"We'll make this thay last Injin Hunt, and we aint agoin' ter take any Injins to the reservation unless'un he gets thar afore we do."

6

A NECESSARY DIGRESSION:
Poacher Control; Your Author's Hands; Silver Bars; Drug Scare; The Wrong End of a Knife (Twice Over); Arctic Ed Joins the Harvest Run; The Search for Dr. Death; Pheasant Killers; Cat Killers; Tylenol Killers; The Tylenol Sweepstakes

Maxwell is working out with weights.

He's fanning them—one, two, three—against his thighs, straight out in a T and above his head until they crack together. It is a soft sound, not like iron hitting iron. The weights are hardly dumbbells. They're silver bars. Maxwell is pumping silver. He's exercising with 100-ounce troy bars. Each bar weighs about eight pounds. Each one is worth about $1,100, depending on the daily silver quote. The suitcase on the luggage rack in the corner is half full with them.

Sunny day in Ukiah, county seat to Mendocino. The pink door to this trashbag motel room is open.

Jumping jacks. He's doing jumping jacks now with the silver.

"God, this is a sleazy motel, isn't it?" says Maxwell. One, two, three. One, two, three.

"Yeah."

"Good thing I like sleazy motels."

"Yeah."

If you're doing all right in the marijuana trade, silver bars are not a bad way to go. I once walked into the office of a small silver

77

dealer with Maxwell. Maxwell sold the man about $25,000 worth of silver. Maxwell and the dealer shook hands. The dealer waited half a second for Max to introduce himself. He didn't. So the dealer didn't introduce himself, either. No last names, no first names. No paper, no receipts. They both smiled, however. The dealer looked over the silver, walked into the back room to the safe, pulled out the money and paid Maxwell in cash.

Max has a grower friend who was called in by the Internal Revenue Service. The friend had stupidly deposited over $10,000 in cash at his bank. Ten thousand automatically flags the IRS. The agents wanted to know where he got the money, and after they examined the rest of his accounts they wanted to know where he got that money, too. He came to Maxwell and they cooked up a good story. The friend told the IRS he had bought silver when it was low and sold when it was high. Simple. No paper tracks. The friend had to pay a capital gains tax on his profits, quite a big one, but he avoided true embarrassment.

Today we're driving east to Oroville, a small city in the Sierra foothills. Maxwell needs to visit Killer Jack, another friend of his. So do I. Killer Jack has some unusual talents. Jack seems to be able to control his adrenal glands. He can marshal great energy and minimize great pain. Jack can let a pickup truck run over his chest. He can push a knitting needle clean through his arm, or his neck, hang a forty-pound bucket from the needle and later close the wound with will power. Pretty neat. The real thing. Not too many people can pull these tricks off. But Jack has a more practical side, which is more in demand in this sad world of ours. Jack is qualified on most small arms weapons in the U. S. Army. He turned in the highest number of sniper kills in Vietnam. Now he guards oil executives and rock groups like The Who. Or he trains other bodyguards. Jack trained the bodyguards for Anastasio Somoza in Nicaragua before the revolution. Cyrus Vance, secretary of state for the previous administration, wrote him a nasty letter calling him a disgrace to the country. Reagan's Raiders don't write letters like this. On his belt Jack wears a custom-built .45. In his jacket he carries a Walther PPK loaded with exploding bullets. And in his pants pockets—for fun, mostly—he hides a few throwing knives. Killer Jack's very good at what he does.

"I like to think of Jack as Dr. Death," says Maxwell packing the silver bars. "Don't call him that to his face, though. Jack's a hell of a nice guy. Wait till you meet him."

I want to meet Jack. I figure he's the perfect person to take combat pistol from. I would like revenge for my hands. I'll settle for preparedness.

"Oh, Jesus, it'll be fun!" says Max, who looks forward to training with the best. He tosses a nine-millimeter automatic on top of the silver bars and latches the case.

Maxwell has known Jack for a while, although not a long time, and he has very carefully worked up a history of himself that holds water but in no way mentions marijuana. Maxwell's a persuasive fellow. Basically, he trades on his Vietnam days. Jack gets a real kick talking about Vietnam. Not many vets still see Nam as quite the barrel of fun he and Maxwell do.

There's a new hand on board for this run. Arctic Ed. Ed has hidden talents of his own but he doesn't talk about them much. Ed's a husky, you see, and truth be told, he could use a little training himself. He's a city dog. Good at terrorizing cats and mailmen, not so good at jumping into the backs of pickups. This is a shakedown cruise for Ed, with much tossing of bones into the flatbed to induce him to make the jump. He'll learn. Any good American learns what he has to.

It turns out Maxwell has several reasons for blasting out to Jack's. First, of course, for the fun of it. Max likes his guns. Second, he views the session as occupational training: poacher control. It never hurts to know how to fire off six rounds in five seconds into two different rip-off artists. (Jack will teach us the Mozambique Drill: "Mozambique, two in the stomach, one in the beak.") Third, like me, Maxwell has revenge in mind. Or, again like me, he'll settle for catharsis. It's a good feeling, being prepared, knowing that if anyone ever attacks you or yours ever again and you're ready, that too tall scumbag is going to *die*.

Maxwell, too, once came out on the wrong end of a knife. I never knew this. He tells me on the way out.

It was two days before the end of the harvest.

Maxwell, Billie and a neighbor were sitting around the table at the hideaway cottage at three in the morning. They were drinking tequila and doing all-night lines of cocaine and, of course, smoking dope, a predecessor to the killer "polio."

The neighbor had been coked up for a day or two. Everybody was going giddy and getting raggedy. It looked to be a good harvest, a very good harvest.

The neighbor had been sleeping with a former girlfriend of Maxwell's, his ex-old lady, in fact, but she and Maxwell had broken up months before, and Maxwell, so he says, wasn't jealous.

Maxwell was mixing the drinks. He was standing with his side to Billie and the neighbor as he cut limes for the tequilas with a butcher knife. Suddenly the neighbor said:

"Maxwell, you're after me!"

Maxwell turned away from the limes. He was surprised the neighbor was shouting.

"I'm not going to let you get me!"

"What?" Maxwell turned but it was too late.

The neighbor grabbed the butcher knife and shoved it to the hilt into Maxwell's stomach—about three inches below and to the right of his bellybutton.

The neighbor yanked the bloody knife out and raised it above his shoulder to stab Maxwell again when Billie grabbed him from behind and smashed him to the pine floor.

The neighbor managed to run outside. Maxwell sat down. He was able to sit down. He had a problem now. He was wounded. Probably wounded badly. But they had the best part of the crop still in the ground. The wound didn't hurt too much and he was able to stop the bleeding with paper towels. He couldn't figure the neighbor. The neighbor must have gone paranoid. He must have been projecting. He must have been so guilty at what he'd done, even though Maxwell didn't care, that he felt he had to strike out first.

The more Maxwell thought about it, the more pissed he became. He grabbed the Colt out of the truck and started up for the neighbor's land. He still didn't feel the pain, and he wanted to have it out.

Billie and some other friends convinced him this would be stupid. They were finishing the harvest. Nobody could risk a killing now.

Maxwell agreed. He chucked the pistol into the bushes and headed up the road with his flashlight. The flashlight was a big six-volt Ray-O-Vac with a handle.

The neighbor was camped out in a little pup tent.

Maxwell jerked on the tent line and screamed for the neighbor to come out.

The neighbor stuck his head outside the tent flap. Maxwell let him have it in the face. The flashlight smashed against his head and the big battery flew off and the glass broke. The neighbor bolted for the woods, screaming to heaven, his face streaming with blood. He was stark naked.

Maxwell spent the next two days bringing in the sheaves with his partners. He watched as his testicles turned black as rotten fruit and the bottom of his stomach turned black, too, and began to swell.

He knew he had more of a problem now.

Maxwell had blood poisoning of the worst kind. He was afraid to go to a hospital. What would he tell the doctors? They would know it was a stab wound and call in the police, and besides, he realized, he was losing it. He was feverish and he couldn't think.

He remembered an old friend. The old friend lived in Santa Cruz, the California beach town south of San Francisco. Maxwell checked into the top floor of a big fun cinderblock Miami-type hotel on the boardwalk, the best hotel in town. Maxwell had lots of money by now, even if it looked like he didn't have much else. The friend's wife knew a nurse. The nurse was discreet. She stole antibiotics from the hospital and shot up Maxwell every day in his suite overlooking the Pacific. Room service came in the morning and the evening and they didn't ask questions because the discreet nurse tipped them very well.

Maxwell recovered, although he's convinced that he is sterile as a result of the infection.

He pulls up his T-shirt. There's the scar. It looks like a three-inch question mark.

"I like it," he says, "the scar, I mean."

Maxwell tells me something else that went wrong more recently: yesterday. Not all the dope he ran out of the hideaway made it to New York. The shipment came out two pounds short. The Preferred Customer claims that one package was missing when his wife picked it up at Emory Air Freight. Very bad news, not so much because Maxwell's going to be out $4,400, which, however, still buys a lot of collapsy tanks and nights on the town, but because it means there is a crack in the system. Maxwell has sent a lot of dope to the Preferred Customer. He wants to send a lot more. Who pulled the rip-off? Two choices and two choices only. Either there's a mole at Emory Air Freight, or else the Preferred Customer did it, perhaps one of his people without his knowledge. Maxwell finds it hard to believe that the Preferred Customer would steal from his own shipment even though the Preferred Customer knows Max will make good on his guarantee to refund the $4,400.

Still, stranger things have happened. Maxwell knows the dealer has been doing a lot of coke lately and that he's been fighting with his wife. The wife has been doing too much coke. . . . On the other hand, maybe the Emory copilot snuck back during the flight and sniffed out the cargo. An amusing thought. More likely, a member of the ground crew, a loader, might have punctured the main package and counted his blessing. Still more likely, the clerk at Emory's San Francisco office may have put two and two together. A lot of Californians are aware of the state's leading crop, and more Americans are corrupt these days than one might hope. Maxwell remembers this woman well. She was wearing an expensive piece of "pawn shop" New Mexican turquoise around her neck and she looked hip. Max had even hit on her a little, joking about this and that as he filled out the forms.

A smart cookie in the San Francisco office of an air freight company could double her monthly salary by stealing only one pound, and Maxwell figures he's not the only grower to use commercial air freight during peak harvest. He's probably one of a thousand. He'll probably never know what went wrong for sure, but if he decides it had to be the Preferred Customer then somehow he'll have to fly to New York for a day. New York is an amusing town to Maxwell. The place is very violent, and he likes watching the women get out of the taxi cabs along Central Park, but this is peak harvest, and the only scheduled diversion is Killer Jack. . . .

We checked into adjoining rooms at Maxwell's favorite sin pit in Oroville, and Max put in a call to Jack. No Killer.

"Ah, he's probably out testing his crossbow," says Maxwell. Jack is developing a new type of metal crossbow that will be considerably more lethal than anything employed at the Battle of Hastings.

Maxwell's beat. He wants to sack out. He's never been impressed much with Oroville. He recommends a suitably sleazy bar that should give me a taste of what life is all about in these parts. We're several hundred miles away from the strange sophistication of northern California.

"Yeah, check out some of these yahoo spud-dinks," says Max. "You won't believe how slow the human mind can operate."

Oroville is a farming and ranching center about seventy-five miles north of Sacramento, the state capital. It sits beside the Feather River, a passable salmon stream, and Oroville reservoir. If Oroville has a claim to fame, it didn't acquire it until three years ago. Two white teenagers (one about seventeen, the other fifteen) went deer-hunting one day. They couldn't locate any deer but on the way back to town they saw a black boy about their age walking along a railroad track. They didn't know him. He was a complete stranger. They shot him. Shot him dead. The cops asked why. "Couldn't find no deer," said one of the hunters. Nice little California town.

Max knows his sleaze. The bar qualified. I had a few beers, shot a half-dozen games of eight ball, chatted up the locals. One guy was wearing an old pheasant hunting coat with the big slash pocket in the back for the birds. The coat was splattered with dried blood across the front. The guy told me he'd just gotten out of prison three days before. Now he was looking for his little brother. The guy had a cat and he had entrusted this cat to his little brother to take care of while he was in the joint. Mr. Pheasant Killer loved this cat more than life and prudence. Something went wrong. The cat died. The Orovillian in the pheasant coat is drinking now. So far, he says, he's drunk eleven beers. He doesn't like what happened to the cat. The cat was the only thing in the world he loved. His little brother killed this cat. When he catches up to little brother, little brother is going to *pay*.

I believe him.

I picked up a six-pack myself at the Go-Getter's market next to the motel. Oroville is the kind of town that doesn't even carry *Newsweek*. The hot-ticket items at the newscounter are *Easy Rider* (the biker magazine), *Soldier of Fortune* and maybe the *Weekly World News*, the paper that took over the gore-and-naked-tittie tradition from the old *National Enquirer*. The new *Enquirer* is too tame for Orovillians. In the headlines I notice that seven people have been poisoned by the Tylenol Killer so far. I'm surprised the Tylenol Killer seems to live in Chicago. I would think Oroville would be more convivial.

"If ever there were a town where America could in good conscience test the neutron bomb, it would be Oroville," Maxwell will say. "I hate the place. Hate it."

Jack is still not answering. Max and I go out to dinner at a steakhouse where the waitresses wear tight brown pants and cowboy boots with fake spurs. Maxwell tells me he prefers to eat t-bone cold and raw but that this has a way of freaking out waitresses. I can't imagine why.

Maxwell keeps ordering Coca-Cola: "Give me a big bucket of Coke, please." Maxwell's been on the wagon ever since that night when he wound up in someone else's sports coat, the wallet in his pocket. He's resolved not to order another drink until he can remember what really happened.

Jack didn't return that night. By morning rain was falling. Rain is the only thing that could make Oroville worse than it already is.

Maxwell is almost ready to leave today but he wants to see Killer Jack if at all possible. To stay active he starts placing calls around the country, checking on things, trying to see what went wrong in New York.

Making the rounds of bars in Oroville and talking to ex-cons about their dead pets gets old quick. I stopped by the Go-Getter's market again to read the rest of *Soldier of Fortune* when I noticed in the daily paper that the Federal Drug Administration was asking consumers to turn in all packages of extra-strength Tylenol stamped with the lot numbers of already contaminated bottles. The FDA needed to make this direct plea, of course, because nearly every market in the country had taken extra-strength Tylenol off store shelves days ago.

I wondered. If any place in the United States still sold Tylenol, it would have to be here in Oroville.

A special excitement gripped me. I dropped the paper and walked over to the drug aisle.

Sure enough: three bottles of extra-strength Tylenol, looking exactly like the bottles pictured on the front page of every paper in the country for over a week, and on television, too.

I bought all three.

When I got to the cashier, the man behind me, who was about sixty-five, said loudly: "Say, isn't there something . . . isn't there something on the news 'bout that med'cine?"

The clerk looked at the three bottles of Tylenol. News to her. The other people in the checkout line peered up at the counter. There *was* something. They'd heard something. But they couldn't place their finger on it. . . .

I turned to everybody.

"I don't care. I don't care if there's *cyanide* in these bottles. I've got such a splitting headache!"

None of the Orovillians laughed. In fact, my little joke made them all quite quiet. They didn't get it. There was something wrong with Tylenol . . . but what was it?

"The Tylenol Sweepstakes!" yelled Maxwell.

He was lying on his back on the motel bed watching the cable news network on TV. He was naked except for a pair of skivvies.

"What do you mean?"

"First person to score a bottle of tainted Tylenol wins."

"What do we win?"

"Well," said Maxwell thinking, "I don't know." He was gripped by the challenge. He jumped off the sagging bed and pulled on his pants. "Okay," he said, "winner pays the room rent. Okay?"

We rushed to the truck, threw Ed, the husky, in the cab with us. No time to reinforce his jumping response.

"Yes, ma'am," Maxwell would say politely as we entered Safeway or Ron's Stop 'n' Shop, "you happen to have any of that extra-strength Tylenol they're always advertising? Gee, my head hurts!"

Nearly every store in Oroville was still selling extra-strength Tylenol although every other town in America had pulled the stuff long ago.

We spent about $100 each.

Then we drove back to the hotel and dumped the dozens of bottles on the twin beds, switched on the cable news out of Atlanta and waited for the poisoned lot numbers to appear on the screen.

"Oh, fuck!" Maxwell started shouting when the numbers came across. "Mah-thuh fuck-ah! I've won! I've won the Tylenol Sweepstakes!"

And he had, too.

He had a bottle from lot number 1766MA. A California copy-cat killer had been at work, putting strychnine into the bottles rather than cyanide.

You don't have to be told where the first bottle of killer Tylenol with this lot number came from. Oroville.

A few weeks later Maxwell had his lucky Tylenol Sweepstakes winner encased in solid Plexiglas like a scorpion. But before he entombed the pills, for days while we toured around talking to growers, buyers and hands, whenever the discussion got tense, for whatever reason, Maxwell would whip out the bottle and say, "Hey, you look like you have a headache. Here, have a couple of my extra-strength Tylenols."

7

THE SEARCH FOR KILLER JACK, PART II:
Doctor Death Himself Blood Drips from the Map of Saigon; The Governor of California Arrests a Grandmother; The Good Doctor Takes a Break from Killing Communists to Instruct Maxwell and Me in the Gentle Art of Firing the Colt .45 Mozambique-style; What Happens to Cubans Who Smoke Dope; The Causal Relationship between Heroin and Beer; Why Junkies and Scotch Drinkers Should Both Be Put to Death; Toad Bile

Three-thirty in the morning. Something wakes me up. There's somebody else in my motel room. I roll off the side of the bed, between the bed and the wall. Voices.

Only the paranoia of the recently injured. The voices are next door, in Max's room.

The Preferred Customer has woken Max up. It's six-thirty in New York. The Preferred Customer wants twenty more pounds. He wants them immediately. He'll wire the money today. He wants to put the matter of the lost parcel on ice for the moment because the rest of the shipment is moving quickly. Great shit. World-class dope. A new experience for New Yorkers.

"You don't seem to understand," I can hear Max patiently

explaining through the thin, fake, wood-paneled wall. "The stuff isn't with me."

The Preferred Customer says he understands that. Can't Max go get the stuff and air express it as he did before?

"You don't understand," says Max. "Look, you're in New York, right? You know how far Miami is, don't you? Okay, you get in your car and you drive from New York to Miami. That's what you're asking me to do. From here to the stuff to the San Francisco airport and back to here is like driving from New York to Miami."

The Preferred Customer finally understands. He doesn't get out of New York much. Max tells him to be patient.

Back to dreamland.

Max bounds into my room. It's eight-thirty now. He stayed up to call Jack at six. It occurred to him that Jack might have a day job in town. Sure enough, someone answered the phone. It wasn't Jack, though. Jack had moved. The number was old. We've spent two days in Oroville for a wrong number. But Max finally did some detective work that he should have done a day ago. He started calling gun shops. He called the biggest one first and they certainly knew Killer Jack. He was their idea of a Preferred Customer. They didn't have his home number, but they suggested a certain class III dealer. A class III dealer is one authorized to sell automatic weapons and silencers, and there aren't many of them in America.

"Of course," explains Maxwell, "I forgot. Jack is writing a manual on machine guns."

Right. Of course.

Anyway, we score. Jack's home. He's not too busy. We're on for his intensive three-day combat pistol course. We're to bring cash. He'll supply the Colts.

At the restaurant where the waitresses wear tight pants and fake spurs is another surprise. The *Chronicle* is giving the president the big front-page play that it did two weeks ago:

REAGAN DECLARES WAR ON "DRUG MENACE"

**More U.S.
Help for
California**

WASHINGTON: President Reagan, vowing to "end the drug menace and cripple organized crime," unveiled a $200 million proposal yesterday to wage a war against drugs with twelve new federal strike forces, including three in California. . . .

Officials said up to 700 new FBI and DEA agents would be hired along with 500 other agents who would work for Treasury Department bureaus such as Alcohol, Tobacco and Firearms and the Internal Revenue Service. . . .

"The time has come to cripple the power of the mob in America," Reagan said. "Our commitment to this program is unshakeable. We intend to do what is necessary to end the drug menace and cripple organized crime. . . .

"Can we honestly say that America is a land 'with justice for all' if we do not now exert every effort to eliminate this confederation of professional criminals, this dark, evil enemy within?" said Reagan, who appeared tired and spoke with little emotion.

"What a beast! What a dope!"

Max means Reagan. He doesn't care if the entire coffee shop hears him. He quiets down.

"You know, the last time I was in New York, the Preferred Customer [he doesn't call him that] wanted me to meet some burglars for a deal. I said, 'Man, burglars are scum, coming into your house and ripping you off. Just because I'm an outlaw, doesn't mean I like criminals.'"

Max says that Jack looks nothing at all like one of the deadliest men on earth.

Jack turns out to be much shorter than either of us, about five feet seven, 150 pounds, personable, friendly, quick smiles (sometimes too quick) clean shaven, black curly hair neither short nor long. He's younger than I expected, twenty-seven. Max is right except for two things: Jack's body and his eyes. Although he carries no body fat whatsoever there is no exaggerated definition to his muscles, either. Jack does not look like a useless weightlifter. He looks like an animal, a panther or a bobcat, and as I watch him do the most simple things–pass a magazine to his wife, pop a cup of coffee into the microwave, sweep up his daughter into his arms—I notice that every motion he makes is studied and contained and yet spontaneous. If someone suddenly broke through the window, Jack would be able to jump three feet to the side and pull the Walther PPK from his pocket at the same time and fire the clip—one-two, one-two, one-two—and reload as he landed back on the kitchen floor. Jack doesn't walk. He glides. Watching Killer Jack go through the daily motions of life is like watching a strip of those ancient kinescope photographs which break down movement into separate parts.

And then the eyes. The eyes have no color yet they are not black like Max's. They are gray or black or green without ever settling on a particular shade. No matter how much Jack's mouth smiles or the little lines around his eyes crinkle, the pupils only stare. It can be very disconcerting to look into those eyes. Especially when Jack jumps into a story.

Like when Jack lived in Washington, D.C. He was bored. And he hated "niggers." He would stuff newspapers under a thick leather coat and walk down the most dangerous, black-only ghetto streets and affect an attitude of *bait:* There's money on me someplace, asshole. I'm lost. I'm drunk. What you gonna do 'bout it? And then when someone did do something about it, some stupid washroom-type of junkie mugger, perhaps, Jack would whip out a cutting knife and, you know, cut the artist to fucking ribbons. For fun. If that is what you call fun. Because that is how Jack viewed it. He would go out night after night in southeast Washington or south Chicago, where he's from, and just . . . do battle.

Jack is like George Patton. He believes he was born to be a warrior. When word came back from the Pentagon that his older brother had been killed by the communists in Vietnam, Jack lied about his age and joined up. The Vietnamese never made a bigger mistake than killing Killer Jack's older brother. Because he made them pay and pay and pay, and he knew how, better than most warriors who have ever lived on this earth. Gentle Jack would be the Sgt. York/Audie Murphy of the Vietnam War if America could stomach a hero from that war at all.

Jack's kitchen looks like a small arms factory. We walk in. We shake hands. Jack picks up what looks like a polished green-black piece of two-by-four and slips it into Max's hand. Max hefts it, almost twirls it like a baton. This hunk of metal, this stick, is some sort of new Finnish machine gun, vaguely patterned after the Russian Kalashnikov, but better, the way laser disks are better than solid-state stereo equipment. The talk this afternoon will be about guns. Every kind of gun from two-shot derringers to helicopter gunships.

Maxwell takes off his down vest.

He's got a clean new T-shirt on today, special laugh for Jack.

The T-shirt has a drawing of Vietnam splashed across it in dark green. At the upper right is:

WAR GAMES
1961–1975
PARTICIPANT
2ND PLACE

A spot of blood drips out of the place on the map that represents Saigon. . . .

Jack smiles but he doesn't really appreciate the shirt. Jack doesn't like losing. He takes the apparel hint, however, and disappears into his big owner-built ranch house. He returns in a minute wearing a duck-billed hat. The hat is pitch black and new. On the crown is a gold marijuana leaf with a diagonal gold bar through it.

This puts the day in perspective.

"Great hat," says Max, who doesn't dare laugh.

This hat is worn by the special marijuana eradication teams in California. George "Duke" Deukmejian, now the governor of America's leading state, wore a hat exactly like this one when he made a famous media bust four years ago. The Duke, then only attorney general of California, jumped out of *Angel II,* the police helicopter, under the blaze of strobes and mini-cams. This was Willits, Mendocino County. The state arrested a sixty-seven-year-old grandmother, but who cares? The Duke looked good on television and he is now governor.

Jack sometimes accompanies marijuana raids as a demolition expert. If the patch is artfully booby-trapped, Jack's job is to defuse the situation.

But this is not Jack's hat. Jack tells us "those marijuana growers" are going to be in for a rough season this year and next. That's what his friends in the raiding forces say. The raiders are going to conduct themselves as if they were in combat. They're going to carry M-16s and they're going to secure perimeters, and God help any grower who raises a shotgun because the raiders are going to be stone afraid and yet getting off on the situation at the same time because from now on raiding pot farmers will be as much a rush as Nam.

Jack does not do dope. He does not drink, not even beer. He does not smoke tobacco. Jack likes to be in total control at all times.

Jack's daughter is four years old and she is all over the kitchen. No matter what she does, Jack does not scold her. He explains. The little girl never touches the guns, even though there are more loaded guns in this room than anyplace outside of an El Salvadorian barracks. Jack's little daughter is a wild creature but Jack's little daughter minds. She takes after him, says her mother. "I hate to think what will happen to the first boy who puts his hands in her pants when she doesn't want him to," says Jack. Jack plans to make his daughter so proficient in martial arts by the time she is fourteen that the first lustful fool who grabs for her zipper will never live to touch another zipper again.

It's clear after a while that we are not going to begin combat pistol training today. We're just going to feel each other out, shoot the shit, establish the ground rules and pay our green's fees.

Jack likes Max and he likes me, too, for some reason. We pay. Three hundred each, two hundred more for ammo. Eight bills.

Jack takes Maxwell aside, but I can hear what he is telling him.

"I won't accept anybody with a criminal record and no political radicals. I mean, I'll teach somebody who's a little liberal. Just don't have them talk politics around me."

Jack has a button he sometimes wears: I'D RATHER BE KILLING COMMUNISTS. You see a button like that on a man with a custom .45 pistol strapped to his hip, holding a Krashnikov machine gun, a Walther in his pocket, and somehow you don't feel like talking about human rights violations in Latin America, you understand.

As we leave, Jack gives me the stare. The colorless, killer eye stare. This stare makes you understand not only that you are in the presence of a man who is five times stronger than you, a man who can toss a knife through your chest before you can think to dodge, who can stop his own wounds from bleeding when you would simply faint, who teaches that neck-breaking is the most underused self-defense motion, who has trained all his life to kill people and enjoys his work. You are meant to understand that if you betray this man's trust in any way, you are one dead mangled American. Not a nice stare.

But I withstand it. What do I have to hide? Only who I am and why I'm here. . . .

Next day, seven o'clock, on the pistol range.

Seven in the morning is perhaps a little stringent for Max, certainly for me, but we must be prepared for more than cowardly nighttime poachers and junkie cat burglars who show up only under cover of dark.

Jack recommends the .45-caliber Colt automatic pistol for home protection and anything else. The Colt was developed in 1911 to replace the .38 used in the Spanish American War. Certain tribesmen in the Philippines possessed the unsettling ability to absorb six rounds from a .38 revolver and still plunge their spears into the startled hearts of America's first imperial soldiers.

The same thing once happened to Jack behind the lines in Laos. "Shot this gook six times in the chest with the M-16 but nobody told him he was dead. Blew out his entire spine from neck to balls and he kept coming. That guy really shook me."

The .45 has real stopping power and no true American should be without one. It is interesting to note that as America becomes a more violent country, as tens of thousands of marijuana growers arm themselves, and several million home owners and apartment dwellers take up arms for their own reasons, our national weapon of choice has been changing from the .38 revolver or the supermacho .357 magnum seen on the L.A. cop shows to the ancient and elegant .45. Unlike the .357, or any other revolver, the Colt is an automatic (really a semi-automatic). You need only pull the trigger and the discharge recocks the gun. Quicker than a revolver. But most police officers, according to Jack, do not possess the skill or motivation to shoot the tricky old Colt .45 accurately. Marijuana growers, mercenaries like Jack, and homeowners are more motivated. . . .

But your young author can't shoot a .45 automatic.

Once again, it's my hand.

The .45, I'm sure you are aware, has two safeties. One is a little twig of metal that is flipped on and off with the thumb. The other is called the grip safety. It's a plate in the handle that must be squeezed strongly as you pull the trigger. The trusty grip safety is a sane precaution against misfires. Let's say you're riding point on Mindinao Island and a Filipino warrior spears your cavalry horse in the haunches. The stallion rears. You tumble off. The pistol slips out of your hand, hits the hard jungle floor and discharges. You certainly wouldn't want to accidentally shoot the horse in front of you in the withers, would you?

The problem with the grip safety from my point of view is that it must be gripped, and the muscles of my palm have atrophied from the operation following my attack. I can't squeeze the release properly when I fire.

So Jack loans me his own gun. Even a Quaker would cream for this pistol. It's beautiful. Polished stainless steel, balanced like Bjorn Borg's favorite tennis racquet and customized for the aficionado: throated, ramped, Packmeyer grips, and silver-soldered sights, completely accurate. And point of it all, the grip safety plate has been pinned tight for quicker firing.

Now we're ready for the fun.

The target range: five human silhouettes, each a torso and head, tacked to a long wooden frame against a sloping hillside. The hill acts as a backstop. Maxwell and I stand thirty feet back since, according to Jack, 90 percent of America's modern gun battles take place within a distance of ten yards. *BAM BAM BAM!* The .45 drives a momentum of its own. You fire. It cocks. And you're on to the next target.

"Okay, Steve, target one and target three in the head, target five in the chest."

Okay. *BAM BAM BAM!* Three very dead muggers, or for Maxwell, poachers. This goes on for hours.

"No, Max, pull back hard with the left hand, push out hard with the right. Cut the diagonal. Push *out* and *up* with the pistol. Quicker that way. Remember, no brandishing. No warning shots. If they keep coming and you've been shooting them in the chest, take off their face. Mozambique: two in the chest, one in the beak. They'll be dead after that."

I've already killed more punks than savage New York City in a week, and Jack tells us that in real life this pistol has served him quite well, too.

So far he's killed six men with this Colt. One in Laos, one in Orange County (a "beaner" who drew on him after the Mexican robbed a liquor store), and four in Angola. The Angola story even relates to this book. . . .

"Me and two others were working behind the lines. We're supposed to destroy some stuff and we have, but we find our way out blocked. These four Cubans are sitting on the bumper of their truck right in the middle of the road that we have to go down. But they don't see us because they're all smoking dope."

Jack stepped into the road.

The Cubans waved for him to halt.

Jack drilled them so quickly, one-two-three-four, a bullet in each one, and then the secure return, five-six-seven-eight, another slug for each one of Castro's soldiers, that none of the Cubans had a chance to raise their weapons.

But Jack's two companions were frantic. They thought the fire would draw reinforcements. Jack was cool. He began to search the dead Cubans.

"Come on, Jack!" the two other mercenaries shouted.

Jack took his time.

He was looking for something. He was looking for their stash. He found it.

"Hey," Jack says today and smiles with this big goofy grin on his face, those silencer earphones that deaden the sound of gunshots strapped to his head, "and it was dynamite fucking smoke, too! Those Cubans were totally stoned the whole time."

War stories. American stories.

Jack was guarding The Who in Los Angeles. A freak on PCP broke through the police lines with a broken wine bottle in his hand. He managed to slash a groupie across the face and then started to escape down a hallway behind the stage. "Freeze, fucker!" shouted Jack. He dropped to his knees, sighted down the barrel of the customized Colt. Keith Moon, the now dead drummer, ran up to Jack and screamed in his hopped-up Brit accent: "Shoot him, mate! Shoot him!" Moon wanted action but Jack didn't shoot. The PCP freak dropped the bottle and started crying.

Jack used to guard the Six Million Dollar Man, Lee Majors, and he even worked for Roman Polanski for one night. Polanski had just been accused of drugging and raping a thirteen-year-old girl in Los Angeles. He was planning his escape to France. Jack and a partner had been hired for the emergency. The next day when they found out who they were guarding they quit.

Jack was called to Las Vegas. A gambler had lost so much money at a major hotel that he couldn't leave town. Jack's contacts were too afraid of the mob to operate in Las Vegas themselves. They needed an unknown. Jack borrowed a helicopter from an oil exploration company and taped over the markings. The pilot dropped him on the roof and landed in the front parking lot. Jack picked up the gambler in the stairwell at precisely the appointed time. The gambler and Jack made for the lobby and the front door. In the lobby they were met by the mob gunmen. Jack slipped one arm around the gambler's waist and with the other he drew back his jacket. Jack showed his Colt, placed his hand over the handle. He smiled. The mob people smiled. They'd been upstaged. The gambler owed something less than a million. The negative publicity which would have resulted from a gun battle in the lobby of the hotel between a man of Jack's skills and ferocity and three

members of the Mafia would have been worth what? Three
million? Five million? Not to mention the unpleasant lawsuits
from the relatives of guests caught in the crossfire. Jack ushered
the gambler out the front door to the parking lot and into the
helicopter. As they whirled away Jack threw the gunmen a kiss.

I have to ask Jack how much he received for a job like that. Two
thousand plus expenses, says Jack. Two thousand dollars. I must
note that Killer Jack does not know how much he is worth—or else
he simply works for love. . . .

Max mentions the time he was stabbed.

Which reminds Jack of a time he guarded a shipment of uncut
diamonds. Certain respectable Americans, hardly drug dealers,
make so much underground money that to avoid taxes they
convert the funds into uncut diamonds, which are as negotiable as
currency. Jack was driving. A partner was riding shotgun. A heist
car pulled alongside and started blasting. Jack gunned the vehicle
to eighty and started firing one-handed, and even reloaded
one-handed (a skill Maxwell and I will learn tomorrow).

"It was pretty funny," Jack says and laughs. "I think I got the
guy. I spiderwebbed his windshield and then he started weaving
across the road."

But his partner had taken a slug, too, in the leg. The bullet had
pierced the door.

Now comes the funny part of the story.

The partner begged to be taken to a hospital.

"No way," Jack told him. "Not with a bad GSW like that."

Even Maxwell must interrupt to ask what a "GSW" is.

"Gunshot wound," says Jack as if Max had asked what USA
meant.

The partner passed out. Jack pushed a couple of pills down his
throat and drove him to a veterinarian he knew.

The vet put the man on animal anesthetics, sewed him up with
animal sutures and provided him with animal tranquilizers after
the operation.

"He treated him just like he would have any other 140-pound
German shepherd. I suppose it wasn't any better or any worse
than the treatment he would have received in a hospital."

I think my favorite was the Flashlight Drill. Jack feels that most
of the drills and moves taught in martial arts classes or by pistol
experts are so much bunkum. "These guys have never had to kill
anyone," says Jack. Jack was a good teacher because he didn't

adhere to some abstract idea of form. He had used the moves himself in Laos or Angola, Las Vegas or New York. (Jack has a one day anti-rape course. He teaches you how to break the rapist's neck. The course would last only twenty minutes, he says, but it takes him seven hours to convince most women it's okay to kill their attackers.)

The Flashlight Drill is very practical.

Let's say some dickhead breaks into your apartment. Well, you don't want to turn on the lights like a dummy and present a clear target. So you hold the Colt in your right hand as you normally would, but you rest your right wrist on top of your left wrist, arching your left wrist so that the backs of the wrists press hard against each other in a stable platform. (Go ahead, try it.) And in the fist of your left hand you grip the flashlight so that you can flick it on and off by the deadman's switch. (That's what it's called: the deadman's switch. I like that.)

You hear a noise. You touch the deadman's switch. You light up the intruder (the poacher?). The light goes off. You jump a yard to the side so that the intruder doesn't shoot you. You make the split-second decision to shoot, drop the safety: shoot.

It was lots of fun, crouching and whirling around an indoor range, firing at silhouettes.

One time I put four .45 slugs through the paper hearts of two silhouette intruders in about three seconds.

"You know," says Jack, "you seem to have some special sort of motivation."

He's right.

Months ago, while I was beginning to research this book, reading up on the silly attempts in the 1930s to outlaw marijuana because Mexican-Americans and black jazz singers smoked it, checking the medical data (neutral to positive, I'm afraid) and lining up my Deep Sources, I went to a showing of *The World According to Garp* with my first wife. We had just broken up. She lived three blocks away from me in a backyard cottage. For three hours after "Garp," we partied around quite righteously in her living room and in her bed, making me think there might be some hope for our marriage after all. At four in the morning I heard something at the window. This window opened above the queen-sized bed in her tiny bedroom.

"It's nothing," says Jan.

"No, somebody's . . . ." I was going to say "somebody's there," but I didn't get the chance. They were already there.

I pushed Jan to the left and we stumbled, naked, through the corner of the living room to the kitchen. The only way out was through the kitchen. When we got there we realized two, not one, have jumped through the window. One of these pricks is tall, about six two; the other is short, about five feet ten. But they're skinny. They feel skinny through their coats.

"Oh, God, don't shoot! Please don't shoot!" Jan is screaming. But as she's screaming, she's trying to get the door unlocked behind her.

The shorter guy is telling her that he is a "police officer." While he's lying, he's strangling her. After it's all over, Jan's neck and collarbone will be ringed with broken blood vessels.

I am screaming and breaking the windows on the door to make noise because I know the landlord in the front house has a pistol. After we somehow guess in the dark that the two don't have guns themselves, I start swinging at the attackers, avoiding the knife, but not perfectly. One of my last memories is wondering why the guy doesn't drop since I hit him square across the jaw. The door flies open and the lights go on between the houses, because the landlord is aroused, and the attackers quit strangling Jan and run off down the passageway.

I stretched out my arm and pointed to Jan, who was covered in black running blood from chin to pubic hair.

"You've been stabbed!"

And then with my arm outstretched I could see the blood was gushing, shooting like a little fire hose from my own wrist, and I said, "No, it's me! It's me!"

And so, you understand, this part of our story, drilling with Killer Jack, takes on personal meaning. I like playing with the Colt, and when Jack shouts: "Mozambique!" I see the two muggers jumping through the bedroom window almost on top of us, and I imagine myself rolling to the side and grabbing the loaded and cocked Colt, like the one Max sleeps with, and I see the faces in the dark, and I imagine the orange flash of the Colt as the big bullets rip off their eyes and noses and chins and they crumble to the floor in a pool of blood the way I looked in the hospital gurney until they stitched me up in seven and a half hours.

And believe me, it's not lost on me what the police will say later: that these two were junkies, and that my ex-wife is a doctor. The junkies thought she might have drugs on her. This oldest of junkie myths is what got my hands slashed. There isn't a doctor in America who keeps drugs in her house. It is, in fact, a rare public pharmacy that will dispense morphine or dilaudid, I will soon discover, even to those who might enjoy the pain being stilled instead of lying in their beds forcing themselves to consider again and again and again what they will do to the next drug coward who jumps through the window. . . .

Consider the irony if you will: a participatory author writing a book on marijuana, toking up himself day after day during his research, barely able to write in his notebook because his hands have been slashed by drug fiends. Instead, he talks into a tape recorder and sends the tapes to a secretary in the city who types up the notes.

Such a person has examined the connection between marijuana and heroin perhaps a bit more closely than Associate Attorney General Rudolpho J. Giuliani, who muses that the one must necessarily lead to the other while he sips Glenfiddich single-malt Scotch. ("I prefer Tab," Giuliani, the real-life model for the prosecutor in the movie *Prince of the City* will tell me later, "but since that would embarrass me at a party, I order the best.")

Heroin I can take or leave. Junkies I don't like. I don't like anyone who can't control their ecstasy. And I don't like anyone who tries to control other people's ecstasy, either. In other words I puke toad bile when Scotch-swilling Republicans tell me I may drink their drug but I can't smoke my own. To me that's unAmerican. Golly.

Mr. Giuliani feels that while perhaps there is not a causal relationship . . . most heroin addicts do start out on marijuana. I've met a few junkies and I can say that without exception every junkie starts his or her drug habit not with marijuana but with beer. Yes, beer. (And Budweiser or Schlitz, not even very good beer.) And so I hope that after the Republicans have tried and failed to root out marijuana from this suffering democracy that they will start on the real genesis of drug evil: beer.

Junkies! Send them all to England where dope's legal. Or why not El Salvador? Junkies don't care if they're loved or hated. They'd be the perfect soldiers. And talk about cheap. Enough junk to boil down all the junkie soldiers in America could be bought for the price of five or ten helicopter gunships. And the government already knows how to manufacture heroin better than the Mafia. CIA mercenaries produced it for years in the Golden Triangle.

Shall we be sensible for a second? Set up a system of child-abuse centers since seven out of ten jailed criminals were battered and beaten as children? Perhaps provide jobs to every kid who might turn junkie, and every other kid and adult, too? We're talking full employment at decent wages here. No, this last would savage corporate profits, not to mention balloon inflation. Can't have that.

So let's just line the fuckers up against the wall and shoot them all down. That's this author's carefully considered solution to the heroin problem.

After that, we'll move on to the hard drugs—like Scotch. I ask you: Who are the most dangerous drug abusers in the world? Scotch drinkers. Who invaded Cuba and assassinated Lumumba and Diem? John F. Kennedy, a drinker of Scotch. Who pumped half a million troops into South Vietnam as if they were so much sewage from under Dallas? Lyndon Baines Johnson, a Scotch drinker. And who's willing to blow us all to Armageddon to secure Christian civilization? Why, George Bush, Cap Weinberger, Paul Nitze and Eugene Rostow, *Scotch drinkers all,* I believe.

This nation has a drug problem, ladies and gentlemen, and I only hope we knuckle down and do something about it before it's too late.

But I thought we were out on a target range in the California Sierras, talking marijuana.

I wanted to mention one more thing. Jack is a bit of a survivalist, like most other people in these foothills, be they mercenaries, narcotics agents, growers or retired folks. They all think either Reagan or the Russians will drop the big one. Maybe both at the same time. And so they've got their bunkers, and their food stocks stored in fifty-gallon drums next to the dosimeters. Jack's got enough ammo to win the Alamo and even a supply of poison gases too. "It's incredible what's legal to buy so long as you keep it separate," he says.

I like Jack. He calls the truth as he sees it and he's intense. Bullshitters waste my time.

Besides, I watched one evening while Killer Jack cleaned his guns in the sink with soap and water. Now who except for Steve Martin would really do that?

8

FLY-OVER:

Nighttime Is for Poachers, Daytime Is for Busts; A Return to The Land Where Imminent Bust Is Imminent and Many Questions Are Asked: Why Did Fireman Become a Criminal? Why Does He Hate the Sanctimonious Mr. Reagan So? How Are Vanessa Redgrave and the Ayatollah Khomeini Alike? Has This Year's Abominable Weather Been Caused by America's Bizarre Affection for Underarm Deodorants? And, Most Importantly, Does Abstinence Kill?

Eight hours away from Oroville. Top of Crystal Peak, looking down on Fireman's and Sarah's forty acres. I let Ed out to chase woodchucks or whatever passes for alley cats in these north woods. Ed is adjusting well to the rigors of country life.

It is a deep-sea night, with 10,000 stars splashed across the sky like islands. The air here tonight is as good as air gets on this earth.

Long way from: Mozambique! Two bullets in the stomach, one in the beak! GSW's, "Shot this gook six times in the chest, nobody told him he was dead!" "I'D RATHER BE KILLING COMMUNISTS." "Oh, God! Please, don't shoot! Please!" As she opens the kitchen door behind her back . . .

But not that far.

Maxwell and I were gone five days. Five days is a long time in the middle of harvest.

There's been a fly-over on The Land.

This is it! fumes Fireman.

Fireman, Lannie and the kids are chowing down on a righteous meal as Fireman relays the news. We're eating a wild dope-growing hippie dish: tuna fish and macaroni with peas, powdered lemonade, canned pineapple chunks, pickled artichokes and Fig Newtons for dessert.

Really it! Six months into his new profession as marijuana grower and he's going to get busted. His wife Lannie will go to jail. ("Oh, come on!" says Lannie serving the artichoke hearts.) The kids'll have to run for the woods. ("Oh, come on!" say the two oldest.) He's never going to pay off the land and trailer.

Fireman passes around a joint of early harvest. It's pretty and green as a beer bottle. Not too bad, a little rocky, but smooth enough considering it hasn't been properly dried. Lannie and I are the only ones partaking. The kids never touch dope and Fireman has sworn off. His chest used to hurt when he smoked. The young doctor at the Garberville Clinic, graduate of Yale Medical School, said it really might be the dope. Fireman quit and the pain in his chest went away. Who knows?

Fireman says the bust will come down tomorrow at dawn. Definitely. That's the hour. Dawn. The Bureau of Narcotics Enforcement buzzed half the forties in the neighborhood yesterday, dipping their Cessna's dragon wings, coming back for a closer look, probably counting plants and gun muzzles. Tomorrow at dawn. The skies will be black with helicopters. This won't be any county bust, either. The feds are in on this one. Humboldt County's on the map now. Life is going to get highly political very quick. Tomorrow at dawn. That's when the Bogies are going to float down.

I wonder if Fireman has a case of first-timer's jitters. No, he says, he's not alone. All over the mountain, growers have been pulling their plants. People aren't bothering to hang and dry. They're cutting and splitting.

"You see any horse trailers on the way in?"

"Yeah."

"See a lot more traffic than usual?"

"Yeah."

"Tomorrow at dawn," says Fireman.

"Shit," says I.

"Shit is right," says Fireman.

Without transition Fireman breaks into another topic. After a few months of chitchatting with the Fireman, I can tell you that busts are only Fireman's second-favorite thing to talk about. Taxes and *Why He Hates Ronald Reagan* are first.

"Reagan!" starts Fireman. He acts as if the president of the United States sits up all night in the oval office personally devising ways to prevent Fireman from earning a decent living.

Fireman quit paying taxes the very night Ronald Reagan appeared on television to tell the nation that anyone who refused to pay every last nickel of his income tax was a gutless criminal sure as the punk who robs the corner liquor store. (These are not Mr. Reagan's exact words, but this is how Fireman recalls the evening.) I remember that speech, too. Mr. Reagan was so sincere with his ingratiating eye twitches, I thought for sure he would arrest his own attorney general, William French Smith, for questionable tax shelters. Fireman resolved never to pay a penny of income tax ever again. In fact, President Reagan wreaked a major change in Fireman's life that evening. The president's speech was the final straw to Fireman, sitting in Uppie's Corner, Boston, nearly broke, two kids fighting on the couch, the baby and the toddler sick with the flu in the bedroom. The speech pissed him off so much that if you ask him how he, an upstanding driver of hook-and-ladder trucks, ever came to grow an evil narcotic like *Cannabis Sativa–Indica,* he'll stand up and shout about the night the millionaire president *whom he voted for* (Fireman still can't believe he actually voted for Reagan) said that schmucks like himself were criminals for fudging on their taxes. If he was being called a criminal, reasoned Fireman, he might as well start behaving like one.

Myself, I'm a little more concerned about tomorrow's bust.

Should I get off The Land?

I would if I were you, says Fireman. He's driving Lannie and the kids to Garberville.

Well, hey, I'm ripped from Fireman's early harvest, and still reverberating from Killer Jack's. It's kind of hard to run into the woods with a city husky, and what if the raiders confiscate my tapes? Perhaps this was not calm reasoning but it affected me. I decided to walk down to Sarah's trailer and warn her and then drive for safer ground. Fireman says Sarah didn't get up on The

Land until after dark tonight and he didn't get a chance to warn her, since they're not speaking.

The kerosene lamp was glowing inside Sarah's trailer but the shadows seemed strange. They batted around the windows. Monsters inside. I imagined shadow monsters fighting in front of the lamp. Then came a wonderful sound. Deep, deep sighing and much rhythm. I walked around to the front of the trailer where there is a little window without curtains. I looked inside. Sarah and Wyatt were making love.

If I stood on the edge of the milk crate that held the cherry tomatoes, I could see their pink asses rising and falling. Wyatt was on top of Sarah but she seemed to be doing all the work. Her head lolled from side to side and her ankles were locked around the small of Wyatt's back. Sarah's legs are as long as Lisa's. I stood and watched. Even hitched up my pants and told Ed to quit pacing. I thought how nice bodies look in the soft yellow light of a kerosene lamp.

Below me to the left of "Sarah's Ridge," as she calls it, the fog was riding up in a wide river between the valley walls. Fog is beautiful until it touches you. Some people are like that. Above, it was a three-quarter moon, so clear you could consider flying up and touching it. Far above us on the mountain, somewhere near Lisa's barn, came the hysterical yip-yip of a coyote. I noticed that Ed did not move with the sound. Must have been a male coyote. Do you remember in *The Call of the Wild* when Buck, the dog, goes off to mate with a she-wolf? Under the whine of the coyote, closer, was the whir and whip of an owl. Owls are the only creatures born old. They always sound like elderly men rasping away in the nursing home, telling the young janitor how things used to be.

I turned back to the window. Sarah and Wyatt were still paying their respects. How was I ever going to warn them of Imminent Narco Assault?

I realized that I had gone without sexual intercourse for twelve days myself. This is the longest period of sustained abstinence I've suffered since age seventeen. No sacrifice too great for Research, I suppose, but I wondered. Would I die? Does abstinence kill? Maxwell says it does. He may be right. (Please pray for me.) I've heard that certain devoted Catholic nuns, like Vanessa Redgrave in *The Devils,* and equally committed Moslems like A. Khomeini have also survived without orgasm for as long as twelve days, but I

don't know. That's pretty hard to believe. Even if it's true, I think
we all understand what damage it has done to their souls. Besides,
abstinence of any kind is just not American.

So I enjoyed this erotic interlude.

The shadows stilled.

I knocked on the thin metal trailer door.

"Hello?"

Sarah, bright and chirrupy. A little bird, tough and rarely
ruffled.

I told them about the fly-over.

They weren't impressed.

They agreed that fly-overs usually meant a bust, but they were in
no mood to be arrested. They were naked. Life was good. The
harvest was almost over. Sarah and Wyatt are different than most
people. They believe that if they remain naked and fucking, the
violent, repressed agents of the law will be kept at bay like
vampires before a crucifix.

Maybe they were right.

But I had my clothes on.

I decided to hotfoot it down to Ft. Seward, a former railroad
station on the Eel about forty-five minutes away to the northwest.
Ft. Seward, if you recall, is the town where Humboldt's white
pioneers and the army incinerated the last of Chief Lassik's
warriors. I preferred to sleep with the ghosts of dead Indians than
with the possibility that adrenaline-crazed Nam vets would pile out
of the helicopters on top of my sleeping bag, little gold marijuana
leafs decorating their combat caps.

I was not alone in paranoia. Even though it was midnight, the
dirt road to the secondary was crowded with worried settlers
packing out the impromptu harvest. Nobody was about to be
caught with their plants in the ground. (I once bought an ounce of
dope in Boston at a vastly reduced price. The stuff was dark-
colored and almost damp. The dealer called it "Helicopter
Green," which meant it had been hurriedly harvested as the
copter blasted over the ridge.)

At the top of Crystal Mountain before the road winds down for
the locked gate, suddenly, the southern sky lit up in a wide white
flash. The tide had gone out of the night. If San Francisco, the
Alameda Naval Air Station and the Concord weapons depot
where nuclear warheads are stored, were attacked by enemy
missiles, this is what the sky would look like to the south of
Humboldt County. I know I was royally whipped on pre-bust

paranoia, but it suddenly occurred to me that Nuclear Apocalypse had at last arrived. When I was a wee-Chapple and followed the daily megatonage war between Khrushchev and Kennedy, I imagined Armageddon a hundred times over. (I have yet to meet a child my age who didn't go to sleep convinced at least one night that he might not wake up, that thermonuclear war would wipe him and his sisters and his parents away before it was time to get up and catch the schoolbus.) Well, here it was. I switched on the radio to make sure. Steely Dan was singing about nineteen-year-olds on coke and Cuervo. I punched the button. Some wild, wooden minister was spieling on about his bizarre God. Another button: advertisements for tampons and chewing gum. In short, everything was hunky-dory in America this night. No atomic death this evening. I drove on to the gate.

Three months ago in the summer, the gate off The Land to the paved road was fashioned of thin pipe and wire, fastened with a small Master lock. Now it is a thick welded affair secured by an indestructible combination lock and fitted between two sunken concrete posts. Poacher paranoia and rightly so. Both sides of the gate are piled high with boulders so that nobody can drive around.

But trouble seemed to be on the inside of the gate. The dirt parking lot was crowded with cars. Their lights were on. The lights cut through the dust. Half a dozen men stood beside the gate. I stopped. You have to stop to fix the combination. I let Ed out with me. Most people are afraid of ninety-pound dogs.

A guy about twenty wearing a blue bomber jacket came over.

"Got any papers?" he asks. He means rolling papers.

He has a Mexican accent, which is definitely out of place here in the mountains. I wonder if he could be either a poacher or a narc.

He takes a casual, but careful, look over the interior of the Incognito Mobile.

"I guess I don't," I say. "You see that flash to the south?"

"Wasn't that something? Musta been dry lightning."

"Yeah."

A four-wheel-drive Toyota pickup pulls around us. The driver looks scared. He wants off The Land. He wants off quick. The windows of the cab have been blacked out with sun screen.

Three does and a buck crash across the road on the turn into Ft. Seward. I slam on the breaks. Ed sticks his head out the window and starts barking. A hundred years ago there were so many deer in this region that the mountain men shot down eighty at a time and stripped them for the buckskin. In 1920 the state of California launched a campaign against deer poachers. The game wardens drove into Humboldt. When they got to Ft. Seward and Island Mountain, the poachers fired on them, mostly over their heads. The wardens turned back for Sacramento. Like county sheriffs today, the game wardens decided it wasn't worth dying for other people's vices.

The river runs through Ft. Seward. I bedded down in an acorn graveyard beside the water. All night long acorns fell into the dry leaves like gunshots. I woke up a dozen times.

Nighttime is for poachers. Daytime is for busts.

I didn't get too paranoid, however. I went to sleep thinking of Lisa wriggling under the quilt in front of the Fisher stove. Such fantasies tend to quell all thoughts of Armageddon.

When I got up, I decided to take a bath. The sun was already warm. I soaped down in the middle of the Alder Point swimming hole. Ed chased mallards for breakfast and went hungry. Nobody minds skinny-dipping in the Alder Point swimming hole. They used to. The county received complaints all summer long. The growers grew bored with the hassle. They got together and bought the forty acres bordering the river. Now decent people can bathe decently.

I drove further south and arrived clean at Sarah's trailer, but chastened.

Already ten in the morning. The great helicopter bust had not materialized.

Sarah's up and smiling, wearing only her red long johns and black rubber boots. She's cleaning. Branches and tops are strung out on lines all over the kitchen of her trailer.

Sarah says Fireman and Lannie worry about everything. They exaggerate the dangers of the trade. Why, two weeks ago, she says as she snips bud leaf beside the breakfast dishes, Fireman and Lannie couldn't sleep because they thought they discovered mold on one of their plants. They decided this one diseased plant would infect the others and their entire crop would go down. They tossed and they turned and in the morning they drove for the local agronomist. This young man, a botany graduate from a place like Texas A&M, turned over the moldy branch in his palm. He wet his fingers and felt the mold. He touched it again with his wet fingers. Then he started to laugh.

"Mud," he pronounced. "It's only mud."

"They spent a whole night not sleeping because of mud mold," says Sarah. "There are some things you should worry about and some things you shouldn't."

"Where's Wyatt?" I want to know.

"Good point," says Sarah.

Wyatt's still asleep on the foam mattress outside. The bed overlooks the mountains. If you sleep on the foam bed, the dawn sun will wake you up and you can stare off fifty miles at the river, the mountains and the redwoods until you are able to recall your dreams.

"Vice squad! Vice squad!" Sarah shouts out the window.

Comes a sleepy voice.

"I didn't do it."

That's Wyatt. He's a funny character.

Sarah has set the date for her abortion.

Wyatt will drive her to the town of Mendocino where the doctors are supposed to be very good. Wyatt made Sarah pregnant the last time, not this time. Wyatt was gone when she had the last abortion. When he returned, he was broken up.

"Why did you do it? Why did you do it?" he asked. "I would have wanted the child so much."

Wyatt is an emotional guy. Whether he is dependable is another question.

Wyatt stands outside the trailer stretching and rubbing the matter out of his eyes. He's wearing a thick, beaver-felt rancher's hat on his head. Except for the hat, he's buck naked.

Sarah's still talking about the abortion.

"You know," says Wyatt, "you have an abortion and that means you can't fuck for a month."

At first Sarah laughs at Wyatt's contribution to feminine medicine, but then, standing tall in her long red underwear and harvest boots, she bristles. Sarah's had four abortions so far in her life. She disappears into the back of the trailer where the boys sleep and returns with a copy of *Our Bodies, Our Selves*. She finds the appropriate abortion aftermath section and reads aloud that the waiting period is only a week.

This is the sort of thing Sarah and Wyatt fight about.

"Look," Wyatt is about to change his position completely, "the book doesn't say a woman can't be licked out the day after the operation. Slowly, I mean."

This meets with approval.

And it's back to the farmer's life: cleaning dope till the chickens fall asleep.

At Fireman's trailer, too, nobody is bothered that the imminent bust did not occur as predicted.

Half a dozen people are cleaning. Lannie passes around a pitcher of orange juice and the subject of discussion is whether the PTA should lobby the school district to start classes for four-year-olds. Some people think it is too young for a child to leave home. Others think that's when little kids learn the best. Another hot topic is the weather. What is wrong with nature this year? Why are the rains so early? Is it abnormal ocean currents? *El Nino?* Sunspots? The ash screen from the Mexican volcano *El Chichon?* Has America's bizarre affection for gas-powered body deodorants pumped too much ozone into the ionosphere? (I like this last explanation best.)

And then a third subject.

Has everybody heard about Kathy Davis? No. Well, Kathy Davis was a director of the credit union. You know, she lived up on Salmon Creek, and last week a couple of poachers beat her head out against the wall of her drying room.

Oh.

Nice thing to talk about before noon. But nobody seems to mind. Everybody in this room, except for the children, is committing a felony offense each day of their lives. Reagan's Raiders would like to put them away for the rest of time. They're outlaws. They admit it. No big deal. You want to live in the country and you don't have money, you grow dope. You have a head on your shoulders, you understand the risks. The risks are two: bust and rip-off. Kathy Davis got ripped off. Bad.

RIP-OFF

9

THE MURDER OF KATHY DAVIS

Kathy Davis lay upstairs in the loft bed wearing only a nightshirt, a gray and blue flannel man's shirt that reached below her knees. She was short, five feet four, and slight, 110 pounds. Her jaw and nose were delicate, her smile small and white. She had dark thick hair and deep eyes and she looked very good in a bathing suit. Women found her pretty and nice. Men wanted to sleep with her.

Kathy Davis was a pillar of the southern Humboldt community. She sat on the county grand jury and she was a director of the Community Credit Union. She co-founded the hospice to attend to people dying slowly and in special pain.

Kathy Davis was reading *The Clan of the Cave Bear,* an engaging saga as popular with country women from Humboldt as it is with women across America. It was only nine-thirty but Kathy Davis was tired. She rose early each day to tend the plants and her animals: six cats, the chickens, her two dogs Pedro and Petunia. Kathy Davis had a child as well, Nan, her adopted daughter. Kathy Davis had just returned from dinner with the neighbors, a lawyer and his wife, and they had spent most of the time talking about her problems with Nan.

This was a period of worry in Kathy Davis's life. Four months ago Nan, then eighteen, had left home to live on her own. Mother and daughter agreed the time had come but Kathy Davis still worried. The girl mattered more than anything else in the world to her. She wanted to do right. Yet, at the same time, they argued too much and she was strangely jealous of Nan's beauty and growing power.

111

Kathy Davis also agonized about her new profession. This was the height of the growing season and she had already been ripped off not once, but twice. The second time she had found a small child's shoe in one of her two patches, and an expensive Buck clasp knife as well. She had placed the evidence in a plastic bag and listed possible suspects in her diary. She stayed up until four in the morning worrying about the loss.

"I've spent all this time growing the plants," she wrote, "and yet they keep getting ripped off. I can't do anything right, even grow pot."

Kathy Davis did not plan to grow marijuana next year. The dangers were too great. She owned only eleven acres and because they were so hilly she was forced to grow close to the house. Even though partially hidden by a little field of corn, the plants could actually be spotted from the road if poachers or sheriffs knew what they were looking for. Confiscation to her was a real threat. She owned the land free and clear and the house was already built. Her homestead was all she had in the world.

Besides, Kathy Davis felt a change coming to the North Country. Humboldt County was no longer the peaceful utopia she had moved to in 1969, almost the first homesteader on Salmon Creek Road, a narrow blacktop that winds into the oak-covered mountains above the little town of Miranda on the Eel River where Lisa and I had watched the Hoopa Indians play the South Fork Bear Cubs. Property lines were patrolled like military perimeters now. Her neighbors had begun to pool resources and hire communal guards, armed guards. Nobody would think to take a long walk at sunset as they used to. Marijuana had started out as a way to get by and do right. She wasn't sure what it had become now.

Kathy Davis had never been a hippie. She had moved out of Berkeley with her husband to try a new life in the country. She had been a social worker. One of her jobs was to match orphans to families. One day a four-year-old girl appeared in her office who was so vibrant and full of life Kathy Davis decided immediately that she would like the girl for herself. Such a thing had never happened before in the dreary adoption agency. Her coworkers told her she was crazy. Kathy Davis did not care. She had a disease that blocked her Fallopian tubes and she was unable to bear children of her own. She adopted Nan. The new family drove north.

Davis became a family therapist, the type of social worker who counsels people in an office like a psychiatrist. She was caring and she was smart and she was discreet. People began to respect her.

But after a few years she grew tired of her new coworkers. At the same time, her own family was breaking up. She kept her daughter. Her husband got half of their twenty-two acres. She became a waitress, working first the Benbow Inn, the *deco* English hotel that is the most expensive establishment north of San Francisco, and then the Brass Rail, a friendly sort of supper club and bar, a hangout for the provincial theater crowd and business people, not growers especially. She helped start the organic pizza restaurant in Redway, Papa John's, and then she decided that working nights was bad for her relationship with her daughter. To stay home with Nan, she knew, would take a little money. Well, she was a natural gardener, and natural gardeners had grown prosperous in the hills all around her. She decided to grow dope. After all, she smoked it and she liked it.

She was a gentle farmer. She hated even to watch her marijuana plants be cut down. If the chickens on the property needed to be killed—and how were they to be eaten if not killed first?—the job would be given to neighbors. One day a little dog of theirs, a short-haired terrier, contracted a painful disease. There were crystals in the dog's penis. They tried to keep the pup alive but there was no way. She took Nan by the hand and they went down the road to town beyond earshot. A neighbor shot the dog.

She was a conscious pacifist. She had boyfriends and if they came to the house packing guns on their belts, she told them to take them off, put them away where she couldn't see them.

Kathy Davis lay under the covers quietly that night, September 29, a few days before Maxwell and I had first visited the hideaway. She adjusted and readjusted the kerosene lamp beside the bed. The lamp was the only light on in the house. She could not see downstairs.

But she heard them enter.

Her house is unusual. It is L-shaped. One leg of the L, the breezeway, is open without doors almost like a covered bridge with rooms attached. You can walk right through this part of the house. Above the breezeway on the right is a loft with a bathroom and bedroom. The bedroom itself is enclosed by French doors. Stairs lead up from the deck of the breezeway to the loft.

Kathy Davis rolled back the covers and set *The Clan of the Cave Bear* on the nighttable. She started through the French doors.

The men were crossing the wooden floor of the breezeway.

Two of them. Disguised. One with a clear plastic mask that distorted his features, the other under a full-head Halloween gorilla mask. Both men were wearing new garden gloves.

The man in the plastic mask caught sight of her at the edge of the loft. He bounded to the stairs and charged up. He shot out his hand and grabbed her tight by the shirt front and he slammed her body against the wall.

"We want your cash! We want your cash!"

He held a .38 revolver over her head.

"I don't have much," said Kathy Davis.

"I know you do! You always do!" shouted the man. He was husky, with muscled shoulders and a paunchy stomach. She did not recognize him.

He smashed Kathy Davis full across the face with the barrel of the pistol. It was no warning blow. It was the beginning.

She told him she had $1,000. Already her nose was oozing blood.

The man pulled her off the wall but he did not let her go. They stumbled upstairs to the loft bedroom. Kathy Davis reached under the bed and came up with an envelope. The man in the mask snatched it from her and ripped it open. She was telling the truth. A thousand dollars in $100 bills. He shoved the money in his shoe.

"There's more! There's more!" the man shouted.

"No," said Kathy Davis.

The man grabbed her by the shirt again. He pushed her toward the stairs. She stumbled down as he shoved her from behind.

At the bottom she saw his partner. He was thinner, slight. Even under the hideous gorilla mask she recognized Rene Palomino. Palomino was a kid, twenty years old, two years older than Nan. He had worked pot for Kathy Davis's old boyfriend, and had used her phone on and off for several years. Once she had fed him and his wife and baby and allowed them to sleep at the house for two days.

"Why are you doing this to me?" she asked Rene Palomino. "I was nice to you."

The man in the plastic mask was Palomino's uncle, Armando Mendoza, age twenty-eight. Mendoza caught hold of her night-shirt again and yanked her, dragged her into the small drying room tucked under the loft. The drying room was hung with pot, festooned with over sixteen pounds. Bud was everywhere and the sweet skunk smell was overpowering. Mendoza hit his head against the plants and shoved Kathy Davis through to the back. She fell hard against the little day bed. Her back hit the wall. Her legs splayed forward onto the floor.

"Please don't do this to me."

One of the men hit her hard with the pistol barrel. The metal sights caught in her cheek and the flesh ripped.

Kathy Davis put her hands above her face.

"Please don't do this to me! Please don't do this to me! Please don't do this to me!"

She kept repeating, crying, begging for her life.

"Come on, man! Let's go!" shouted Palomino. "Let's go!"

But Mendoza was wild, according to his nephew. He struck Kathy Davis across the face again and again and again, faster and faster, until blood splattered the wall behind them in streaks. Palomino jumped across the room, he says now, and grabbed his uncle's left arm. His hands slipped in the garden gloves. He couldn't hold on. Mendoza swirled and cracked him across the head. Palomino fell to the floor, his lip split. Mendoza turned back to Kathy Davis, and this time, according to his nephew, he hit her so hard that he opened a wide hole clean through her cheek above her teeth. (According to Prosecutor Mike Mock, Mendoza denied smashing Davis with his nickel-plated .38. "However," says Mock, "the hole in Davis's cheek was consistent with the shape of the .38 barrel. The .38 was probably rammed clean through her cheek.") Blood was everywhere, over everything now. Davis was hit once more so hard that the butt of the pistol broke. Part of the handle was later found in her hair. According to Palomino, Mendoza clutched Kathy Davis by the neck with both hands and started to strangle her. Palomino tried to get up. Then Kathy Davis started to urinate from under the nightshirt.

The nephew knew it was all over now. He was sick to his stomach. He couldn't take it. The smell of the pot, the urine, the sweat. He pulled himself up and ran through the breezeway. He ran for their van.

Mendoza dropped Kathy Davis's body on the bed.

He ran outside, too.

Outside someone screamed: "Halt!"

Guards.

While they had been inside, guards from up the road had discovered their van and shot out the tires. This was standard procedure on the road at this time of night.

With his .22, Palomino fired a shot at the guards or over their heads.

Mendoza and Palomino ran for the front of the property toward the pond and then they split up. Mendoza cut left, down the steep hill to the bottom while Palomino cut right across the road in front of the guards and then down the next ridge to Salmon Creek. They scrambled for their lives, smashing into rocks and branches all the way.

The three guards rushed into the house.

Pedro and Petunia still barked hysterically. They had barked all through the murder. Kathy Davis lay in her blood.

The guards had a major problem. This was not the end of harvest along Salmon Creek Road. This was not the beginning. This was peak. Thousands of plants were within days of final maturity. The little female hairs were almost golden brown. If the sheriffs roared up the road, dozens of growers would freak. People were sure to be busted, and more growers might die in the confusion. Kathy Davis was dead and nobody could bring her back. If they just buried her, she would not be the first body to be discovered two months after harvest.

On the other hand, this was Kathy Davis. Not some transient trimmer. People would miss her, and . . . the discussion blasted around the blood-splattered house for over two hours. And people loved her, too. These pricks could still be caught. They were on foot. It was four miles down the mountain to Highway 101. If they called the sheriffs in Garberville, the sheriffs could block the bottom of the road and cut them off. Meanwhile the guards could gather an armed posse and fan down the ravines after the killers. Former Humboldt District Attorney Bernard DePaoli believes the guards warned as many people up and down Salmon Creek as they could before they called the Garberville substation at 3:45. According to Prosecutor Mock, the guards may not have debated what to do, however. Because Kathy Davis's body was in the storage room, they might not have been able to find her immediately. Mock believes the guards came back to the house three times before they located Davis, and that confusion, rather than indecision, may have accounted for the time lapse.

At any rate, the deputies jammed out immediately after calling Eureka.

At 7:05 a neighbor on a motorcycle caught up with Armando Mendoza. The neighbor had a .45 strapped to his leg, and he marched Mendoza up the hill to the sheriff.

At eight o'clock, DePaoli and his senior investigator arrived from Eureka, sixty miles north. DePaoli was armed with a six-inch .38 Smith & Wesson revolver on his hip and a nine-millimeter automatic tucked into his boot. He set up a command post at the Davis house and called for the California Highway Patrol helicopter in Redding. The copter arrived within the hour and now all hell broke loose. There had not been time to warn everybody. The copter blasted up and down the canyons fifty feet above the ground, searching for Palomino, but dozens of homesteaders assumed the bust was on. They heard the WHOOPA WHOOPA WHOOPA WHOOPA and dodged out of their houses with shears and machetes in hand and slashed down their crops.

The CHP helicopter landed in one yard, according to DePaoli, that was flying an enormous thirty-five-foot-tall American flag, "a flag as big as the flag over the courthouse." A short-haired man wearing a baseball cap stepped outside his trailer cradling an Israeli-made Uzi machine gun, a .357 magnum pistol on his hip. The helicopter pilot, laughs DePaoli, granted this pot patriot "instant immunity."

Everywhere the copter landed the police granted immunity. The sheriffs stumbled through patch after patch and walked into sheds and houses festooned with drying bud. They told the growers they were only hunting Kathy Davis's killer. Nobody believed the promise of immunity would last long, and they were right. DePaoli decided to go back the next day to bust, and this time when the copter sashayed low, all the plants had been harvested. In one day Salmon Creek had completed its harvest.

Three days later the Humboldt sheriff's department received a long-distance call from Modesto, 250 miles south in the San Joaquin Valley. The caller was Rene Palomino. He wanted to turn himself in.

This had been their third trip up Salmon Creek. His uncle had forced him, said Palomino. His uncle had beaten him. His uncle beat people bad when he got drunk. His uncle had been paroled from San Quentin three months before from a burglary conviction. They had been heading up the road past Kathy Davis's but the road was blocked two hundred yards from her house. They'd been drinking beer and whiskey all the way from Modesto. They did not want to leave empty-handed. No way.

But they did leave empty-handed, except for the cash. The surge of the killing had become the thing. Mendoza and Palomino ran out on over $20,000 in marijuana, which had been theirs for the taking.

This account of Kathy Davis's murder comes essentially from descriptions by former District Attorney Bernard DePaoli, Prosecutor Mike Mock, the attorney for Rene Palomino, William Connell, and Mendoza's attorney, John Young. Nobody but the murderers will ever know who did exactly what that awful night in Kathy Davis's house on Salmon Creek Road. Palomino and Mendoza blame each other. Rene Palomino turned state's evidence and testified against his uncle.

"As far as who is most culpable, it was Rene Palomino," said John Young after the trial. "He had lived at Miss Davis's home. He ate her food. He ripped her off on at least two previous occasions. She was on to him. Armando Mendoza had never been on the mountain before. He had never met the lady before. If Palomino's hand didn't kill her, he is still culpable."

The trial had its share of errors. Mendoza's clothes were contaminated by sheriff's personnel and rendered inadmissable evidence. According to Prosecutor Mock, the state would only have been able to prove that Kathy Davis's blood spattered the clothes of Rene Palomino. This would have made their star witness look bad so the prosecution declined to enter the bloody clothing from either man. The error also influenced the state to reduce the charge against Mendoza.

Mock joined the prosecution months after the arrest. He is still angry that a plea-bargain was struck with Palomino. "The deal hamstrung me. It wasn't necessary. . . . The tragedy of the case, in my opinion, is that they both were not brought to trial for first degree murder."

Armando Mendoza pleaded guilty to second degree murder, with no use of a weapon, and was sentenced to sixteen years to life in state prison. He will be eligible for parole in only seven and half years. Rene Palomino was allowed to plead guilty to a charge of accessory to murder after the fact. He received only one year in county jail, much of it time served.

It is the saddest of wakes in the most beautiful of places.

Twenty people have left the pond where 120 mourners linked hands and bent their heads and sang "Amazing Grace."

The day is hot. People are stunned. They are stoned. They are drinking.

Twenty people follow Kathy Davis's daughter Nan up the path from the pond, through the front yard past the bathtub rooted to the front porch, a homemade hot tub with copper piping winding around the porcelain. The house is handcrafted of natural beam and cedar shake, the breezeway open in the center. It's clean now. We file through in order to exorcise the killing and start the house over. It is a hot fall day. From the rakish hill beyond the breezeway you can see for miles. The valleys come together in a bowl while rivers of dark, bushy oak trees line the ravines. You can trace the route that Kathy's killers must have taken.

We all sit down against the hill. Twenty feet below on the lip of the steep canyon, Nan holds a white box in her hands. The box is square and it is crossed with ribbon. Nan looks younger than she is. She looks fourteen. She is wearing a yellow print sarong with an open back. I've watched her walk among the mourners. She's smiled. She's been gracious. She's been the solemn host.

She walks the gift box over to a sickly apricot tree. Two feet beyond the tree the land drops 400 feet.

She pries away the ribbon, pulls at it, slips it off the strange Macy's housewares box.

Nan is crying now.

She kneels and pops the lid off the box and slowly pours the ashes into the weeds around the listing little apricot sapling.

The box is full of the cremated flesh of her mother. It is not fine like cigarette ashes, but thick, thick as thumb nails. Potato chips. Broken, ugly, chips of flesh. Then Kathy Davis's daughter falls to the ground and manages to sit. She's crying louder now, no longer the contained host, and the only sound in the valley is the sound of her weeping. Then, far away across the bowl, beyond miles of yellow grass waiting for the next winter rains, comes the sound of gunfire. Gunfire. Somebody is shooting. The shots are loud, from a 30.30 maybe, a powerful rifle, but they do not come one after another as if the person is target practicing. He is shooting at something. Deer? Poachers? The shots ring out and everybody refuses to look across the valley toward the sound. The daughter of Kathy Davis is crying now and she cannot stop herself. Everybody on the hill is crying. I'm crying. It's the singing that makes you cry, I think. Down at the pond I can hear the dull sound of singing, far away. They're singing "Amazing Grace" again:

Amazing Grace, how sweet the sound
Who loved a wretch like me,
I once was lost but now I'm found,
Was blind but now can see.

The only people who do not cry today are the little children, who run circles around the pond and throw duckweed at each other and laugh.

Kathy Davis was a hopelessly unhappy woman. When Bernard DePaoli, the DA, reads passages of her diary to me after the funeral, the words become spooky. She seems to have lived her last year like a patient in the hospice where she worked, a dying woman foretelling her own death.

"I have lived on the edge for years. I will go crazy soon or die."

"Oh, God, I am tired of working. I want to lay down, go to sleep, not wake up, and have everything taken care of. The time is coming."

"I don't know anything about happiness, joy, contentment, satisfaction. I only know about pain, unhappiness, sadness, confusion. . . . Oh, God—help me before I die."

Kathy Davis drove north to paradise, but she never shook the loneliness she brought with her.

I left the wake with Sarah's Wyatt. Wyatt wanted to leave early. He wanted a real drink at a bar. Wyatt hasn't been drunk in three days. I asked him if he knew Kathy Davis well. Wyatt looked at me with his recessed blue eyes over his Dodge City cheekbones. "Sure, I knew her. Yeah. I knew her well. I loved her," he said. (Six months later he will tell me he had two very slow dances with Kathy Davis at a party a year before she died. He'd wanted to go home with her.)

Four months later Nan sits on the curb outside Papa John's Organic Pizza in Redway. She is slightly taller than her mother, perhaps five feet six, with long, dark hair, a long nose and a lithe body. What is strange is that she looks like Kathy Davis, although Kathy Davis is not her natural mother.

She speaks quickly, forcefully and neutrally. So far, nobody in the hills of Humboldt will talk about who Kathy Davis really was. Her daughter plunks herself down on the curb, eighteen years old now, wearing new jeans, new red leather hiking boots and a clean flannel shirt under a green down vest. She speaks about her mother so quickly that she gives a week of interviews in ten minutes.

Nan buried Kathy Davis at the base of the apricot tree, not because the little tree overlooked the beautiful valley but because this tree was always dying. This tree was a problem tree. It produced half the apricots it should have, and then the week before it was to be harvested, raccoons would arrive and devour the fruit. It was sickly. It did not respond to sun or ferti-lizer.

I ask Nan if she thinks the ashes of her mother will help the tree.

"Sure. Sure they will. That's the point. That's why I put them there. That was Kathy."

Kathy Davis was involved with death all her life. Nan believes she knew what was coming the night of the murder, when she was being beaten with the pistol.

"Kathy was not in her body. She had studied Kübler-Ross. She watched dozens of people die. She knew how to separate her mind from the pain of her body and I believe that at some point she just left."

What amazes Nan is that two months before Kathy Davis died she told a friend that she wanted to be cremated and she wanted her ashes to be spread at the base of the sickly apricot tree. This friend was in Mexico when Kathy Davis was murdered. She missed the funeral. When she finally got back to Humboldt, she took Nan aside and told her she had done exactly what her mother had wanted: Have a big party for me and spread my ashes under the apricot tree. It was exactly what her mother had wanted only her mother had never discussed her wishes with her.

Kathy Davis was radical.

What does "radical" mean to an eighteen-year-old in 1983?

"Kathy got into conflicts with the more traditional medical people, the nurses, after she started the hospice. One man couldn't eat. He was dying of throat cancer. He was in a great deal of pain. She fixed him a marijuana tea from the sun leaves."

Sun leaves?

"The sun leaf is the leaf that gets the most sun and is usually the largest. This man did well with the tea. He had approved of the marijuana, of course. The tea took some of the pain away and for the first time in a while he was able to eat and drink and laugh and he appreciated the medicine a great deal. The nurses hated her for what she had done."

Her mother was not lucky in love, says Nan. She picked the wrong kind of men.

"Kathy was not a funny ha-ha sort of person. Kathy was an intense personal relater," Papa John, an old boyfriend, will say.

Kathy Davis took up with some very tough big-time growers. Kathy Davis took up with some very nice, soft, personable men. Kathy Davis was never happy with men. One man whom she loved very much left her when he realized she was unable to bear his child. He returned to his former wife. Kathy Davis blamed herself for her medical inability since if she had gone to a gynecologist before she turned twenty-five the condition, a cyst, might have been reversible.

Bernard DePaoli, the DA, told me Kathy Davis was a major grower. I'm surprised when Nan agrees.

"She was as major a grower as any grower on Spring Creek Road and everybody is a major grower there."

How many plants?

"Twenty-seven. Her marijuana had the best taste. It was the stoniest. It was the best on the road."

Kathy Davis loved her daughter. She loved her animals. She had one hobby: raising iris bulbs. She planted twenty-six different varieties this year.

Nan looks me in the eye but I could be anybody.

"Kathy didn't live to see them come up. I will."

The Salmon Creek growers held a community meeting after Kathy Davis was murdered.

An old man stood up. He said he had operated a still on Long Island during Prohibition. He said everything had gone fine until the outsiders arrived. He cautioned the group of young people. When you harvest, he said, when you plant and when you clean, don't hire anybody you wouldn't consider family. Most people on Salmon Creek Road took his advice if they hadn't already thought of it themselves long ago. But now they went one step farther. They blasphemed Kathy Davis's name. They bought guns.

The guards had been right that night, at two in the morning, October 1. Kathy Davis was not a migrant farmworker. Kathy Davis was one of them.

Something was happening. Something was changing. Was the old back-to-the-land paradise ending, killed by the same marijuana that had helped to float the dreams?

The letters shot into *Star Root,* the alternative paper to the Redwood *Record* and the Eureka *Times–Standard.*

One was long and passionate in its logic:

I did not foresee the degree to which (marijuana growing) would impact on our dream—the dream which I perhaps deluded myself into thinking we had. Now we see violence, greed, murders and perhaps worst of all, complete alienation from each other—millions of gates, a complete breakdown at certain times of the year of everything beautiful we had—cooperation, trust, interdependence, a real love and openness. . . . Was it worth it? I ask myself as well, for sure—the Goddess knows, I wanted money, too. But how much do we need? What are we willing to give up for it . . . ?

Because marijuana is illegal, whole groups of people, particularly women, are deprived of civil justice. Think about it. Can you sue a grower up front for child support? Alimony? Palimony? What if you worked as hard being a housewife as he worked being a grower, but he thinks the investment is his because he was in the patch? And you didn't get legally married because of your existential love of freedom? Can you get even the justice mainstream American women get in the courts, common-law or legally married? Even that? What about the workers? Can you sue a grower for unpaid wages? Breach of contract? Can you join the farm workers' union or create one for pot-growing workers? Unemployment? Disability? Workers compensation? If you get busted in the patch, who pays legal fees? What about neighbors' arguments over water and road access? Tenant farmers and rent disputes? Because marijuana is illegal, the real facts cannot be brought up in court, therefore conflicts are settled by vengeance, blackmail, stealing, violence of all kinds, vandalism and mayhem. . . .

If it were legal, it would be grown much more efficiently and much less wastefully—water lines, little-bitty isolated patches, how environmentally sound is all that? Grown properly, marijuana could be . . . more sound . . . than . . . logging. . . .

I don't mean to be at all self-righteous, but I believe the death of this community lies in the continuation of the greed brought about by the fact that illegally grown marijuana sells for more than legally grown would. Aren't we sick of it? Aren't you? Can't we get rid of the gates and find each other again? What's the cure for this sickness? Legalization is one.

Someone else was quoted: "Salmon Creek has turned to marijuana economically and spiritually. I don't want to paint a golden picture of Salmon Creek in the food-stamp days, but I felt something die when I couldn't walk where I wanted when I wanted. Business is good, but, God, we pay a terrible price for living outside the law. Now we live under the powerful rather than the just."

And Kathy Davis's mother, Bertha Crowell, wrote:

She never willingly hurt any thing or person! She always collected stray, unwanted animals as a child and the same kind of people as she grew older! . . . I'm struggling with enormous feelings of hate for her killers, which is a strange and horrible feeling for me to have. I taught her nonviolence because I believe in it. Yet there is evil in the world which she and I find hard to see. I believe even as they killed her she forgave them as "crazy. . . ."

It is my feeling that big growers and greed in your community are what brought in the criminal element, which Kathy just didn't want to believe. . . .

It is not greed as such that brings in the rips. It is the widespread cultivation of marijuana plain and simple.

"I've talked to convicts in San Quentin and Folsom," says DePaoli, the DA. "The word is out. If you want to make some money when you're released, go north and grow or trim—or rip someone off."

Few urban criminals feel comfortable traipsing around the backwoods. They stand out like TV dandies and they don't know what they're doing. But some, like Mendoza, manage too well.

Ironically, the tales of marijuana wealth often emanate from the larger operations, but the family grower is the vulnerable one. Small-timers are less armed and rarely hire guards. A sleazy rip may rod up to Humboldt with wide eyes on taking down a hundred plants, but people who grow a hundred plants (or 500) aim to harvest their own and they usually pack the firepower to prove the point.

The Davis murder forced every grower to look at his or her own operation. It was a gruesome killing but marijuana farmers are good at facing facts. I asked Sarah what she thought of Kathy Davis's murder. They had met many times. Her reaction was quick. Sarah had only one line.

"She knew the poachers, didn't she?"

Maxwell never met Kathy Davis, but like Sarah he looks at the situation with a cold eye.

"Look, she was unarmed, alone, no guards. Her plants could be seen from the road and the road was paved, with no gate. She was the easiest target in the area, plus she knew the rips. Right?"

Maxwell shrugs. Kathy Davis went out in the worst way possible and he feels sorry for her. But he shrugs nonetheless.

"You know," says Maxwell a day later, Kathy Davis still on his mind, "I used to have a little scene down in Arizona, in the middle of nowhere. A neighbor comes by for dinner one night and he pulls out a couple of those Whammo slingshots. He'd just bought them in town. He turns to everybody—this was long ago and there weren't too many rip-offs—and he says, 'This is all I'm going to need to protect my crop.' I guess he meant he'd use the slingshots to scare away deer. He always thought we were too gung ho.

"A couple of months later I get this call from him. 'Maxwell, you've got to come up here. You've got to bring guns. Bring people. I'm being ripped off. God, you've got to help me!' I mean, he was *highly* concerned.

"So I go on up the mountain to his place. He and his partner are scared. They're lying back in their cabin doing nothing. They knew the rips were outside waiting for dark, but they didn't know what to do. So I broke out the weapons. Jesus, we had rifles, a couple of shotguns and pistols. My partner had a machine gun he'd smuggled back from Nam years before. I mean we were ready. Exactly at sunset we ran out on the porch and started firing into every nook and cranny. Oh, fuck! Did we let 'er rip. Full rock 'n' roll. Twigs and branches are flying off all over the place. Orange flames everywhere. We're screaming and hollering, 'Come out you sleazy motherfuckers! You dogs!' We just had a great time! And after we'd fired that off, we hit the booze and we got stinking drunk on Jack Daniels until midnight, and every so often we'd run outside and fire a few clips into the mountain and scream, 'You scum bags, you scummy fuckers, you come on out!' It was one hell of a morale booster, let me tell you, and the rips never did come back."

Too bad Kathy Davis never knew Max.

BUST

10

AT LAST THE NARCOS, EVIL AND AWESOME:
Greed Grips an Amateur; Automatic Bust
Bait; May I See Your Warrant, Please; "Go
Back, Pickles"; Inadequate Guard Dogs;
The Soft Drink Situation at the Eureka Jail
. . . Parrot Fish and Brahms; Rabbits and
Deer; A Stray Herd of Moronic Cows
Chews Off a Crop; Pauline Kael and John
Leonard Appear at an Aging Hipsters Para-
dise to Discuss Japanese Buddhism

When he finally heard it, Fireman was roofing a new house miles
away from his own land. He was straddling the cornice, a hammer
in his hand, three galvanized nails sticking out of his mouth like
toothpicks. *WHOOPA WHOOPA WHOOPA WHOOPA WHOO-
PA.* The sound was low yet strong, as even and rhythmical as a
synthesized drumbeat. And then, suddenly, it was on top of them,
sidling evil and awesome over the final ridge, like a giant wasp. At
last, after all those false runs. Oh, God, the narcos, Reagan's
Raiders in, yes, the fuselage gleamed, it was two o'clock, the sun
was full and hard—a red-white-and-blue U. S. Customs' helicopter, a blood orange stripe down the side. The real thing, no
white-knuckle fly-over far away in the sky. This was it.

The big machine skimmed the tree tops fifty feet above the
closest clump of redwoods, closer, coming for them, and Fireman

could see men inside clutching their weapons. Fireman touched the tip of his tongue to the roof of his mouth. His tongue stuck.

The copter spotted them.

It dropped into the clearing and began to circle the house.

Somebody on the roof shouted out: "Let's split!"

The owner answered through his teeth: "Don't fucking move! Don't act guilty! They want to see if we'll run. My plants are out of the ground."

Mine, too, thought Fireman, and he broke into a crazy kid's smile.

They stayed put, three growers building a house, helpless on the roof.

Suddenly, the big helicopter let out a long fart of a backfire, a thirty-foot trail of black exhaust. Fireman and the others went hysterical. They started laughing so hard, scared and excited at the same time.

"It's a missile," screamed Fireman.

"No, man," said the owner of the new house, who was a combat vet, "they're landing."

"It was like Vietnam!" Fireman will say later. "My stomach was churning."

In northern California, when the helicopters come down, there are only two reference points. If the grower is a vet, then, "It was just like Vietnam!" If she isn't, then, "It was just like *Apocalypse Now!*"

But the helicopter was not after Fireman and the others. It rose off the house and dished below the next ridge.

The raiders circled a large green modular trailer, the nicest home for ten miles, the only place with electricity and a telephone, the one homestead that stood out cleanly from the rest, the elaborate prefab house with fuchsia-covered trellises that I had admired the time I took the wrong road out of Sarah's and Fireman's forty, the suburban house of George and Trudy Ralph, the retired couple.

George Ralph heard the helicopter. He walked across the living room and watched it through the kitchen window.

George Ralph knew why the copter was coming down. He knew it was law enforcement. But he was mad. They had no right to come onto his land. He opened the door and strutted out of the house. He intended to confront these illegal invaders.

Where is your warrant? May I see your warrant, please? This is what he planned to ask them.

George Ralph was wearing a charcoal-colored car coat, a nice zip-up sweater, clean blue jeans and black rubber boots. Except for the black boots, he looked out of place in this land of combat lace-ups, camo caps and checkered wool jackets.

The pilot picked a flat spot a hundred yards southeast of the house.

George marched across the field he considered his front lawn. He marched straight for the settling helicopter.

He stopped. The wind from the rotors whipped at his trousers and blew dust in his face. He smoothed his hair. The grass flattened all around him.

The rhythm of the blades frightened George Ralph and for some reason thrilled him as well. In eighteen months in the wilderness this was the loudest noise he had heard.

He took another step and then he froze.

The machine was still ten feet off the ground.

George Ralph could see the men in their green and black uniforms. He could see their faces.

The door opened slowly, with effort, like a freezer door.

The copter still had not touched down.

A man bent low and then jumped.

The man was wearing black coveralls and a black cap. He clutched an M-16 combat rifle to his chest with both hands. The man hit the ground in a crouch. He grunted so loudly that George Ralph could hear him above the whir of the rotor blades.

The man ran for George Ralph.

"Down! Down!" the officer in the black coveralls screamed.

George Ralph did not get down. He did not move. He could not move.

The raider caught up to him.

"Down! Down on the ground!"

George Ralph dropped to his knees but that was all.

"Hands behind your back! Down!"

The raider, Sgt. Richard Cairns, on loan as a consultant from the San Francisco Police Department to the California Bureau of Narcotics Enforcement, aimed the barrel of his M-16 at George Ralph's chest.

"All the way! On the ground!"

George Ralph wobbled. He lowered himself onto his shoulder. His chest pushed into the dirt. He put out his hands ahead of his head. He was not afraid but he felt the dirt under his fingernails and he could smell the green winter grass.

Sgt. Cairns kicked George Ralph's legs apart and frisked him. A man fifteen years older than himself, Ralph was not armed. Cairns bent over and handcuffed Ralph's hands behind his back.

Behind them, the helicopter was on the ground, blades still twirling.

One raider sprinted for the main house. Two more ran down the hill to secure the greenhouse. Two others charged into the woods to the right of the greenhouse.

Cairns left Ralph cuffed in the field and ran up the knoll to the house, too.

"Police! Come out! We have a search warrant!" he and the other officer yelled.

The agents were amped out. They were hyped. They imagined the growers inside going for their guns.

Inside, Trudy Ralph did not know what to do. She put her hands over her head. Noises came out of her mouth but not words. Trudy Ralph was forty-nine years old. All her life she had been an elementary schoolteacher. The two children started bawling. Trudy Ralph put her hands over her ears. Two women guests were up for the weekend. They started crying along with the children.

Sgt. Cairns pounded on the door.

"Come on out! We have a warrant!"

The women filed out before the children and the officers handcuffed them.

Mrs. Ralph's thirteen-year-old schnauzer, Pickles, was last out. Pickles is about twelve inches high and rather bald for a dog.

Sgt. Cairns could see there was nobody else.

He started to smile.

"What kind of guard dog is this?" He pointed to Pickles.

Sgt. Richard Cairns is five feet ten, curly haired, broad-lipped, strong, and average-looking.

"There was a man," he says, "his wife, two kids, and two other women. The guy was mellow. He was down in the dumps that his crop was being ripped off. Then he started yelling and hollering. He seemed spaced to me. The woman kept calling us fascists. We had pictures of the land and buildings and a layout of the place. Everybody knew what they were going to do. There were six of us in the helicopter. Two of us were to go to the field, two of us to the house and two of us to the greenhouse. It was run as a military operation. The man was in the field. I jumped out of the helicopter. It was ten feet off the ground. I didn't want him to get to the house, in case he had guns there, because it could have turned into a siege. I ran him down in the field and handcuffed him."

In the woods near the greenhouse were two open, uncamouflaged patches of full-grown marijuana plants. But the greenhouse itself was screaming with dope.

"The guy had $75,000 to $100,000 plainly," says Cairns. "There was pot drying all over the place in his house. The plants in the greenhouse were monsters. They were twenty feet high. I'm serious."

Outside, the children kept crying and there was no way to stop them.

The raiders brought chainsaws and machetes from the helicopter and cut down the plants in the forest and at the greenhouse. All told, they harvested 172 mature marijuana plants. Inside the house in the closets they found plastic bags stuffed with manicured bud.

The agents sat the Ralphs, the children and the guests in kitchen chairs while they clumped the plants in the center of a twenty-foot rope-mesh net. They hooked the net to a cable which hung from the belly of the helicopter. The copter lifted straight off the ground and hovered while the agents cinched the net. The bundle was as big as a full-sized American pickup truck. And then it was gone—up, up and away, easy come easy go. George Ralph's first-time crop flew off like Dumbo the elephant, and George would have cried on the spot, except that like old Dumbo he was a little smarter than he looked. The raiders hadn't gotten it all. . . .

The strange green parcel was towed north for miles to Alder Point, where I had gone swimming the morning after the fly-over. It was lowered into a ten-wheel dump truck at the Louisiana–Pacific two-by-four mill, and then driven to another L–P mill at Samoa, near Eureka, the Humboldt County seat, and burned in a high-intensity pulp mill boiler. Unlike consumers, the government burns wet pot and requires a hot flame.

When the helicopter returned from Alder Point, the raiders started to load up Mr. and Mrs. Ralph. They left behind the children and the two women, a lesbian couple.

Trudy Ralph was in tears as the agents marched her to the helicopter. She had never felt handcuffs before. She had never been arrested. Trudy Ralph is short with dull blond hair, the color of old uncut wheat. She was wearing blue polyester pants and a dark cotton blouse with big golden pheasants stamped across the front and back. She bit her lips throughout the arrest and she wondered what would happen to them, to her, after it was all over.

They would be marked for life, wouldn't they? She had been a schoolteacher. If she went back to work and they were convicted, wouldn't the state take away her license? She remembered the words "moral turpitude" in the boiler-plate contract she signed every year. Wouldn't a conviction for marijuana cultivation constitute moral turpitude? She was furious at George for growing this stuff. She didn't smoke it herself.

Trudy's little dog Pickles trotted after her as she was led to the helicopter. Pickles barked and whined, and the sound of Pickles made Trudy cry harder.

"Go back! Go back, Pickles!" Trudy Ralph kept shouting as she wept. "Stay! Stay! Stay! Stay!"

Trudy Ralph was dreadfully afraid that Pickles would be killed by the helicopter as it lifted off.

"Please, please take my dog back to the house," she begged the deputies. "Pickles will be hurt. She's thirteen years old."

The agents held their M-16s and told her to climb into the helicopter.

Trudy Ralph, who had never been arrested for anything in her life, refused. She refused for her dog. She fell on her face in the dirt with her hands cuffed behind her back and she cried, "Please, please take my Pickles back to the house! Somebody, please!"

The agents were embarrassed.

One of the narcotics officers was a woman, a deputy sheriff on loan from Humboldt County. She put her arm around Mrs. Ralph's shoulder and asked the other Humboldt deputy if he would carry the little dog back to the house. The deputy grabbed the dog. Trudy Ralph picked herself off the ground, still sniffling, and climbed into the helicopter.

The Ralphs were flown to Alder Point where they watched their crop being hauled away in the National Guard dump truck. They were searched again in Alder Point, and then driven by car to Garberville. In Garberville they were patted down a third time and driven to the county jail in Eureka, an hour and a half northwest. There they were searched a fourth time, but now the procedure became lax. They were booked together as man and wife, and then told to walk down a jail corridor and lock themselves into a cell. George didn't bother to lock himself up. He found a phone and called friends. He wanted a lawyer, fast.

After he dealt with the lawyer, he traipsed back to the booking desk and asked if they had a Coke machine. He was thirsty.

"Coke machine? Coke machine?" the deputy asked and rolled

his eyes. "Where do you think you are? Everybody in this jail would get strung out if we had a coke machine."

George liked this touch. He liked it a lot. It was the only part of the bust that he found funny.

George Ralph is a fifty-two-year-old hipster. He's aging but he's aging well, with his own brand of humor. He has all his hair, which is still thick and red. He is a tall, almost gawky person. He stands about six three, and his eyes and Adam's apple both bulge a little too much. He looks like a hayseed, which he is not, or exactly like, if you will, a gentle, misplaced trumpet fish cruising the wrong reef.

Trudy Ralph is wearing the same blue polyester pants and pheasant print blouse she was wearing the day she was busted.

Their house is an elaborate three-part mobile home, but it is carefully put together. It looks like a factory-built prefab, the kind of house whose components are brought in by flatcar. No railroad reaches into these hills. The Ralph home was trucked slowly over the narrow blacktop from Eureka. The house cost $41,000; the fifty-five acres underneath it, $55,000.

Inside, the walls are paneled with plastic wood, imitation oak. Thick brown carpet covers the floors. The sofas and chairs are striped brown, blue and beige. The lamps could have come from any Holiday Inn. The living room ceiling is beamed with thick wood, darkly stained. An inexpensive chandelier hangs in the dining room. The kitchen is large and well-designed with a counter and chopping block island in the middle.

Trudy Ralph has prepared a full dinner for us: pork roast, cauliflower covered in Kraft cheddar cheese, white rice, a salad of apple bits, raisins and chopped celery. The meal is good. Before dinner, George offers a special Mendocino sherry he has discovered; with dinner, Carlo Rossi rosé. All night long we drink rosé until between the three of us we have killed a gallon. Every quarter-hour or so, George leaves the room to change the album. George likes Segovia and Brahms.

The view out the dining room window is as wild as it is outside Fireman's or Sarah's trailer: hills of long green grass spotted with black oak and holy madrone, dropping to gulleys thick with muddy winter runoff, rising in the east to saddles of clean white snow on the mountains.

The house of George and Trudy Ralph is a blue-collar Shangrila.

Trudy comes from Philadelphia, a solid if restrictive Catholic home. Her father was a high-school principal. Her parents tried to stop her from going off to the University of California at Berkeley for college. She went anyway and she wrote them once a week. She still writes them once a week.

George was poorer, a bright, ex-Navy man, Korean War vet, almost a conscientious objector, but not quite. He was extremely curious to see Japan and the Navy seemed the easiest way.

Both were attracted to the fun of the beat scene in San Francisco. Jazz thrilled Trudy. They met one night on the long line outside the Black Hawk, the premier underground jazz club of the time. Virginal with a taste for the wild, Trudy seemed very pretty to George. George was authentic. He had a goatee and he'd been all over Asia, and that very night he made Trudy laugh and laugh. Nobody had laughed much back in Philadelphia, not in her parish.

They took an apartment in North Beach, at the top of Telegraph Hill, which was dirt cheap then. The City Lights Book Store and the Co-Existence Bagel Shop were blocks away. They stayed up late drinking jug wine and discussing Japanese Buddhism while they listened to FM radio station KPFA, which featured a wacky Pauline Kael, who was to become the clever and rarely wacky film critic for *The New Yorker,* and John Leonard, who became the book critic for the New York *Times.* George and Trudy felt that San Francisco in the 1950s was the center of culture for a de-culturized nation, with Joe McCarthy frothing in the Senate and Dwight Eisenhower golfing in lederhosen on the capital links.

George didn't play the saxophone. Trudy didn't write poetry. He became a union truck driver, she a schoolteacher. They moved south of the city to the peninsula. They wanted to start a family. They still followed jazz, and they joined the Bach Dinner and Dynamite Society.

Times changed and George and Trudy did little changing with them. But they followed along. George, at least, never quite went straight. Throughout the 1960s he experimented with uppers and downers, amphetamines and Seconal, and also the psychedelics like marijuana. He tried LSD once and did not like it. He was given some heroin and for half a year he sampled that, too, careful to snort only once a month. He did not tell Trudy for several years.

Trudy was serious about teaching. She volunteered at an almost all-black school in the Fillmore, the ghetto, and then she worked at the San Francisco school district's first "free school." The day she was hired, the principal interviewed her with an unlit joint of

marijuana cradled in his hand. Trudy was bothered by the free
school, not so much by the principal's use of marijuana but by the
lack of discipline. The children did not seem to want to learn.

At home, their neighborhood was changing. It had never been
expensive to begin with and now blacks were moving in, displaced
by high-rises and urban renewal downtown. George and Trudy do
not believe they are prejudiced, but they noticed that once
minorities moved into their neighborhood, their house was broken
into three times in three years. Trudy was attacked one day in the
school cafeteria by two black teenagers. Her eye was blackened.
They wondered about moving to the country, but they decided the
schools would be better near an urban area.

They had one child, a son. The boy was bright and straight-
forward. He developed the best qualities of his parents. He was
neither slightly frightened by the world, like Trudy, nor alienated
like his father. He was a child of the 1960s but he never did drugs.
He studied and he dated girls and in the late 1970s he enrolled at
Laney Junior College in the East Bay. He said he wanted to be a
biologist and he was reasonably good at computers, too. His one
passion was motorcycles. When he was nineteen, he was riding his
used Honda down the Bayshore Freeway to a night class. A light
rain was falling. The driver of a semi-truck changed lanes and did
not see the boy. Their son was killed instantly.

George broke down.

He began to show up late for work. He sat around the living
room for hours. For a year and a half he became "physically ill."
Doctors found nothing wrong.

He and Trudy flew to the Caribbean to try to shake him of his
depression. They began to eat up their savings. Nothing worked.
They thought of moving to the country again. That might bring
them happiness. Nothing tied them to the city any longer.

They drove the backroads of California and Oregon looking for
land. Few places were affordable. One of them was Humboldt
County.

They fell in love with their fifty-five acres. For months they
camped out in a Sears' umbrella tent. Camping at last brought the
blood back to George's heart. He loved it. The smell of the grasses
and the dirt, the tan oaks, the manzanita, the Douglas fur. They
gathered arrowroot, mint and bay leaves for soups and drinks.
George saw bobcats early one morning, first one, then another.
He'd never seen bobcats before. He'd only read about them. He
watched deer every night and his wife set up a salt lick. George

was from Michigan and he longed to shoot a buck for the table with the ancient World War II carbine he owned, but Trudy put her foot down. No deer were to be killed on their land. They saw rabbits and quail. They marveled at the taste of unchlorinated well water. Most of all, George liked to sit in front of the tent in an old canvas chair and look out across his land at sunset. *His land.*

He began to recover.

And with his health, his hipster's yen for experimentation returned. This land, he realized, would be ideal for growing marijuana. He knew that the younger people in the hills were growing dope, although he had no idea how many were, or what kind of people they might be. He rarely talked to his neighbors. They drove by so quickly that Trudy put up a SLOW CHILDREN sign. They noticed that carloads of people drove by their land in the spring and summer, and that they were gone by winter. One day some cows wandered onto their acreage. Trudy went next door to find out who they belonged to. The neighbor on the right told her they belonged to the neighbor on the left.

"Poison the fuckers," advised the neighbor on the right. "That bastard lets them run free and they might eat your crop."

Looking back on it all, George and Trudy admit they were curiously naive.

But, George told himself, wasn't he rolling joints with sax players when these kids were in elementary school?

So he took out a subscription to *High Times* magazine and mail-ordered manuals on marijuana cultivation. He decided a greenhouse would be foolproof. How could anybody see what was growing inside? And if the sheriffs couldn't see inside, they would have no grounds for probable cause. They would not be able to secure a valid search warrant. George even hired a friend to fly over his land from different angles. The friend told George the big greenhouse looked like nothing so much as a small pond or a sheet of glass. George was excited by this. It never occurred to him that any greenhouse in Humboldt or Mendocino County was viewed as automatic bust bait, as Maxwell says. There were few legitimate hothouse farmers anywhere in northern California.

George was getting greedy. He was stoked now. He knew people in the city who might unload his crop. He wondered if they would pay as much as the listings in the "Trans-High Market Quotations" published in *High Times,* maybe $2,200 a pound, perhaps $2,500. He would be sure to get the best seeds. In one year, he calculated, he could make more money than he had earned in his entire life! He built the greenhouse, and then he decided to risk the two patches in the forest. He row-cropped them like corn. George even today has never heard of *guerrilla growing*.

A week before the bust a fixed-wing plane dipped low over his land. This plane was taking photographs of his two patches to make sure they had not been harvested. The BNE already had preliminary photos of the patches from their earlier fly-over when Fireman and so many growers on the other side of the wide valley had panicked and pulled. The day before the bust, the phone rang and George answered it. The caller was a man. In a formal, businesslike tone, the caller asked if he, George Ralph, planned to be home the next day. George said, "Yes." The man hung up. The next day, the day of the bust, in the morning, not even the early morning, the Customs' helicopter flew a preliminary trip low over their land. Neither George nor Trudy thought to run.

"What could we have done?" Trudy asks even now. "We had the children and our guests, and there were all the animals. We had to stay."

11

BUST GIDDINESS:

Skies Black with Helicopters; Twenty-four-hour Colonics; Once More, Cocaine Abuse; The Talking Eggplants of Murrish's Market; Ronald Reagan and *Psycho;* The SAC Headquarters of Humboldt County; Wounded Eagles and Dead Sheriffs; You Haven't Seen Anything Yet . . . THINK ABOUT CHANGING YOUR LIFESTYLE; What to Say If Your Lover Does Not Get Along with Your Corgi . . . Sarah Completes the Harvest; Lisa Meets the Naked Grower; Billie Mimics Gene Kelly; Maxwell Quotes from Ecclesiastes; Fireman Takes on the President . . . The Government's Price-support System for Marijuana . . . Growing Dope Is Not for the Faint at Heart; Marijuana Orchids; Keep Your Wits About You; Splintering Duck Decoys with the Uzi . . . Graves Registration and The Honest Count; Ida Murphy Gets Busted by the Granite City (Illinois) Police Department . . . Toe-sucking and The Great Lumber Strike of 1935 . . . Let's Dispense with the Rumors, Shall We?

The big raids started quietly in Del Norte, the depressed logging and fishing county north of Humboldt, bordering Oregon. The helicopter swept south down the back country for several days before growers realized what was going on. Then, instantly, the number-one question in northern California became: Where would the raiders hit next?

Farmers poured into Garberville until the little town, marijuana capital to the continental United States, screamed and bristled and laughed like a gecko.

In one day every motel room from Eureka to Ukiah was occupied, and more marijuana will be manicured this week in front of color TVs tuned to "Different Strokes" and "Family Feud" than gets processed in a month on Colombia's Guijara Peninsula.

The simple signs of Bust Giddiness are everywhere. Flash fights over the pool table in the Cellar, open coke abuse in the Greyhound bus depot (a hill exile splitting for San Francisco pulls out a vial and a spoon and offers the clerk a heady snort). Conversation is goofier than usual as some real space-cookies abandon their barefoot plantations and seek refuge in the hot tub at the Sherwood Forest Motel. A twenty-two-year-old hill woman in a T-shirt, no bottom, straddles the Jacuzzi jet: "So we stay here a week. So what? I'm going to fast. I just did a twenty-four-hour colonic anyway." Groans from everybody else in the tub. "Hey," says space-cookie, "it really grossed me out at first, too, but the idea is to get rid of all that shit, right?" Right.

And in the vegetable aisle at Murrish's Market I run into Marty, the friend of Lisa who had played host to the naked cleaning ladies. Outwardly, Marty is playing his usual Lower Manhattan neurotic cool. "Where do you think they'll bust next, Marty?" "My place," says Marty. "If I were the cops, I'd bust me next." He shrugs his skinny shoulders. "I've got shopping to do." No big deal, these raids. And then Marty turns back to me. "Did you see those eggplants move? The eggplants, they're moving." We both stare at the enormous pyramid of fat purple eggplants. The eggplants are not moving. Marty shrugs again. So the eggplants are not moving. Eggplants don't have legs, right? He turns. With an earthy thunk like a copter crashing on soft ground, the entire pile of eggplants suddenly comes crashing down all around us. "Hey," shrugs Marty for the last time, "what I tell you?" Marty maintains.

But the Cheyenne Mountain, the vibrating Strategic Air Com-

mand Headquarters of Incoming Rumors is Janey's Cafe. Janey's
is the gossip center of southern Humboldt. When things are
happening, there's no need to pick up the phone or watch the
news. Go to Janey's. They already know. If they don't they'll make
it up.

Janey's is a tiny cafe across the street from the post office in
Garberville. People pick up their mail and walk across the street to
read it at Janey's over a cup of coffee or a chocolate malted. Janey
doesn't make mere shakes or frappés. She makes malteds. There
are a thousand Janey's Cafes across the Midwest. The farmers
come in and share the news with their neighbors. This is Humboldt
County, California. The farmers grow dope and the news today is
the bust. Over the counter is a framed movie poster of Ronald
Reagan pulling a six-gun. "When Ronnie was governor," Janey
once told me as she turned three cheeseburgers, "the caption we
pasted on the glass said, 'Tax Everything.'" Today, the day the
word of the raids has hit Garberville, the cook, who is eighty-two,
three years older than Janey, says the balloon out of the president's mouth should be changed to read: "Screw Everybody."

Janey's also functions as the library annex. There are two wire
racks full of used paperbacks. No need to pay. Borrow and return,
or replace the book with one of your own. Titles like *Mandingo,
Tales of the South Pacific, Psycho, I Never Promised You a Rose
Garden,* true classics of pop lit. Janey also collects magazines that
she thinks will be of particular interest to her customers. An article
I once wrote for *Mother Jones* was "cussed and discussed," and
today she has a spin-off piece, the current *Newsweek.* The
Newsweek is marvelously timed. It came out yesterday. Already
Janey's backup copy has been stolen. This one has been encased in
plastic like an airline magazine. The cover: a North Carolina pot
farmer standing in a field of marijuana holding a pitchfork in one
hand and a Colt AR-15 in the other. The title: "Grass, Guns and
Money, America's Billion Dollar Marijuana Crop." The colors:
garish. Yellow background, green plants, black-and-red ski mask
over the grower's head. This is a definite sold-out issue in northern
California this week and Janey is guarding her remaining copy.

I sat in Janey's for most of the afternoon. The conversation,
condensed, said it all.

A young logger wearing a red-and-black wool jack shirt, dirty
boots, five-day beard, funny eyes, one askew. He's waving the
day's San Francisco *Chronicle.* Everybody reads the *Chronicle* in
marijuana country. Marijuana growers, the professionals like

Maxwell, like to laugh at the news. The way they earn their living
is so unreal that the New York *Times* would seem like fantasy to
them. The *Chronicle* is the sort of paper that would rip the news of
World War III out of the UPI wire machine. But they would send
out their best two reporters in a helicopter of their own to cover
the Wild Busts in Humboldt.

Brandishing the *Chron,* the logger quotes from the front page to
anyone who will listen and even if they are already talking
themselves, the patrons at Janey's are capable of listening at the
same time.

The logger reads a quote from an hysterical grower: "The cops
are dropping in on the growers, pointing their guns at them and
making them lie spread-eagled while they cut down the crops.
They're cocking rifles at people's heads and hitting places without
search warrants. They've blackened the skies with helicopters."

"What?" asks Janey. She's reading another newspaper, a local
one, the Redwood *Record,* to see if she knows anyone who's been
arrested so far.

"Blackened the skies with helicopters," repeats the logger.

"I wonder how many helicopters they really have?" asks Janey.
"Some say four helicopters. Some say two. I say two."

I love the way Janey talks. She has no idea whatsoever how
many helicopters are being used by the BNE, yet she always
sounds so sure of herself, so logical.

Janey puts down her paper on the counter. She lays her bifocals
on top of the paper. She looks first at the cook who is spreading
chopped onions on the grill, then at the logger, then at me.

"You know," says Janey, "they're riding the nets."

"Riding the nets?" asks a blond woman about thirty-five with a
little dish nose and teased hair, the kind of woman cowboys fight
over at closing time, the sort of young American who might have
lived in Malibu for a summer with the fantasy of becoming a movie
star only to be knocked up by a kid surfer and have an abortion
that didn't work out quite right. An American with something
missing.

"Yes," replies Janey, completely sure of herself. "The agents
ride these nets. The nets are hung from cables. The cables are
attached to the helicopters. They ride in at tree level, and they are
ready to kill, believe you me."

Janey says this as calmly as if she had seen the raid on the
Ralphs' herself. It's clear old Janey imagines Sgt. Richard Cairns
to be naked to the waist, like Conan, The Barbarian, gripping the

copter cable with his left hand, clutching his M-16 in his right, hollering "hi-de-ho" over the madrone ridges at 120 miles per hour, the rifle open to full rock 'n' roll so that he can spray the women and children who run screaming from solarized cabins.

The young logger is still reading the incredible *Chronicle* article.

"A sniper shot at and hit an airplane being used in the raids. San Francisco head of the BNE Jerry Smith said that the report was in but could not be confirmed."

"Shooting at helicopters!" said somebody standing behind me.

"The National Guard is involved," says the Malibu blond, "like, out in Hawaii."

"There're roadblocks in Alder Point."

It's the old cook speaking. I know he hasn't been in Alder Point since the summer.

A minute later someone new says that L–P, the Louisiana–Pacific timber company, is tight with the narcs and is letting them use the Alder Point mill as a staging area.

I love all this bullshit. And then comes the live voice of approximate reality.

A cheap little Panasonic radio sits above the stove. The voice on the radio has been talking without inflection all the while. Suddenly, there is a pause and then a wild crackle like the aftermath of the Hindenburg explosion. The radio station, KERG in Redway, a brand-new radio voice, has opened its talk show to news of the raids. Sixty growers have called in already today but this one is different. Looking back on it, I think the deejay opened the pots, the controls, so that the sound came in twice as loud. The burst of static silenced even the patrons at Janey's.

It's a grower on the front lines.

"You want to know what's going on?" asks the grower. "Turn up your fucking radio!"

Janey doesn't touch the radio but everybody is as quiet as toast. *WHOOPA WHOOPA WHOOPA WHOOPA*. It's the frightening sound of a large helicopter. No mistake about it. This crazy grower is being busted right now. He's called in to KERG and left his receiver off the hook.

The sound of the helicopter fills the little cafe.

Irrationally, everybody is scared. I'm scared. Another long crack of static. The live, busted grower goes off the air. We're all quiet as ice cream.

"Golly!" says Janey finally, and she is as articulate as anyone in the room.

Growers will jam the KERG talk show for the next three days and the station will cancel normal programming.

An attitude of bemused hysteria has gripped Janey's Cafe, and northern California, too.

Several thousand homeowners begin to complain that the narcos have cut the phone lines. Nobody denies the agents jam Channel 9 on the CB when they make their raids but Lew Florence, manager of Continental Telephone, refutes reports that phone service is being cut during these raids.

"Absolutely untrue," he tells the Redwood *Record*. Temporary outages are occurring because too many people are trying to use the lines at the same time. Presumably to warn neighbors and find out what's going on.

The idea that marijuana growers have the outrageous *hutzpah* to call into radio stations and the major California newspapers and protest the raids galls certain representatives of the North County establishment. Like Gene Cox, Humboldt County sheriff, who will be leaving office in January.

"These guys are a bunch of phonies. They're blowing smoke, buddy. If they are such heroes, how come there are five dead people this year directly connected to narcotics, mostly in Humboldt? Is this what America wants? These guys won't admit they are doing something illegal. And yet they don't want it legalized. There's too much big money in it right now. They're hollering like a wounded eagle right now, because they are getting hurt in the pocketbook."

(Gene Cox was a wild man. One wonders, had he not been a sheriff, and had he been twenty years younger, perhaps he might have become a marijuana grower himself. In late fall, Gene Cox was murdered by a man recently discharged from a mental hospital. The man was shooting people at the Eureka trailer court owned by Cox's father-in-law. Sheriff Cox appeared after work to straighten out the situation. . . . Humboldt County, ask Chief Lassik, is a rough place to operate out of.)

Even the running congressman gets into the act. Gumball-faced, bald-headed, seven-term Republican Representative Don Clausen tells reporters from the *Star Root,* "You better start thinking about changing your lifestyle. You haven't seen anything yet." The rather pro-marijuana publication prints Clausen's picture under the caption, START THINKING ABOUT CHANGING YOUR LIFESTYLES, and some will say on November 3, less than two weeks away, that Mr. Clausen went down as much to his support of the marijuana raids as he did to unemployment and his gung-ho backing of the MX missile.

I love Janey's but I left a few hours before dark. I considered driving the ninety miles to The Land.

I ran into Sarah at the Beacon station.

Sarah was not worried about the raids. Sarah was worried about her relationship with Wyatt. Wyatt did not get along with Sarah's aging corgi, Amelia. The man at the Beacon station who had filled her propane tank had told her that it was a bad sign if a lover did not get along with a woman's dog.

Anyway, forget the raids, she was going to the movies. Garberville has only one movie theater. The matinee was *Heartland*.

So, after a long lunch at the Woodrose, the cafe with the best food in town, but a cafe where some of the waitresses may be so slow the question of brain damage may honestly be raised, I was surprised to run into Sarah a second time and hear that she had decided to drive out to The Land and harvest her remaining plants.

Someone in the theater had whispered to her that the raiders had popped the Ralphs. Sarah is nobody's fool.

We drove the long road together.

The Land was very beautiful. The fog was crab-walking up the valley. Eight mountain peaks are visible from Sarah's trailer. The mountains are green, blue or brown depending on light and rainfall. Twenty miles to the south, rain is falling but the sun is shining on top of us here. We feel lucky. Sarah always feels lucky. We stand on Sarah's Ridge and watch the blue rain crash and drench a hundred other growers. It is cold today, even under the late fall sun. The air is arctic air. It has never been breathed before. A tan mountain lion could amble across the tip of Sarah's Ridge. One did last week, and there are few mountain lions left in California or America. But I have a feeling that no mountain lion will come out today. Sarah and Wyatt are fighting, and pumas are sensitive creatures.

(One hundred and fifty miles south, Maxwell is harvesting his last thirty ditch-riders. Sarah may be an unreconstructed hippie and Max may be a vet philistine, but they are both equally shrewd cookies, and you don't have to be overly shrewd to decide to finish your crop when the evening news is screaming the narcos will if you won't. Max tells me later that they had a grand time. Billie was coked and he started singing "Singing in the Rain," like Gene Kelly. Dancing like him, too. It was raining over the hideaway.

Max got into the spirit. He called the harvesters over to the papa
pickup when they were done and he delivered a brief, mock
oration. He quoted Ecclesiastes. All about harvesting the herb
and sowing the seed. We shall go rejoicing, bringing in the
sheaves. "Hey," says Max, "I look at the Bible every night. Only
the cover, of course. But they seem to have a Bible in every motel
I've ever stayed in.")

I broke out some sardines and Sarah brought out some Triscuits.

As we sat on a stump, Wyatt skidded down the steep hill. He
was carrying a fourteen-foot marijuana plant across his shoulders.
One of Sarah's leggy *Sativa* crosses. What a monster. What a
beauty. There is a small bundle of roots at the bottom. Marijuana
has a small root ball. Wyatt had yanked this plant, the last one, out
of the ground without bothering to cut it. He tossed it across the
trunk of the Incognito Mobile and began to clip off the branches.
He stuffed the branches into a green garbage bag.

Sarah is still more concerned with Wyatt than with the final
harvest.

"You either have to live by yourself or you have to compromise.
There's no other way."

Wyatt ignored her. He clipped the big branches and he stuffed
them in the bag. Wyatt wanted to be done and off The Land.

We're munching. Wyatt's clipping. The view is cold and beautiful, and then Fireman came down the hill. After all, half the forty
belonged to him and Lannie.

Fireman was a little embarrassed. He hadn't been speaking to
Sarah. But this was serious. For weeks, Fireman had been trying
to set up a meeting with Sarah. Sarah had been leaving her stalks
in a big garbage barrel in front of her trailer. The green stalks
could easily be seen from the jeep road. Fireman imagines that any
poachers who sawed the lock at the gate and went blasting by
would rightly assume that pot was drying in her trailer. Then, after
they had looted her trailer, since she was rarely there, they might
climb up to his and beat in Lannie's face the way those prick-bags
had beaten in Kathy Davis's.

Fireman is on a roll. He would have made a good old-time
newspaper man. He always says what he's thinking and he's always
thinking something.

"This Reagan running around making out like all these family
growers are in the Mafia. It just ain't so. What's he going to do
when everybody finds out the truth? I hear the raiders are coming
in without warrants. Pitch and bitch, pitch and bitch, you can pitch

and bitch all you want but it's not going to do you any good. They're not arresting people. They're just taking the crop. So what are you going to do, sue? It's bad business. These raiders are afraid to go after the heavy scenes. There's people in this county with Uzis, M-16s. The raiders are going for convenience. For the statistics. What they want to do is get as much marijuana in as short a period of time with 'X' amount of money so they can go before Congress and say, 'Look, this is what we did in two weeks in Humboldt County, California. If we had ten times as much money or a hundred times that much, think what we could do! We could begin to put a dent in the marijuana problem.' It's all politics. It's all part of something big."

Sarah could care less.

"Hi," she sparkles to Fireman.

She looks at everybody.

"Well, this is a day of celebration for me. I've got all my plants out of the ground."

Lannie, Fireman's wife, climbs down the hill. She's puffing. She's got a cold. She says she's going to quit nursing the baby today or tomorrow. Still, she's cheerful enough. She says she was in the country store this afternoon after they busted the Ralphs. She was in line at the checkout counter. Two old ladies stood in front of her.

"Just think," said the first old lady, "when that helicopter passed over, the net must have shook enough to seed the whole town."

And the second old lady replied, "I wouldn't mind if a few seeds landed in my yard. Those volunteers are the hardiest plants."

To Lisa, the busts constitute a price-support system. The system is a bit more exciting and violent than the government's subsidy for corn or soybeans, but it leads to the same result: prices are floated artificially high. Marijuana is a weed. Retarded alcoholics could grow it. If it weren't illegal, why would America's hedonists be so willing to pay $2,200 a pound? That's how much Lisa got this year. A representative of sorts from the L.A. music industry drove his rented Blazer all the way to her door. She didn't have to risk Emory Air Freight like Maxwell. And it's nice, smiles Lisa, to hear the results of your labor on the radio. . . .

Nobody relishes the bust season, but most realize it's a necessary part of the game. "Growing dope is not for the faint at

heart," says Maxwell. The professionals take the necessary precautions, and trust to Jah and Jack Daniels to see them through.

Lisa, Maxwell, Sarah and Fireman all follow at least the basic
rules of guerrilla growing. Don't get greedy. Don't grow in the
open. Scatter the plants. Tie down to manzanita and holly. Hide
the plants under fir and madrone. Accept a lower per-plant yield.
Bury the grow lines. Do not build a greenhouse the size of the
infield at Shea Stadium.

Lisa, Maxwell, Sarah and Fireman are not even state-of-the-art
growers. State-of-the-art growers in the hills might be the ones
who buy used semitruck trailers and bury them in the hillsides.
There's no way to see these growhouses from the air. In the cities
growhouses have a weak point. They use a lot of electricity.
Narcotics enforcement goes to the electric companies, and the
utilities provide them with kilowatt data. Lofts and warehouses
that suddenly consume the electricity of aluminum refineries are
easily singled out. But the state-of-the-art rural growhouse may be
powered by banks of solar cells or by heavy-duty Honda genera-
tors.

My favorite advanced outdoorsman has suspended 200 plants in
plastic buckets rigged to ropes and pulleys under oaks and
redwoods. These plants live fifteen feet above the ground like
certain Hawaiian orchids. To water them, the grower bought a
secondhand Cal–Trans tanker truck. The plantation lies along the
banks of the Eel. The truck sucks itself full from the river. Then
the workers drive it around under the trees and spritz the plants.
(This from Maxwell. I've never seen the operation myself, so we
must, adhering to the rigid principles of journalistic integrity
followed so far, label this only a good anecdote.)

Besides guerrilla growing, common sense and a willingness to
defend the crop, the last precaution the good grower takes is
intelligence. It doesn't hurt to acquire a DEA manual. It doesn't
hurt to drink a few rounds with a secretary from the sheriff's office.
In my talk with Bernard DePaoli, the bitter, ousted district
attorney from Humboldt, I am told there were no less than five
secret investigations of sheriff's department secretaries, sheriff's
deputies and clerks in the county assessor's office where the raiders
pinpoint ownership to secure their search warrants.

Lisa points out that the busts are coming at the tail end of the
harvest. The main event was over ten days ago. Most everybody
has pulled and sold or stored by now. She wonders how the raiders

could have so little knowledge of how marijuana is grown. Or is it that they have no contacts at all in the grower community? The raiders seem to be hitting the newer subdivisions. The farmers getting popped are very often first-timers. First-timers and stupid. Like the Ralphs.

The professionals appreciate the George Ralphs of the marijuana frontier, because the George Ralphs run interference for the Lisas and the Maxwells.

They erect wartish greenhouses. They snake yards of plastic pipe across the wilderness. They row-crop and they row-crop big. And when the *WHOOPA WHOOPA WHOOPA WHOOPA* finally sounds across the ridge, they don't even think to run.

The George Ralphs are bust bait. Not too many smart farmers get arrested. Knock on wood, barring fate, pray to the goddess, don't get cocky, too loud, too drunk in the wrong bar, piss off the former partner or sleep with his wife while he's passed out in the other room. You know, keep your wits about you.

But the other side appreciates the George Ralphs just as much as Maxwell does. Losers bring an easy bust. An easy bust is a safe bust. Maxwell or Fireman would never shoot at a uniformed raider. They're armed for poachers, not police. The media view of the violent grower is mostly myth. "If they ever caught me unawares," says Maxwell, "like asleep in the field, I'd bury my pistol and come out with my hands touching heaven. That's what lawyers are for."

In a review of the Drug Enforcement Agency's 1982 report on its Domestic Marijuana Eradication/Suppression Program, *High Times* magazine made an interesting comparison:

> In the course of raiding 4,657 pot plots and arresting 2,512 'subjects,' (agents) confiscated only 785 weapons. That means they found a gun—or some sort of weapon—in only seventeen percent of the raids, or in thirty-one percent of the arrests. According to the National Rifle Association, fifty-seven percent of the households in rural America own firearms; so it would seem that pot farmers are much less prepared to defend their property with guns than are most rural Americans.

On the other hand, certain badgers, pushed to the edge, snow-snotted with coke three days running until as the fourth dawn peeks over the ridge, they wander out to the pond to splinter duck decoys with the Uzi, such alienated Americans can tend to make an error in judgment, and errors in judgment are what kill narcotics officers.

The George Ralphs allow the narcos to chalk up easy points.

Here Maxwell draws a comparison to Vietnam.

Maxwell once was given a distasteful job in the Army. A job he's never forgotten, just as he's never forgotten the horse-people at the Colorado State Mental Hospital.

The job had a name: graves registration.

It was a simple job. Max would go out after a battle and total up the dead. Hey, hey, LBJ, how many gooks did we kill today?

First time out, Max kept an honest count. Then he tried an experiment. There's a head. There's a leg. There's another leg. How many bodies we got here? Well, three. I mean, who's to say for sure? Nobody's going to stitch the gook back together, are they? Three Xs on the clipboard. Three dead bodies in that quadrant.

Maxwell's creative zeal paid off. The captains always picked Maxwell for grave registration. He delivered the most flattering count. A good count meant a good fight. America's plowboys had not died in vain. No way. They had killed X number of gooks. The body count proved that. Maxwell's body count. Graves registration.

So when the raiders pounce a greenhouse in Whale Gulch in the middle of June and rip out 600 ten-inch plants called starts, half of them males, the other half females, that's 600 marijuana plants period. How much dope do you get from 600 marijuana plants? Well, two pounds per plant. That's what the DEA says. Two pounds times 600 plants is 1,200. Well, at $2,000 a pound that's $1.2 million at the wholesale level; call it a conservative $3 million on the street. No matter that half the plants must be culled out as males, many will die, others will be eaten by rats, mites and deer, and most of the plants will be nurtured under conditions of guerrilla growing and yield far less than a whopping two pounds per plant.

The newspaper account will read: "Agents from the California Bureau of Narcotics Enforcement (BNE) in conjunction with Mendocino County sheriffs and observers from President Reagan's new Strike Force Against Narcotics destroyed an estimated $3 million worth of marijuana in a predawn raid in Whale Gulch, Mendocino County, California, on the state's rocky northern coast."

Graves Registration. The Body Count. The Easy Bust.

Of course, in all fairness, the agents must rip off the Ralphs. They're so obvious. Neighbors complain. Good citizens . . . who drink Cutty Sark. . . .

Not every bust is an easy bust. Some busts look easy but present hidden problems. Other collars must be worked for. And some busts turn out not to be busts at all.

Take a bust with unexpected problems. *The Okra Bust.* At about the same time the raiders descended on Humboldt County, a truly serious narcotics investigation took place in Granite City, Illinois. It was dark. The sun had set. An unnamed officer responded to a complaint from an unnamed citizen. The citizen reported a field of unabashed *Cannabis* growing behind his apartment building. The officer showed up. No warrant. No matter. He ripped up the ninety-four marijuana plants. The plants were very healthy and each was four feet tall. Only problem, they weren't marijuana plants. They were okra. Okra, that hardy, eccentric, southern vegetable. The okra belonged to Ida Murphy. Ida Murphy woke up early the next day, went out to water her okra and—no okra!

"It's embarrassing," says Captain Robert Astorian of the Granite City Police Department. Okra "resembles marijuana somewhat. Of course, the lady was upset. I called her up and apologized and told her to contact our city attorney about damages."

I don't know: Did Ida Murphy claim $2,000 a pound for her okra?

Not every bust is as easy as Ida Murphy's or George Ralph's. Lisa told me about a bust far to the south, in a county where marijuana is not yet the leading crop. Wine grapes present the main competition.

The sheriff had targeted a major bust. This bust looked juicy. The sheriff was up for re-election. He invited in the leading television station to witness the raid. The raiders found real marijuana, not okra, but they had a worse problem, considering the glare of the mini-cams. The legally targeted, warranted, bust yielded only twenty plants. Twenty plants does not impress the prime-time viewer. What to do? The sheriff was a quick thinker. He stepped into the helicopter himself and they rodded up and down the canyon. The sheriff had no additional warrants. He didn't care. He told the growers to produce pot and produce it quickly. The growers complied. Americans are not stupid. When the bust was over, the sheriff exhibited a major haul. The television station was pleased. A thousand plants. One grower. Four million dollars wholesale. The news changed to flooded Mormons in Utah, hurricanes in Tonga.

Of course, the bust would not stand up in court, but that was not the point. The point was to look good. The point was to re-elect the sheriff.

But my favorite bust of the harvest season was not a bust at all. Money is made in strange ways in the United States. Porno actresses draw salaries just as surely as Nancy Reagan's appointment secretary. San Francisco is the capital of porno films because the judges there all belong to the American Civil Liberties Union and the weather is suitable for filming most days of the year. A solid "X" actress had decided to have a child with another open American. This man was a sensible person. He loved orgies and he loved his child. He bought land in Humboldt because he figured anything goes north of San Francisco. He brought the child with him.

After several years the actress changed her mind about the child. She wanted custody. So she hired a private detective, and the private detective hired a helicopter, and the helicopter winged its way low across Humboldt. Its mission: to land on the father's land and steal back the child.

The male porno actor did not grow dope. He did not need to. He only appreciated the freedom of the region. At the same time, all his neighbors wore clothes to their work. They were familiar with helicopters and helicopters meant a different thing to them. Helicopters meant a bust. Or a very creative rip-off. Daytime is for busts. Nighttime is for poachers.

The helicopter came in low over the ridge. Growers ran to secure their crops. One farmer grabbed his shotgun and hid. The copter hovered and then landed behind the actor's cabin. The grower could see that the passengers were private, not law enforcement. He showed himself and his shotgun. The detective was gung ho. He pulled out a pistol. The grower fired a blast over the helicopter. The detective and the pilot decided they had made a serious mistake.

The actress never did recover her child. She was persuaded that the father was the more gentle parent after all. The detective wound up in court in Eureka. But the actress still wanted visiting rights. She bought forty acres at the bottom of the mountain. Lisa once visited her to get her opinion on a matter of concern to the

fire committee. Lisa is chairperson of the volunteer fire department for the mountain.

The actress welcomed Lisa. The actress was outside tending her
garden. Zucchini and coyote squash. She was dressed for Humboldt, with a cartridge belt around her waist, a Colt .45 tucked in
the holster and a fancy lady's Stetson. Nothing else at all from
instep to Stetson. Unless you counted her hoe.

Lisa liked the actress.

Months later in San Francisco, Lisa went to a movie the woman
starred in. It wasn't too bad, said Lisa. Lots of toe-sucking in the
boys' locker room after football practice. It reminded Lisa of high
school. Not that the production values were the best. . . .

Once in a while busts come down on the most sophisticated old
hands, hardly the George Ralphs of the world, even though these
commercial growers have taken every precaution, created the
Perfect Set-up, in fact.

Oh, God, the Perfect Set-up! The one big score.

A friend of Max's once had the Perfect Set-up. He owned 160
acres in an isolated area of the Sierra foothills. The growers put
the pot on a steep hillside that was topped with a bank of large
overhanging madrone trees. They dropped the grow bags in the
scrub so that they were all surrounded by manzanita and holly.
Because of the camouflage, the location and the steep bank, they
knew they wouldn't have to worry about fly-overs. There was only
one way onto the property, across a bridge over a sixty-foot gorge.
They installed a metal gate that cantilevered six feet over the gorge
on both sides, and they surrounded the gate with a special barbed
wire, concertina wire, that would slice intruders into tuna sand-
wiches. If you blew away the lock and got inside, the gate was
designed to still close automatically behind you. Now you were
facing another problem: two rotweilers. Rotweilers are the
Roman–German dogs that Doberman pinschers have been bred
from. Rotweilers make Dobermans seem like froufrou poodles.
Naturally, these rots had been trained to eat intruders from nave
to chops. So nobody figured they'd have to worry much about
poachers. The perimeter was also patrolled by two ex-Green
Berets. They lived in a trailer overlooking the plants. The boss,
who had been a lieutenant colonel, stayed in another trailer with
his wife. The Perfect Operation. The trailers were fitted with video
machines and the colonel belonged to a mail-order tape club.

Everybody agreed to stay on the land for ten months without leaving except when absolutely necessary for supplies. The Perfect Set-up. One big score. A million plus. The American Dream. The vets had thought of everything, and some growers spend months in places like Bali, Belize and the Costa Brava thinking everything through. But a few weeks before he had decided to grow dope— just one more crop, you understand—the colonel loaned a couple of down-and-outers near the land about $5,000, a man and his wife. Their child had been born deformed. They had medical bills.

The couple ratted on the colonel. They figured if the colonel were in jail they wouldn't have to repay the five grand. So the colonel went down from being too nice.

He got off, however, because the warrant was improperly written. The cops claimed that they had seen the dope themselves. But there was no way that was possible. The colonel's lawyer proved that an informer must have tipped the narcotics agents, the judge was forced to agree and charges were dropped.

The Perfect Set-up. These stories take on the trappings of Greek tragedy. Some trifling mistake, some act of *hubris* finally queers the deal. To quote the buzzcocks: Something's gone wrong again.

The Dairy Barn Disguise, for instance.

The father of a Pennsylvania pot farmer raised dairy cows. Prices were no better for milk and beef in Pennsylvania than they were across the country in California. The middleman always seemed to wind up with the profits. So the family built a second barn inside the first one. The outside barn housed cows as it always had. The inside barn, built on the second story behind the old walls, housed marijuana, 800 plants in growbags. They cut the roof off the center of the barn because the narcos don't fly over the Pennsylvania Dutch yet. They installed switches and a warning bell inside the second floor growhouse so that the pot hands would know when outsiders were in the dairy barn below. Business was conducted as usual. They missed only one thing. The 800 growbags were placed on sheets of corrugated steel set at an incline so that water would run off into troughs and from there into underground pipes. That way nobody could see grow lines coming in or out of the barn. Then a freak Indian summer hit. The temperature rose and rose. Special precautions were taken. They watered the plants around the clock to prevent evaporation. They spritzed the leaves. No matter what they did, the plants began to die. Eight hundred marijuana plants shriveled before their eyes. Until it was all over they didn't realize what had gone wrong. The roots had been fried. The corrugated steel had gotten so hot that it had burned the roots through the plastic growbags and each and every plant had wilted.

One man in Mendocino almost had the Perfect Set-up, too. Bruce Perlowin. In an article titled "Secluded 'Fortress' Hides Bizarre Horatio Alger Tale," the Los Angeles *Times* quoted an associate of Perlowin's who said that the then 30-year-old "marijuana kingpin" "netted $16 million in drug profits after expenses that ran as high as $500,000 a week." "There were nights I couldn't give the baby a bath because the tub was full of pot," the *Times* quoted his former wife. Perlowin had the Perfect Defense, too. He built a $200,000 stone wall around the property that he controlled on Robinson Creek, added a chain-link fence topped with barbed wire, installed a steel-lined, bullet-proof command post that contained a 14-line telephone system, a computer and radio equipment. Best of all, I think, was the spiral staircase to the master bedroom. It could be "electrically charged to repel intruders." Perlowin also had plans to install a "laser immobilizer."

He had the Perfect Set-up, and the Perfect Defense, but in the end he had too much of a good thing. Specifically, too many $5, $10, and $20 bills. Perlowin allegedly set up an elaborate money-laundering scheme with a Las Vegas casino. According to federal agents, the small bills, suitcase after suitcase full of them, would be traded for $100 bills which were sent out of the country to Luxembourg, then transferred to bank accounts in the Grand Cayman Islands, and finally returned to the United States "as legitimate, non-taxable offshore loans." Perlowin was an alleged marijuana smuggler, however, not a marijuana grower, and smugglers usually have a different psyche than growers.

Perhaps Maxwell or Sarah could be persuaded to abandon guerrilla growing and go for broke, but I wonder. First generation farmers like to keep the feel of dirt between their fingers. If they did switch from production to distribution, however, I imagine they would blow the first $16 million. Sarah would have the text of the Nuclear Freeze delivered to the front door of every American home. Maxwell would buy up all the brothels in France and then retire to his private pistol museum in Reno.

But it's time to dispense with the rumors of the Big Bust. The talk at Janey's Cafe in Garberville was more off than on.

The skies of Humboldt were never blackened with helicopters. There was only one. It was not a National Guard helicopter like

those used in Hawaii, Georgia and Arkansas. It was a Customs'
copter, as Fireman had said. Six people rode the copter not
including the pilot. Some twenty others worked ground support,
drove the dump trucks and burned the dope.

Most of the raiders wore flac jackets. Only two were permitted
to carry M-16s. BNE Field Commander Pete Mouriski picked
them with care: "They were SWAT team and they had experience.
We don't give automatic weapons to just anyone. The M-16s
belonged to the Customs' service and came with the helicopter.
Some others had twelve-gauge shotguns, not riot guns, and
everybody carried their normal sidearm. I carried a .45 revolver."

No raider even considered riding the mesh nets that towed the
marijuana, as old Janey had claimed.

"Shit," Sgt. Cairns told me, "I ain't going to get in no nets! We
used the nets to haul out the marijuana."

The alleged pot shot at the airplane, presumably the Cessna
used to photograph bust sites, was enigmatic. No pilot, no agent
knows who told the reporter that a plane had been fired upon and
hit. The claim made very good copy and was picked up by
television. So far as I know, nobody has ever shot at a narcotics
helicopter or photographic fly-over plane in California. At least
half a dozen Californians fired upon helicopters spraying malathi-
on on the dread medfly. Two helicopters were hit. Somebody did
shoot at a helicopter working marijuana in Oklahoma. The copter
crashed. They lack mellow in the Midwest.

The issue of search warrants is a hazy one.

"We try to get search warrants for as many places as possible,
but in some cases no warrants are necessary if while flying over an
area we spot marijuana that's being cultivated," said Jerry Smith,
agent in charge of the San Francisco office in the middle of it all.
"In that case a felony is being committed in the eyes of the officers
and no warrant is needed to confiscate it."

Well, if three policemen break into a St. Louis apartment with a
proper warrant to search for hothouse marijuana, and once they
reach the patio, they take a gander across the courtyard and spy
marijuana growing on the patios of three other apartments, they
are not exactly empowered to break down the next three doors
without first acquiring new search warrants from a judge. Green
plants growing in the ground are not the same thing as armed
robbers fleeing the Tick-Tock liquor store. Not yet. Correct me,
Justice Rehnquist, if I err.

The California raiders struck middle ground. One of the two

Humboldt deputies recognized a middle-aged deer hunter during a raid. The man was a judge. The raiders asked if they could confiscate whatever pot they saw.

"The judge wrote us more warrants from the field," says Mouriski.

One rumor that was fought on television across northern California turned out to be true. How true was a matter of some concern.

Louisiana–Pacific, the giant timber, pulp and plywood concern did, in fact, allow the raiders to use its Alder Point mill as a staging area.

So what?

Well, Humboldt County gets very hot in the summer months. Wood burns quickly, even living trees. Louisiana–Pacific owns a whole lot of living trees in the Northwest and arson has become an increasing problem. Resentful growers could presumably do great damage to Louisiana–Pacific forests because trees do not fly back to San Francisco, Sacramento and Washington, D.C., the way marijuana raiders do.

Spokespeople for L–P appeared on television and told the newspapers that the corporation was not in any way responsible for the raids.

"I don't want no retaliation," says John. John is the assistant mill manager at Alder Point. He hitches his pants. "They didn't burn a lick of dope here, not a twig. If you don't believe me, look at the rust on the burner." He points to a big metal tepee burner, twenty feet tall with a screen nipple over the top. The burner is layered with brown and red rust. "If we'd burned it here, most of that rust would be gone, wouldn't it? I don't want no retaliation."

John is a large shovel of a man. His triceps are as big as his biceps and his chest is too big to shove into a fifty-five gallon drum. John says Alder Point was a year-round plywood mill until three years ago. Now there's not enough work to take the mill through the fall, and that with a short crew. John doesn't mind marijuana. Marijuana helps the economy.

"First it was sheep, then it was lumber, now it's marijuana."

He knows the old-time ranchers. They grow. What he doesn't like much are growers who use public forest land—and L–P land. A buddy of his carries three guns when he goes hunting: a rifle for the deer, a pistol and a pocket gun, too, in case he runs into someone's patch by mistake. John smiles. The L–P surveyor was already run off L–P land this year.

The BNE did not tell John they were coming. He heard the rotors and ran out of the mill. He couldn't believe it. Later the manager told him the raiders had called the company but he, the manager, had been told to keep the arrival a secret.

John didn't appreciate the secrecy. Already he was worried about retaliation. He marched down the hill to his house. His wife was in the kitchen. He told her to go in the bedroom and pack.

"You're taking the kids to grandma's."

His wife did not ask why. He would not have told her, he says. Sometimes when he's plain in a piss-poor mood he tells her the same thing. This time, however, he was afraid for their lives.

"Lots of people have been killed the last couple of years over marijuana."

The raids have already been going on for five days. He won't let his family return for ten more.

"I don't mind a family farmer putting a little extra money together. That's okay by me but these commercial growers who come in from the outside destroy the people around them. They're just like big business."

He lowers his voice and glances behind at the dead mill, at the brown river rising behind the mill, at the wild green mountains across the water.

"I guess," allows John, "L–P didn't get where they're at without treading on a few toes, too, but that was what you might call competition."

Well, yes, I do remember reading a commemorative article in the Eureka *Times–Standard*. The "struggle" to unionize northern lumber mills, said the paper, was "populated with lumber barons, hired thugs, communists, club-wielding vigilantes, trade unionists and tear-gas-shooting police." On the big day of the Great Lumber Strike of Humboldt County, 1935, one man was killed outright, two more were "mortally wounded," "the county hospital was jammed" and 114 people landed in jail. One cop had even turned a submachine gun on picketers. Not full rock 'n' roll. The clip jammed after a few rounds. But that's what you might call competition. Alder Point is seven miles from Ft. Seward where Chief Lassik's men were shot and cremated by ranchers and soldiers. That was what you might call competition, too. Raw place, America.

12

THE RAIDERS:

Sgt. Cairns and Field Commander Pete
Mouriski; Dash and Derring-Do . . . Cold
Beer and the Gutter Irish . . . Do Narcotics
Agents Look Nice Like Kurt Vonnegut or Do
They Actually Have Eyes from Duluth? . . .
Toting Up the Bust . . . Are Marijuana
Growers Russians? Do the Russians Smoke
Dope? Then Why Are U-2s Flying Over
California?

Sgt. Cairns rocks back in a cheap green chair behind a cheap
battered desk in a back room of the vice crimes division at San
Francisco police headquarters. A sign down the hall reads:
RESTRICTED AREA. BY ORDER OF CAPTAIN DIARMUID PHILPOTT. There is
a two-way mirror in the wall of this unused acoustic-tiled interro-
gation room. The mirror has the oil of human faces smeared across
it. On the desk between Sgt. Cairns and myself is a foot-thick mug
book that I paged through before the sergeant arrived. It holds
picture after picture, mug shot after mug shot of girls and women
and some boys busted for prostitution in previous months. Some of
these women are smiling coyly like lawyers' wives at a cocktail
party. Some you know are flipping the bird off camera. Some look
degraded or scared. Most of them look like you or me.

Sgt. Richard Cairns was the officer on loan from the SFPD with the M-16 who busted George and Trudy Ralph. Three months later, he remembers them well.

"Those people were living in their own little world. We were told that no police had been in that valley in four years."

What was it like for Sgt. Cairns to leave the sleaze and grit of his city narcotics beat?

"Hey!" he says. "It was a wonderful change of pace. You were out in the helicopter in the wide open spaces. It was an adventure. Exciting. A bit of dash and derring-do!"

"You know," says Cairns, "there's nothing I can do about heroin coming out of Mexico or cocaine smuggled from the mountains of Peru. In Humboldt, I could chop down three or four tons of that shit myself. I put a financial hurt on somebody. I ruined their day. Why should some grower be making all this money tax-free when we can get it?"

He rocks back. Kicks his cowboy boots over the edge of the battered desk.

"In San Francisco we're fighting a losing battle, at least with consumers. It's like fighting Prohibition."

Was he ever scared, jumping point out of the helicopter?

Sgt. Cairns has been fourteen years with the San Francisco Police force, eight of them as a tactical policeman, the last four in narcotics. He was a combat MP during the TET offensive in Vietnam.

"I wasn't paranoid on the raids," he says, "but I've been a policeman long enough to know that a fifteen-year-old kid with a .22 can kill you. You prepare for the worst."

Sgt. Cairns is busy today. He's heading up a task force to defend the Queen of England who will be visiting the city tomorrow, along with President Reagan. Mostly, Sgt. Cairns is worried about Irish protesters, those Irish who did not become cops or presidents.

Sgt. Cairns is wearing a brown polyester shirt, polyester tie, a gold watch with a gold band and gold bracelets on both wrists. Cowboy boots.

What do you drink when you're not on duty?

"You want to know what I drink? Put me down as a cowboy beer drinker. I've got my cowboy boots on today."

Special Agent Pete Mouriski of the California Bureau of Narcotics Enforcement also drinks beer, "cold beer, especially on those hot marijuana raids."

Pete Mouriski was field commander for the big raids, Sgt. Cairns's boss.

Off duty, Bailey's Irish Cream wfth coffee is his favorite drink. "I drink in moderation too much of the time. I smoke ciga- rettes." He taps the pack of Lucky Strikes in his pocket. "But I've never taken drugs. Never have. Never will."

Pete Mouriski sits in a clean, sunlit office near the fashionable tourist piers of downtown San Francisco. The Golden Gate Bridge, entrance to the dope counties of the north, burns primer red through the window. Pete Mouriski is better dressed than Sgt. Cairns—not Ivy League by any means, but stylish, with a red- spotted tie from a downtown department store, black Florsheim loafers and good slacks. Like most narcotics officers, Mouriski does not look the part at first glance. He's tall, six feet two, thin like a steak knife and topped with a barely contained white man's Afro. He looks a lot like Kurt Vonnegut would if Kurt Vonnegut were thinner and didn't think about things so much. Except for his—can you see this coming? His eyes. They're frozen. Eyes from Duluth.

Mr. Mouriski sits in an office decorated with the accoutrements of the trade, a hookah and a hash pipe. Quickly, he runs through what really happened in northern California.

Funded by an end-of-the-harvest grant from the Drug Enforce- ment Agency in Washington, the California Bureau of Narcotics Enforcement decided to sweep the four northwestern counties of California: Del Norte, Trinity, Mendocino and, especially, Hum- boldt. The BNE felt more marijuana was being cultivated in Monterey and Los Angeles counties to the south, but media attention, including *People* magazine, the television show "Sixty Minutes" and an embarrassing article in *Life* titled, "Where the Law Winks at Pot: California's Failing Fight Against Marijuana," had drawn the attention of letter writers and policy makers to the North Coast marijuana frontier.

The DEA grant, for only $25,000, was intended to explore alternative ways of busting pot farmers that would not rely on expensive full-time state or federal agents. Part of the problem with marijuana is that it is after all a farm product. The govern- ment realized they were wasting a lot of money paying detectives to harvest weeds like so many coolies. The DEA had tried National Guard reserves and, in the South, convict laborers but both groups tended to secrete confiscated bud on their persons.

This dismayed federal officials. American drug enforcement operations must not come to resemble *Federales* sweeps where Mexican soldiers soon sell confiscated marijuana on the streets.

The grant was given to test the concept of mixing state agents with off-duty deputy sheriffs from the infected counties. Of course, the state agents would pick the targets and run the operation.

"The whole thing was an experiment in terms of the sheriff's departmental reserves," says Mouriski. "We wanted to try different situations, drive-ins and helicopters, combo raids, without using on-duty deputies. It worked. The different deputies worked well together and the counties liked it because there was no county overtime."

The raiders never made it to Mendocino.

"The rains brought us down. Rains and fog. The helicopter was due for maintenance anyway."

All the media hysteria was over thirteen raids. The raiders seized a total of 2,227 plants in the ground and 1,186 pounds of processed sinsemilla. Grand total, wet and dry: 9,099 pounds.

Four and a half tons. The Eureka papers came up with the figure seven tons and this exaggeration played on the national media. In the beginning of the raids, Bureau Chief Jerry Smith had been quoted as hoping the raids would slash the harvest by at least fifteen to twenty tons.

In the midst of the hoopla one Humboldt deputy sheriff named Lonnie Lawson, who was unconnected with the main raids, noticed a truck and horse trailer sway across a lane marker near Willow Creek, eleven miles below the Hoopa Indian Reservation.

Mr. Lawson pulled the truck over.

The deputy smelled the pungent odor of marijuana.

His nose was true. Seven hundred and fifty pounds of processed pot lay bundled in the back, a hundred more pounds of untrimmed bud crammed into plastic buckets. The driver and his sidekick were packing a semi-automatic rifle and a nine-millimeter automatic pistol. Both weapons were loaded.

One to two million dollars would be a fair estimate of the worth of this bust. In one hour a sheriff's deputy had accidentally stepped on almost as much prepared bud as twenty-six raiders had in ten days.

When it was all over, the raiders admitted they had not even dented the harvest. A Humboldt lawyer estimates that law enforcement never gets more than one percent of the crop. My feeling is that only one in a thousand growers gets popped. I never would have thought this a year ago. I wonder, who smokes all this dope, Russians?

Mr. Mouriski stares out the window toward the Golden Gate Bridge, Hawaii and Japan. "It's tense doing this work," he says, tired. "You're so exposed. God knows the lessons from Vietnam. You're so vulnerable." Mouriski was a Marine sergeant, Ninth Marines, Third Battalion. He fought at Phu Bai south of Da Nang. He could care less about busting other vets. Why should he? "If I have the information, and they're committing the crime, I'm going to attempt to arrest them." Parenthetically, he adds, "I joined up with my older brother. He was wounded twice. He fought at Starlight in sixty-five."

Like the Depression and the Civil War before it, the Vietnam War never seems to go away like a good little boy.

Mouriski has no problem remembering the Ralphs, either, perhaps because they were two of only eight people arrested during the entire sweep, and two others of those eight were let go in the field because they could not be easily transported to jail.

"The grower was hostile. He kept saying nasty things to the officers. So did his wife. They called us 'Gestapo.'"

For three years Pete Mouriski has headed up the largest marijuana eradication campaign in the United States. Next year he's leaving marijuana. Today he sounds just a trifle bored. The total tonnage didn't impress him much, either. It was a late-season, half-assed effort that made good headlines and proved a bureaucratic point: that deputies from four different counties could be thrown together and do a credible job under state and federal direction. Mouriski agrees. It wasn't much, but it was a job, a program. Perhaps they'll receive more money soon.

And, sure enough, next year they will. The DEA will allocate $200,000 for U-2 overflights of not Russia but northern California.

I was sitting in a motel room with Maxwell when the news came over late-night TV.

"U-2s! U-2s! U-2s!" shouted Maxwell.

Maxwell, I thought, was being a little emotional. U-2 overflights at a cost eight times what the federal government had provided the entire previous year made perfect sense. Certain defense contractors would receive a great deal of money, high tech would be propitiated, and nothing at all would be accomplished. Although who am I to say? Perhaps the president of the United States finally got a look, individually, at each marijuana plant being grown on

Maxwell's, Lisa's, Sarah's and Fireman's land, and at all the rest of the pot grown in the northern sector of the state he used to govern, too.

Aerial surveillance is the one topic that makes Special Agent Pete Mouriski sit up a few inches. Aerial surveillance is the technical foreplay to the proper bust. Mouriski discounts all the elaborate precautions and disguises taken by guerrilla growers.

"Marijuana is the easiest stuff to see in the world. You can't hide bright green shiny plants next to holly or manzanita or other greenery. We fly at 1,500 or 3,000 feet, although a helicopter as opposed to a fixed-wing aircraft may go five feet above the ground if it wants to. Our fixed-wing aircraft fly at ninety miles per hour. Spotting the plants is not difficult. Going back and determining the specific property is the hassle. We use compass coordinates and photographs but the spotter is using his naked eye. Then we go to the county assessor's office and the hall of records. We get a warrant to search for those plants we've spotted on our coordinates. The first fly-over is for the warrants. If it's been a long time, we refly the day of the bust or the day before to see if the plants are still there."

Officer Mouriski runs on in a calm, radio announcer's voice, the modulated tone of a trad-jazz deejay. He wonders why a member of the working press is pressing him so. Marijuana is an illegal drug, a narcotic.

"I think the growers are crooks. I think I'm helping society," he has said. "I'm anti-dope. I believe weed is evil, and I love what I do."

13

THE RAIDERS WITHOUT BENEFIT OF FLUORESCENT LIGHTING:

Blood and Milk at the Palace Hotel; Narco Groupies; Mrs. McNab's Single-shot Water Buffalo; Cowboy John's Nose; The Clean Stink of Good and The *Odeur* of Evil; DAs vs. Narcs; Everything about the Narcotics Agent; Why They Hate Marijuana So; Their Tipping Behavior; And a Question—Do Narcotics Agents Resist Temptation Less Well Than the Rest of Us? . . . Crazy Jim Watt's Man in Mendocino, the Dreaded Mr. Bill Stewart; Arctic Eyes Are Not Smiling; Hair of the Frog

Ah, but it's no good interviewing a narcotics agent in an office. The talk becomes all bust stats, aerial surveillance, technical considerations, the safe quote. The only tension is caused by the crackle of the fluorescent lighting overhead and the ever present dislike of the press. Cops like squad cars and helicopters. Action. That's where the fun and stink is. They hate their offices. Offices are for filling out reports, paperwork. At the office they turn into bureaucrats with a rolodex in front of them, and that's how they talk, like bureaucrats. Their balls are elsewhere.

No, the place to interview cops is inside a good bar. Bars serve beer and beer is blood and milk to cops. Especially narcos. Narcotics agents live to drink. Hard to say why. Must release those sweet endorphins, keep 'em loose, offer forgetfulness from the awful responsibility of running down marijuana terrorists in forest and field.

Best bar in northern California is the Palace in Ukiah.

Table to the left of the fireplace is loaded with narcs. Four of them, plus me and the woman lawyer who invited me to sit down. The lawyer and I are the only ones without a pistol under our coats.

"Hey, Ace," says cowboy narc, taller than John Wayne, "the three of us have horses. How come you don't?"

Ace, goggle-eyed. "Whores? You talkin' whores?"

"Horses, talking horses."

"Whores. My wife. She lifts her tail and opens her neck. She's my Arabian. Arabians're the best. They win all the races."

Ace is being oogled. He's not bad-looking: rugged face, Killer Jack body, twenty-four-hour intensity. Two narco groupies, each maybe thirty-five, tight pants over loose butts, nice breasts in open polyester blouses, primped hair and sweet, desperate faces. They follow Ace from the adjoining table for the rest of the evening.

"Ace," says John Wayne, "when was the last time you saw an Arabian run a horse race?"

"I've bet on them," says Ace. Ace is from the city.

"You never bet on an Arabian, Ace. Arabians can't run diddlysquat. Arabians are for A-rabs. What you see on the tracks is quarter horses and thoroughbreds."

"Fuck, your shorts."

"Your shorts got flowers printed on them."

"Suck my ass," says Ace.

"Can't do that, Ace. God gave me a nose."

Now that's proper narc talk, five beers in. Another round arrives. They can buy me beer. I can't buy them beer.

Three of these gentle Americans are from the BNE, state narcs. The fourth is the local fireman, head of the narcotics division of the Mendocino sheriff's department. The local boy and one of the state agents look urban, new leather coats, shiny shoes and scruffy beards. The other two are the real cowboys: six three, one, six four, the other, plus hats, Stetson and Resistol. They ride rodeo in the off months. Very hard to spot, these two. Lot of rancher growers have gone down to their folksy ways. Far as I can tell, only one thing sets them apart from the rest of us: their eyes. I don't

know. There's something about narco eyes. I know a San Francisco madam who says you can always spot a cop by his shoes. Narcs
are more subtle. You must look into their eyes. You won't see
anything. Except blue ice. Narco eyes: straight from Duluth, you
remember.

The Palace has the enormous stuffed head of a water buffalo
jutting out from the mirrored back of the bar. Mrs. McNab,
former owner, killed this poor buf with one shot.

Below the dead buffalo the prosecutor of Mendocino County is
explaining something to the new district attorney, Vivian Lee
Rackauckas. Rackauckas is the only woman DA in California.

This being the Palace, capital of Mendocino County, and a
Friday, too, the prosecutor is discoursing on the difference between good and evil in a voice loud enough for all of us to hear.
The prosecutor knows a certain amount about good and evil
because he spent two years in a federal penitentiary for draft
evasion during the Vietnam War.

"You can spot evil. Evil is a vibration. Certain people give off
the odor of evil. You can actually smell the difference—I can—
between fools who're in over their heads and evil people who will
rape and rape, kill and kill, burgle and burgle."

The narcs don't like to hear philosophy. Philosophy smacks of
ambiguity. Tonight the Palace has ambiguity enough. Against the
wall, in the booths, are two sets of Americans, everybody is
wearing dirty duck-billed caps, including the women, long hair,
old-fashioned beards, combat boots. Not the looks of people who
usually pay two dollars for a Budweiser. Growers. The narcs know
it. The growers recognize the narcs. That's the Palace.

John, the supercowboy narc, turns to me. John Narc was once a
schoolteacher. He says he's seen kids who wanted to do no more
with their lives than smoke the next joint. "If you invent a way to
keep kids off dope so that it's only adults smoking, you'll make a
fortune. Who gives a fuck what adults do?"

Now he stares me down. Freezes me like kryptonite.

"Do you understand what it means to be on our side?" he asks.

The local narc, the Mendocino man, can't handle this. John is
going to get frank. He can see it coming.

"Who *are* you, man?" The Mendo narc rises out of his seat
across the round table. He means me. *"Who the fuck are you?"*

My friend the lawyer has introduced me as a writer. I don't look
much like a writer to Mendocino's leading narcotics agent. The
beard, the hair, the glasses. Hey, I realize the glasses are tinted.

I've just woken up. Long days are behind me. If I'm a writer, Local Boy is telling me, I sure as fuck know more growers than I know cops.

The two cowboy narcs don't care. This is fun. They're drunk. Good time. They don't get much chance to chat with the press, especially wayward members of the press who know the difference between a .45 and a .44, and maybe puke on everything they stand for. They can respect that. They like that. If you don't like intensity, you shouldn't be a narcotics agent. Narcs like the fast current.

A few months back a narcotics agent was in a little fight with a politically prominent DA in northern California. It was a long, drunken night. The agent ended up warm and naked next to the DA's girlfriend, not his wife. The DA was tipped off. He broke into the room. He didn't go for the agent. He grabbed the woman and started bashing her head against the wall. The agent went for the DA. The DA pulled his gun. The agent grabbed for his. Stand-off. Quick thinking. By both parties. Scene defused. Later, the DA rang up Duke Deukmejian, then attorney general, now governor of California. The narcotics agent was slapped on the wrist, forbidden to set foot inside the DA's county.

Who am I?

I hold up my right arm and pull back the sleeve. It's tawdry, I know, but I'm going to trade on my knife slash. Hey, I'm about to say, I know what the fuck junk means—a junkie cut my arm. It's such a cheap gesture, all I have to do is make it.

"Fuck, he's been cut!" says Ace. "Oh, fuck."

Wrong end of the knife. Narco's worst fantasy.

John is earnest, "We don't like to do marijuana. No agent does. It's dirty. It's dangerous. You gotta get up before dawn to hit these farmers. Who wants to climb up a mountain with ninety pounds of dope strapped to your back? And they're armed. They're much more armed than heroin dealers are now. Can you believe that? They've got Uzis and M-16s and Colt AR-15s converted to M-16s."

Ace and the Mendocino narc are wriggling in their seats. Quit talking, they're trying to signal John the cowboy. They think I'll remember everything. John hopes I do. He wants me to put it all down in the Sony after he leaves. He wants me to get it right.

A man steps up to the woman lawyer. The lawyer, by the way, is Susan B. Jordan. Susan Jordan used to be the pre-eminent feminist attorney in the United States. She saved Evon Wanrow, a Spokane

Indian, after Wanrow had been convicted of killing a white child molester. She got Inez Garcia off after Garcia blew away the man who had raped her. Susan B. has defended a lot of marijuana growers. ("The days are gone," she says, "when you could plea bargain the usual cultivation felonies down to a misdemeanor. There is a real attempt now to discourage the big commercial grower. If the farmer has a wife and three kids and he is an unemployed logger and he's growing fewer than 50 plants, that's one thing. If he's got over 100 plants, it's hard to call it personal use. That grower might be facing 12 months in the county jail, although it's still very rare to do state time.") Tonight, Susan Jordan is dressed in designer jeans and high heels. Her friend looks out of place in the Palace. He's got on a white shirt and sports jacket, corduroys and hiking boots. He looks soft and intelligent. He does not look like the sort of American who has ever emptied an H & K Binelli riot gun on another human being. He's picking up Susan and they're going to his house for dinner. This man is a doctor. They leave.

John leans across the table to Ace.

"Why is she with that faggoty guy?"

Ace shrugs.

The narcs are checking out.

So am I.

I forgot. I paid for my first beer at the bar with a twenty-dollar bill. I've got fifteen dollars in change coming. The Palace bartender has the money carefully folded beside the cash register. Palace integrity. I gave him a couple of bucks tip.

"The entire sheriff's department was in here tonight," I said.

"Oh," he says, "you know, they never tip. They drink all night and we wait on them for hours and they never leave us a dime."

Narcotics agents. What a strange job. Out there in the wilderness all alone. Things go wrong on the enforcement frontier. Rudolpho J. Giuliani, who heads up the drug war for the Reagan administration, made his reputation by helping to indict fifty-two of seventy New York City special narcotics agents. Narcotics officers are always on the front line of temptation. Bust a dealer and you and your partner are first on the scene. The dealer is a fast talker. "There's $120,000 on the table. Take sixty grand, officer. Leave me the rest. I'll be gone forever." Maybe the agent makes a lone bust of a hundred pounds of processed marijuana. The grower is halfway over the far ridge. Is it possible, perhaps, to unload the bud on one's own? Who's to know?

Some agents, though, stay to the straight and narrow, and they are the scariest of them all—the Saint Justs who believe in what they do. Interview one of them, and there's no need to get drunk at the Palace. They break the rules. Talk to them anywhere and ice blows out of their eyes.

Bill Stewart, for instance. The man has antifreeze in his veins.

Bill Stewart used to be the head narc here in Mendocino County. He moved on to flashier pastures.

Bill Stewart is the raider Maxwell once fixed in his sights during a bust of a friend's plantation.

I interviewed Bill Stewart last year a few blocks from the bar at the Palace Hotel. Bill Stewart restores my faith in America.

Mr. Stewart looked me over in the modern anteroom of the county sheriff's office. He was wearing tan cowboy boots, bell-bottomed jeans, a black satin baseball jacket, a digital watch with a gold band and two gold rings. His beard was cropped and tawny, his hair blond and wavy. Two straight scars ran down the right side of his face. Like the narcs in the Palace, Stewart did not look like a cop. He looked like Willie Nelson's younger brother. Except for, yes, his pale blue eyes. Less than alive. His back was as stiff as a 30.06.

"How long is this going to take?" Stewart asked. His voice was a monotone only a little higher than a whisper.

"Fifteen, twenty minutes," I lied.

"Good," said Stewart, waving me into a chair. "I have no liking for press people. Half the fucking reporters smoke dope." He fastened on my Moose River hat, the lipstache I sported then. "These stoners will print what they want no matter what I say. I don't think they should be allowed to write the stories."

Stewart was already moving on to Oklahoma, where he wouldn't be just another flashy deputy sheriff. He was going to be a senior agent with the state bureau of narcotics enforcement, although at a lower salary.

("Bill," I wanted to say, "it's stoners like me who are going to make you famous. Somebody who knows Crazy Jim Watt is going to read this page and say, 'Now there's a mean, clean, fighting machine. We need a boy like this on the federal level.' Bill," I'm thinking, "once you learn not to say 'fuck' to the press, maybe you could become the Gordon Liddy of our generation.")

"Have you ever smoked to set up a bust?" I asked. "Or perhaps out of human curiosity?"

Stewart looked through me with his state-of-the-art narco eyes. With those eyes he could look through my skull, through the brick wall, out the building, around the curve of the earth and back into his own brain. That was probably what he was doing.

"I've never used marijuana. I don't intend to use it. It's a clandestine drug. You never know the THC content. Small kids can OD on it."

"Do you drink?"

"After work I hit a bar with a friend and have a pop or two." His voice was still a whisper.

"Do you feel it is fair that you can seize a man's pickup truck when he's on his way to work because you've found a joint in the glove compartment?" Stewart had led the entire state the year before in such confiscations, which are perfectly legal, though rarely so zealously enforced.

"That man should have thought of me before he hid the joint."

"Let's talk about what you call 'cold hits.' Is it true you enjoy working up conversations with strangers in bars, then ask them where you can get some smoke? And that you hitchhike along the roads in the off-season when the harvest is over and bust the people who give you rides if they offer you smoke?"

"People in bars agree to sell me dope. I bust them. You got the hitchhiking story backwards. We pick up a hitchhiker on the way to Willits. We ask him if he wants to sell a pound of good shit. He says yes; we go to his house; we bust him. That's legit."

I don't know. Interviewing Bill Stewart is like being raped in the ass. You feel very bad afterward—and very strange, too.

Later I asked him about stories that he stays only a frog's hair inside the law when he busts people.

"No one is ever bullied," Stewart said. "We never destroy personal property."

CELEBRATION

14

LISA'S BRIEF VACATION:
The Air Goes Out of the Sack; Gophers Copulate; Men Balance Badgers . . . The Intense Search for the World's Largest Marijuana Plants . . . Tossing Pot to Cons . . . Ed Eats the Orphan Babies; Newt Mating; The Cancer Dad Attacks from the Hot Tub . . . Lisa Smiles

The big raids had come in Humboldt and the rest of northern California, and the big raids had gone. The raids were flamboyant this season, the publicity even more hysterical than in past harvests. Strangely, however, real damage was less. This year—for whatever reasons, perhaps politics, perhaps the departure of Bill Stewart to Oklahoma—the local sheriffs seemed to have slacked off, taking easy busts that looked good on paper, like seedling confiscations, but that meant little to most growers. The U-2 overflights were to become bizarre reality, but they would be viewed as no more than live science fiction. Certainly the spy planes could photograph the numbers on license plates from 80,000 feet. They could watch gophers copulate, too. So what? Who would drive up the roads to make the arrests?

The air was out of the sack in northern California by the end of October, and everyone was breathing easier.

Lisa put in a call to Astral Travel in Garberville and reserved her flight for Papeete. I tried to tell her the outer islands were less crowded this time of year but Lisa had had enough of rural living. Tahiti first, then the Tuamotus.

Lisa won't be shoving off for a couple of weeks but she's ready to slip out of her paranoia suit right now. A brief vacation. That's what's called for. Everybody swears the helicopters are grounded but Lisa wonders if the local sheriffs might decide to conduct a mop-up operation on the ground. Lisa is young and freshly moneyed. She sees no reason to stay and suffer through the tail end of the harvest jitters. Or the worst of the Humboldt rains. God, the rain. People are losing their hair. Their toes are webbing, pupils becoming stationary, skin moist to the touch. My God, we're all turning into salamanders! Trapped like ferns on a sponge!

Besides, Lisa has a mission. She wants to find some special beads in San Francisco. I'm not sure why. Lisa's not exactly the moccasin-sewing type. Perhaps it's her sense of accumulation. The beads she's looking for are called white hearts. They're red with a white center. "White hearts are what the Indians traded Manhattan for," explains Lisa. As a native New Yorker she thinks the Indians got the better deal.

I have my own mission to pursue in the southland:

A NEW HIGH
IN MARIJUANA

SANTA CRUZ: Nonplussed Santa Cruz deputy sheriffs found marijuana plants nearly as tall as a three-story building while raiding a farm in the mountainous redwood forest behind this seacoast town, authorities said yesterday.

"You've heard of *Sequoia sempervirens?*" Santa Cruz county sheriff's Sergeant Carl Kuebler asked. "Well, we've got something else—*Sequoia sempercannabis.*"

The giant marijuana plants, seized at a remote mountain farm near Bonny Doon last Friday, measured more than twenty-five feet high.

They had fourteen-inch trunks and seven-foot limbs, and each yielded three pounds of powerful buds.

The raid, in which nine alleged growers were arrested, netted $1.9 million worth of marijuana and boosted the fall harvest seizure to $13 million since September, deputies claimed. . . .

A ground search revealed 203 pounds of processed high-grade sinsemilla worth an estimated $500,000 ready

for market inside the twenty-five-foot-high greenhouse—
and the pot trees.

Santa Cruz is a big beach town sixty miles south of San
Francisco with a boardwalk and an old fashioned roller coaster.

Fourteen-inch trunks! Twenty-five feet tall! I called the sheriff's
department from Garberville. Confirmed. Still, I'm highly suspicious. Twenty-five feet tall is tall for a marijuana plant. Twenty-
five feet tall is four naked weightlifters standing on each other's
shoulders, smoking cigars and smiling Maxwell's regulation smile,
the topmost balancing a full-grown badger on his head. Twenty-
five feet tall is THE WORLD'S LARGEST MARIJUANA
PLANT. Twenty-five feet tall is a mission few authors are entrusted to investigate in their own lifetime. Tall.

It occurred to me that the whole thing might be false. The Santa
Cruz sheriff department's idea of a joke. With all the media
publicity about pot these days, maybe the narcos were getting in
on the act. Narcotics officers are not your normal breed of cop,
and California narcotics officers are not your normal narcos.
Sometimes they exhibit a sense of humor that is, well . . . bent. I
suppose they have to now and then. Comes with the territory. . . .

We started down the big road, Highway 101. The highway is a
raging eight-lane torrent in the San Fernando Valley north of Los
Angeles. It's called the Hollywood Freeway in downtown L.A.,
and in San Francisco, the Bayshore Freeway. But for a hundred
miles below Garberville, almost all the way south to Ukiah,
Highway 101 is little wider than a spring creek. You can just hang
your left foot out the window and stick a quart of beer between
your legs and sail. It's a very American road, with big trees and
tourist traps ("Drive Thru Tree," "The Skunk Railroad," "Trees
of Mystery!" "Visit the House Built from a Single Log!") with a
few recent kinks.

Here and there along the side of the road are convicts. Members
of the Eel River Conservation Camp crew, all men, more than a
few unlucky to get topped in past busts. Even if they're picking up
Coca-Cola cans beside the road because they were dumb enough
to try to shoplift *Soldier of Fortune* from a newsstand in Oroville,
they're still smart enough to know where they are. When Lisa and
I drive by, they all look up and put their fingers to their lips. This
signal means, "Come on, bro, toss a joint. It's hot/wet/cold/
ridiculous out here."

Here's what happens to the tenderhearted grower willing to

share the surplus as he drives by. He's not treated like the government handing out free cheese and butter:

Redwood *Record*
November 25

BUSTED FOR TOSSING POT TO CONVICTS

A forty-four-year-old Miranda man has been arrested for allegedly tossing a small bag of marijuana buds to convicts working alongside U.S. 101.

According to reports from the Garberville sheriff's sub-station, a work crew from the Eel River Conservation Camp at Dean Creek was on roadside detail, about a half-mile north of Sylvandale on Highway 101, at 12:45 PM last Friday when a plastic baggie was thrown from a passing vehicle's window. The bag, which contained slightly over four grams of marijuana flowertops, landed at the feet of the inmates from the minimum security prison, the sheriff's office said.

The pot was confiscated by camp officers, and a description of the vehicle and license number was provided local authorities.

Lisa is a good woman to travel with. Like President Reagan, she doesn't believe in the fifty-five-mile-per-hour speed limit. Lisa believes in the ninety-mile-per-hour speed limit. This is reasonable, at least in the Incognito Mobile. And on curves.

But she likes to make frequent stops.

First stop is Orr's Hotsprings. Orr's is a steamy little resort tucked in a narrow canyon on the Comptche Road between Ukiah and Mendocino. The Orr's clientele has its good and bad eggs. It's a mixture of growers cooling out from the battlefields to the north, quiche and Volvo types from San Francisco, Los Angeles, and points east and traditional health faddists searching for The Cure, any cure.

They have their rules at Orr's. You leave your car in the parking lot and handtruck your luggage on a little wheelbarrow. No drugs, no liquor, no dogs. We left Arctic Ed leashed to the bumper in the parking lot. I thought this was cruel. Ed howled. He continued to howl. No reason to leave him outside the grounds. He's not dangerous. He's not mean. He's a husky; he loves people. If you've ever hugged a living creature on this earth, you'd like Ed.

Plus he's small, only ninety pounds, and he'd already been fed back in Garberville.

Lisa can be a loner. She went for a walk along the creek, possibly to hunt for newts. The California newt mates at this time of the year, so many of them so thick they cover the ground like worms on a rainy night and Cal–Trans puts up signs that say, NEWT CROSSING, with a little squiggly picture of a newt underneath the caption.

I opted for the sauna.

The sauna is beautifully fashioned of white birch. A blue stained-glass window looks out on the stream-filled swimming pool. I was a little embarrassed. I was the only man. Behind me were two women, about twenty-two, unGodly healthy, thighs of Athena, Jane Fonda smiles. I let the birch heat take me over. Ten minutes later I slide a glance behind. The women are on the top bench. They're not kissing, just talking. The woman on the right has a top of black curly hair, splayed legs and sweat like oil everywhere. Her hand is between her legs. She's fingering herself. Just like that. God, I love it! Life.

I was not alone in the hot tub, either.

There's this guy, late thirties, red hair top and bottom like the Naked Cleaning Lady, muscled but atrophied in some undefinable way. Very talkative. He starts telling me why he's here. He has cancer. He's from Missouri. The doctors in San Francisco think they can cure him. He has a blood cancer. So do his two little daughters. They've just been in the hot tub and now they're off to the sauna with mom. Dad is not sure the family cancer is curable. He has a different theory than the doctors. He thinks it's communicable, like AIDS. Myself, I don't like cancer a whole lot. My brother died of cancer two years ago. My father died of cancer twelve years ago. When those about you are dying . . . you tend to want to live faster. This tactless dork is splashing his cancer-ridden ass inches away from me. I'm beginning to get as paranoid as Fireman. If his cancer really is as communicable as he says it is, then, GOOD LORD, THINK HOW FAST IT WOULD TRAVEL ACROSS HOT WATER AND THIS WATER IS HOT!

Finally, Cancer Mary decided to transfer to the sauna. Five minutes later or so, Lisa decided to rejoin the lonely.

It's been seventy-two hours. Seventy-two hours. Abstinence kills much quicker than cancer. We've gone over the topic, I believe. . . .

Lisa has this little gnat's behind you can't help but cup your hands around. I could feel her oily juice under the water with my fingers, and so we managed to consecrate a few minutes to life before the Angel of Death returned from the sauna with his mutating leucocytes. He brought the rest of the family, too.

Second stop is San Francisco General.

Dr. Markison, the hand surgeon, says I'm a highly motivated patient. I'll be able to bowl and thread a needle in no time. Eighteen months to two years. Great. Be sure to keep doing your exercises every day. I do my exercises in a white veggie bucket filled with hot water. Lisa uses these 2.5-gallon buckets to pack dope. Down the hall, the physical therapist fits me with an electronic device about twice the size of a crushproof cigarette box. This little octopus wraps my right hand in electrodes two hours a day even when I'm driving, and delivers the class of shock that makes our prisoners in El Salvador admit they do what they do because Yuri Andropov told them to on the wireless. With me, it's supposed to promote nerve growth.

On to Santa Cruz.

Sunset over Seal Rock. The seals are barking like trained asthmatics. We've made an eight-hour run in six hours including stops.

We checked into the best hotel in Santa Cruz, the same beachfront hotel where Maxwell recuperated from his harvest stabbing. Lisa paid in cash.

I called the narcotics division. Pushing it. Almost closing time. The arresting officer is supposed to meet us at four-thirty.

Immediately, we run into a problem. The arresting officer, a lieutenant, is at home, sick. The police operator patches me into his house, and now we have a second problem. The lieutenant has forgotten all about our appointment. He begins to describe the bust. The bust sounds interesting, as eccentric as the plants themselves. Then we get interrupted. The lieutenant has two lines, and the police operator is patching through a second time.

"Hey, bud, gotta putcha on hold," says the lieutenant.

Lieutenant comes back on.

"Bomb threat."

"Yeah?"

"Yeah."

"Too bad you're sick."

"Yeah."

This lieutenant seems awfully down-to-earth for a narco.

"Hey, you wanna meet for a beer? I guess I'm going to have to go out and defuse the bomb no matter what."

A beer. Blood and milk. Another bar interview. We're in luck.

"Sure," I say.

"Lighthouse Bar at five," says the lieutenant.

Who am I to bring up a seeming abuse of county sick leave?

(It turns out the bomb is a wimpy Coke-bottle affair discovered in a cabinet of a high-school chemistry class in Watsonville, twenty miles away.)

The Lighthouse is a New Jersey bar lost on the surfers' coast. Clerks from the nearby police station are slamming bull dice cups on the bar, padded vinyl seats and a big poster on the wall advertising the upcoming Amarillo Slim Crap's Shoot-out at the Sahara Hotel in Las Vegas.

Naturally, I am shaved and besuited for our rendezvous. These *Cannabis* oddities are serious business to my way of thinking. Nothing must stand in the way of the lieutenant producing the pictures of the plants. Lisa wanted a look at the pictures, too. She's a little nervous, of course, she being a grower and the narcotics lieutenant being a narcotics lieutenant, but Lisa is a bold sort and I'm afraid she wouldn't be the first to go down to curiosity. She's got a green dress on and she's carrying two cameras. Lisa's going to be the photographer with the writer.

The lieutenant takes one look at the both of us, corduroy suit and dress notwithstanding, and he becomes *very* nervous. He doesn't want his name mentioned and, of course, I agree.

He launches into the tale of Gargantua. Real life follows Rabelais. The bust was all coincidence. They descended on the wrong acreage. The sheriffs had, of course, plotted out the address in the bleached ocean hills north of Santa Cruz using a combination of aerial photographs and assessor's data. But somehow they blew it. They were creeping up a drainage ditch on Bonny Doon Road when a grower high in what the lieutenant calls a "gun tower" shouted a warning to a second grower on the ground. The grower on the ground starts running at the cops and this boy is armed. The sheriffs drop to crouch position and the lieutenant pulls his service issue .357.

"Call the police! Call the police!" The grower is screaming.

"We *are* the police!" shouts the lieutenant.

"Oh, fuck," says the grower from behind a bush. "You're the police?"

"We're the police," says the lieutenant.

"Great," says the grower, coming out with his hands up, "we thought you were pirates."

So the deputies scoured the plantation. Remember, now, they were at the wrong place the whole time. Once they'd walked around a bit, the lieutenant realized his error. He got on the phone to the judge.

"Look," the lieutenant tells us, "this was an honest mistake. It's not like we're wandering down the highway. We have a warrant. It's just to the house next door. That's what we tell the judge. The judge says, 'Okay, keep going.'"

Next door were THE WORLD'S LARGEST POT PLANTS.

This place was operated by a bunch of white Rastafarians. Rastafarianism is the ganja religion of Jamaica. The white Rastas proved just as friendly as the growers up the road. They showed the cops everything, including, says the lieutenant, a four-foot-long dog bed fashioned of Thai stick. Marijuana has a number of medicinal uses. Perhaps it banishes fleas as well.

I ask the lieutenant an insider's question: "How come, Sir, if these plants were twenty-five feet tall, that the newspaper says you estimated only a three-pound yield per plant? Isn't that just a little skimpy?"

"The buds were only at the ends of the stems."

This reply doesn't make sense. At best, it is thin reasoning. I know it, and he knows I know it. So after the next question the lieutenant gives the definite, the-interview-is-now-over answer.

"Lieutenant, is the grower profile different here in the southern counties than it is, say, in Mendocino? What does a marijuana grower look like down here?"

"Oh," says the lieutenant, who's a pudgy, curly-haired beach blond, possibly the hardest-to-spot narc I've drunk with in weeks, "typical grower around here could look like anybody. Probably be wearing a brown corduroy suit and big felt hat, most likely."

Lisa sucks her body in.

It takes me a second to get it.

"Nice talking to you two," says the lieutenant, and stands up.

After he left, Lisa said, "No way I'm spending the night in Santa Cruz."

I called the lieutenant several times the next week requesting the pictures. He never sent them. So we still don't know for sure whether the genetic bizarrities were real or the fantasy of a sheriff's press officer.

Okay, so maybe we got a little wasted on the way back to San Francisco. After all, Mission Accomplished. But, hey, very little separates the average narcotics officer from the farmer opposition. Lisa is a charming American just like the lieutenant. She broke for a fifth quicker than the bibulous Mr. Mencken. Myer's rum, though. I don't know if the lieutenant has discovered Myer's dark yet.

The rest of the evening became a traditional blur. I'm sure James Watt and Jimmy Falwell spend nights like this one all the time. The press is just too cowed to print the truth.

Halfway through the bottle, somewhere near Pescadero, Lisa decided it wasn't fair for us to be having such a good time while Ed languished across the back seat. We stopped at a butcher shop and purchased a t-bone for Ed. The meaning of our mission suddenly became clear to Ed and the husky was on board for the evening.

We took Highway 1, the coast road, back to SF. Highway 1 is the discreet way to go, with no highway patrol on the coast route. I once drove Highway 1 from Noyo to Bolinas between midnight and dawn shepherding a friend of Maxwell's, which is a bit like eating breakfast in Skowhegan, Maine, and lunch in Cecilton, Maryland.

By Daly City, the bottle was dead.

In San Francisco, Lisa treated me to a dinner at Squid's. Mostly they serve squid at Squid's. I ordered halibut.

Then we went crosstown to the Adler Museum Bar. The Adler is the best bar in San Francisco, possibly in America. We drank Myer's doubles, sticking to the regimen, you understand. The Adler closed its doors. Now we had a problem. A complex of problems. Where was the Incognito Mobile? I'd forgotten. Lisa was in no condition to remember. How could we manage to start back for Garberville even if we did find the car?

Lisa began to debate the question Carol had raised long ago at Maxwell's hideaway. Resolved: Does the Modern Woman End Up Sucking More Cock Than the Modern Man Eats Pussy? A vulgar proposition, yes, but that hasn't stopped us yet, has it? I, for one, thought the great debate could be resolved once and for all, a couple of John Dewey Americans coming to a pragmatic solution, if only we could locate the Incognito Mobile and get to a motel.

"Where are we?" asked Lisa.

I peered around. We were on Washington Square Park across from the cathedral, catty-corner from the Washington Square Bed & Breakfast Inn . . . the Washington Square Bed & Breakfast Inn.

Solution.

We checked in. The night clerk was tired and gay and could have cared less. He put us on the first floor. (Ed was still in the car.)

Lisa pulled back the covers but her mind was wandering. There may be too much Irish behind Lisa's deep-water eyes. Lisa had already moved beyond the serious question at hand.

"Why do we have hair on only two parts of our bodies?" asked Lisa.

"What do you mean 'we'?"

"We humans."

"What about our underarms?"

"Not counting that."

"The idea is to cover mind and body at the same time, Lisa."

That's how the rest of the night went.

I like waking up in motels as much as Maxwell does but at checkout time we had further problems.

Lisa had spent all her cash on the rum and the steak, at Squid's and Santa Cruz. I was already broke.

"We can't go out through the lobby," I said.

I love the way Lisa smiles. It's a slow starter, for a smile, but once it gets going, it takes you there and back.

"This is the first floor, isn't it?" asked Lisa.

She pushed open the window, hiked up her green dress, brazenly folded two hotel towels under her arm and jumped to the street below.

Me, too.

15

PARTY NIGHT IN GROWERVILLE:
> Billie Buys a Yacht; His Father Is Provided with a Demonstration . . . A Grower Prepares for Armageddon with Solar-powered Jacuzzi Jets; Elizabeth Kübler-Ross Kills a Good Time . . . Please Don't Loft or Bounce the Ball, Thank You; Punk Meets America . . . Night of the Living Dead; Any Port in a Storm; A Stepmother Has a Good Time; Billie Cashes Out

Growers from as far north as Eureka and Hoopa, as far south as Ukiah and Lakeport, are dropping into Garberville this evening. They're streaming out of the hills and filling the motels for two big dances tonight: the annual benefit for the Redwood Health Center and "X" at Pyramid Pins.

Garberville is a marijuana town—lock, stock and barrel. Ukiah and Eureka are much larger but Eureka is a college town with Humboldt State so nearby in Arcata, and Ukiah has never managed to offer a spectacular Saturday night, even though it is chock full of bars. Marijuana people don't feel completely at home in Eureka or Ukiah. They feel at home in Garberville at harvest time the way horsebreeders feel at home in Louisville at Derby time. If you want to party in northern California in the fall, you come to Garberville.

And the place is just a little one-shot piss pot of a town, a main street lined with three gas stations (Shell, Chevron and Beacon), half a dozen steak-and-egg cafes, a gourmet deli or two, the hot-tub establishment, more store-front real-estate offices than seems probable, a Radio Shack, the Greyhound station, a few farm and garden supply stores and a slew of motels—one where the narcs always stay and the rest for tourists and growers.

People are getting giddy now. Most folks have their plants out of the ground. There's still a good deal of trimming to do, but many people have already sold or buried their bud in Ziploc bags and veggie barrels in the forest, waiting for prices to rise in the spring after the harvest glut has been smoked up in San Francisco and New York, Denver and Baton Rouge.

Billie is definitely giddy tonight. Billie is Maxwell's lieutenant but he's on his own tonight. He's taken his split, sold some of it, farmed out some more to distributors here and there and buried the rest.

Billie's spent the last two hours close to the drain at the Humboldt Hot Springs Corporation, soaking off the bush grime of the last two months and most of the paranoia, too. His straight cowboy hair is slicked down. His face is clean-shaven. His smile is working overtime around his big teeth. Billie's got on a new black shirt with mother-of-pearl snaps and his wallet's stuffed with twenties and hundreds. Billie's alive, clean, moneyed and smiling overtime. Billie's ready to party.

After the harvest he's sailing for Australia. Got the boat picked out already. Twice he's dropped down to Sausalito, but negotiations are proceeding slowly. He's buying the little yacht from a classics professor at the University of California. The professor's a little strapped, what with Reaganomics and the freeze at the university. Billie's not strapped but he's only twenty-two years old and the professor can't believe a twenty-two-year-old cowboy is able to buy his boat. He doesn't want to believe it. The professor wants to see every penny up front and Billie is still a grand short.

"Hell," says Billie, "I wish I could just give him a half-pound and let it go at that."

The yacht broker is a little hipper than the professor. Yacht brokers in California, or Florida, are not naive people. Billie senses the broker would *definitely* take eight ounces of good sinse in trade.

So to satisfy the stodgepot professor, Billie is going to bring him the pink owner's slip on his best motorcycle. The classics professor does not appreciate the power of this Kawasaki since the professor has never been on a motorcycle in his life, but the professor is not a total cretin and he knows the wild hunk of metal is worth the last thousand. And then, day after tomorrow or the next day if he can swing it, Billie's off to Sidney.

Billie bailed out of high school at fifteen in Decatur, Illinois, soybean capital of America. He knocked around, worked at a McDonald's in Louisiana, did a term in the Navy. "I used to ask myself, 'When am I going to get a break?' Now I look around and I think: Hey, I'm living close to paradise." Billie doesn't seem to mind that he sleeps every night under the plum tree with the machete. He hates to go home to Decatur or even to visit a city at all. He looks at all the poor dumb suckers frying burgers at McDonald's and he counts the hours until he can return to California and kiss a redwood.

Last Christmas, the last time he was in Decatur, Billie told his father what he did for a living. His dad didn't offer to return the benchheld power saw Billie had given him but he did start screaming. His father drinks a lot of whiskey. Likes rye. He told Billie only dope fiends smoked marijuana. Billie calmed him down long enough to assemble a demonstration.

Billie took a tumbler glass full of his father's whiskey. He placed it on the dining room table next to a similar glass full of water. Into the water he submerged three inches of primo bud, Maxwell's polio.

Then he plucked a goldfish from the living room aquarium and dropped the little fish into the whiskey. The goldfish died in seconds. It went belly up on the bottom. Billie netted another goldfish and dropped it into the glass with the marijuana. The fish swam round and round and round.

Billie laughs. Big smile. Teeth everywhere. His dad was not impressed.

"He's a thick old fuck," says Billie.

We'll start out slow tonight, Billie and I. Hit the health center dinner first since we haven't eaten, then head over two blocks to catch "X" at Pyramid Pins. Why "X," the premier underground punk band in America, is playing in Garberville at all is somewhat of a mystery but Garberville has always shown affection for the unexpected.

The health center was jammed. Perhaps 300 adults, even more kids. Hippie Mormonism, I joke to somebody. She doesn't get it.

The feed is good tonight—organic spaghetti and Indian curry. The food line curls out the door but the beer line is empty. Billie and I took turns tanking up as we waited for dinner.

While Billie was gone I got into a conversation about "Self" with a former computer programmer from Texas. The computer programmer says that Self is neither Mind nor Body, and once you realize that, you can no longer be hurt. She's probably right. Killer Jack might agree, too. I remember this woman from Kathy Davis's wake. The woman once had a four-year-old boy who died of a slow disease. Kathy Davis had counseled her.

"It must have been awful, having the little boy die," I think I had said back at the funeral.

"No," the computer operator had answered, "those were the best four years of my life."

Then I started talking with Jasper. Jasper is one of the most respected growers in the county. He's a single parent. Jasper was traveling through Ecuador a few years ago with the kids. He always travels with the kids. He thought he might want to settle in a certain mountain valley there where everybody is healthy. Since the valley sits on the equator there is less gravitational pull and, supposedly, less of a strain on the hearts of those who live on the valley floor.

Now he doesn't want to leave America. Where else could he do what he does?

One of Jasper's brothers is a millionaire who advises other millionaires what to do with their money. The brother believes that after a brief comeback, the economy is going to plummet. There will be rioting in the cities and perhaps civil war. Jasper can't imagine civil war in the United States because, he says, people are too dumb here to realize that the big rich control their lives. Even so, he has put away a roomful of fifty-five-gallon drums filled with beans and rice, enough to last a year.

Jasper would rather talk about his bathhouse. The boy's got a sauna, a wood-fired hot tub with solar-powered Jacuzzi jets. Now that's grower decadence. I've heard that steelworkers in Pittsburgh are lined up in front of Catholic missions but who can believe it? Jasper's got solar-powered Jacuzzi jets in his hot tub, and like Billie, he once worked at McDonald's. The American Dream: can't beat it with an axe handle!

Jasper doesn't get off his mountain much. The health center is one thing he believes in, however. Since he doesn't pay normal taxes, he makes sure to contribute the proceeds of three plants to the center. That's about $6,000, no fake count, because Jasper grows good plants. Jasper must be one of the few Americans who follows Ronald Reagan's exhortation to fund charity from the private sector.

We finally get our curry.

For entertainment the health center is allowing this strange woman in purple leotards to combine a trapeze act with a reading of Elizabeth Kübler-Ross, the German death aficionado who wrote *On Death and Dying*. First the woman in the purple leotards climbs up on her flying trapeze and floats above our curry. Then she puts her feet firmly on the plank floor and reads a passage or two from Kübler-Ross.

What does this have to do with debauchery and getting laid?

Not nearly enough.

I'm bored. Billie's face is falling into his curry.

Time to check out the "X" concert.

First we stopped off at the Branding Iron for a couple more beers. The Branding Iron must be one of the few country-western bars in America that plays jazz.

Out in the street again, Billie offered me a little mound of cocaine from the back of his palm.

"We're not doing much coke down at the hideaway," says Billie, testing his gums. Billie wants to set the record straight. "Maxwell gets uptight. Shit, he's never on the land. He's only been to the hideaway four or five times and then he always sleeps in motels."

Pyramid Pins used to be a bowling alley. The name is almost perfect Humboldt County, a little joke that refers as much to the power that certain fried minds attribute to the shape of the pyramid as it refers to the number of pyramid symbols used in bowling, the set up of the pins, their shape, the Brunswick logo. No matter. A former bowling alley makes a terrific dance palace. The floors are so hard and smooth. Naturally, the floor has been raised level but a sixty-foot sign still hangs along the far wall of the enormous room: PLEASE DON'T BOUNCE OR LOFT THE BALL. THANK YOU. Behind the dance floor is a stage, and, way at the other end, a jumble of tables, videos and foos-ball machines, along with a burger and malt snackbar.

Billie and me ambled in 'bout midnight.

The Pins was boppin'.

Place was on fire.

Full-tilt ooze.

Good rockin' 2-nite.
House party at Haney's Big House.
Bring your cheap sunglasses.
Oh, Lordy! I forgot my underwear!
Are we not men? No, we are Devo.
Don't stop me now, I'm halfway to heaven!
The local punkers crowded the stage: kids with strip-dyed orange hair, jack boots, black strap motorcycle jackets and studded epaulets. The sons and daughters of hill hippies, the kids, fourteen years old, wore their leathers over farmer's overalls, makeup, earrings, boots, their fashions fashioned from MTV, Music Television, because how often does Mick Jones make it to the redwoods? Oh, Lawdy, someone pass Mick some teeth!

Punk alienation must only be imagined from the moss depths of the redwoods, although, I suppose, it's possible to be real lonely anywhere. . . . Half the leather jackets were slam dancing and the speakers vibrated the cheeseburgers 120 feet back at the grill, but the dancers were upstaged by their twelve-year-old sisters and brothers who weren't old enough to copy their costumes from television. Slam dancing, pushing, shoving, pile diving, slap-slap-mock-slap, crash car into one another, because what is more perfect for slam dancing than the emotions of a twelve-year-old?

The moms and dads of the punkettes formed the next ring, unreconstructed hippies in Abe Lincoln beards, the women, some of them, in harem pants, with gold jangling bracelets around their ankles, bare feet, toe rings, rings on their toes. I'd never seen toe rings before. I'm standing next to a woman who's standing on a chair clapping her hands. She's got toe rings round her little toes. Lawwwwdy, Miz Clawdy, suck that toe ring!

Farmers in green-and-black swirled caps and camo pants. Bare chests. Motorcycle mamas, with red-lined amphetamine faces, San Berdoo colors across raggedy vests, tits showing, where'd the last twelve years go, huh, honey? A few carefully dressed L.A.–types in $200 French aviator glasses and safari jackets, buyers. Cowboys in point-'em boots, snap-button shirts and tight jeans. Loggers in wool caps and STOP POLLUTION: CHOP DOWN AN ENVIRONMENTALIST T-shirts. Indians. Gays dressed as Indians, loggers and cowboys. Lesbians in leotards and square dancing dresses.

My favorite costume was left over from Halloween last week: Ms. Marijuana Bust. She was about twenty, skinny, and dressed as she had been a week ago, in a pair of blue satin cheerleader shorts and an old Playtex bra. Get it? For those who didn't, she had painted two wild green marijuana leaves across her breasts. In the dazzling line-up of Coneheads, Draculas, Werewolves and Reagans singled out for their costumes at the Halloween dance, Ms. Marijuana Bust had seemed maybe a little bit amateurish to me. No way, Jose. She was shouted into first place by an adoring audience, and no werewolf came close.

The real youth contingent crowded the foos-ball table at the back. Or played Asteroids and Cobra Gun Ship on the video machines, like one of Sarah's boys. No age limit at the Pins. Must prove you're twenty-one to buy beer, which is all they sell, but any American who wants to party is let in the door.

I asked the doorman how many people they had tonight.

"Thirteen hundred and counting," he said.

"X," the punk band from Los Angeles, ("the most acclaimed new rock band in America," the L.A. *Times* is calling them) these wimpy outsiders can't believe it. Talking New Wave. Talking alienation. Talking cool. So who are all those bearded men out there pogoing with little babies on their shoulders? Twelve-year-olds with their fists in the air, drunken farmers—*farmers* for fucksakes—Americans who grow plants in dirt! The farmers are screaming for "Louie, Louie." "OH, NO! WE GOTTA GO NOW! LOU-EE! LOU-EYE!" Who *are* these people? "X" was still in America but they sure weren't playing to Santa Monica, and it wasn't the East Village, Philadelphia or Texarkana, either.

Exene, the lead singer, was a Westside L.A. Poseur, the type of wuss who keeps $4,500 James Dean lithographs in her Malibu cottage and creams for bondage photographs. She couldn't handle the excitement. She kept brandishing a little red-and-white can of Budweiser and protesting after songs like "Wild Gift" that she didn't smoke marijuana. Nobody cared. Half the room had consumed more Budweiser this night than Exene could drink in a month. The farmers just rocked back in their overalls and beards and screamed at the stage and LUSTED AFTER EXENE'S PUNK ASS IN THOSE SLICK BLACK LEATHER PANTS, oh, God, oh, God, KEEP FUCKING SINGING, MAMA!

Punk comes to America.

The rest of the band, however, the bass player and the lead guitar, was swimming with the scene. Babies, farmers, sixteen-year-olds rubbing titties, forty-year-olds whale kissing with their tongues hanging loose, the eight-year-olds dropping cheeseburgers on the video consoles. What was going on? Something's happening, Mr. Jones, but you don't know what it is. Punk had met

America for the first time. The bass player tendered a dedication to "the farmers in the audience," and the roof lifted off the Pins. This was no wimpy, sexless New Wave club. Who *were* these people?

Billie dances with everyone, so long as they're good-looking and female. He's very polite, the young cowboy, and he scores medium well. The problem is, most hill beauties standing around waiting, are only waiting for their Johnny-Be-Goods to come out of the *pissoir*. It's still the Wild West north of San Francisco, men and boys, three to one.

Usually, the dances at Pyramid Pins go on to four in the morning, or dawn. At two the management turns on the lights. Everybody tosses their empty Buds in the trash and helps to clean up. Then the lights snap off again and the band jams for hours. Pyramid Pins is the strangest and probably the best after-hours club on the West Coast. But Exene and "X" were running scared. They checked out early at two o'clock.

Garberville was all dressed up with no place to go.

Billie and I started for the Sherwood Forest. I already had a room. The Sherwood is a little plastic but the narcos are afraid to stay there and its hot tub is heated all winter long. Every motel in Garberville was full. Billie was planning to crash on the floor. Five years ago motels in redwood country shut down for the winter. Now the rainy months are sold out. In October the cleaners pour in from San Francisco, Sacramento, L.A. and the East. By the end of November growers slide down from the hills, park their pickups outside and spend hours taking hot showers and watching color television while they coke up. I was lucky to have a room at all.

As we passed through the redwood arch to the Sherwood Forest, the main street of Garberville looked like the climax from *Night of the Living Dead*. The streets had come alive. People charged out of the bars and dance halls for their motel rooms. The Sherwood Forest has about forty-five rooms. The place was dark when we passed under the arch. Ten minutes later, all the room lights were on, cassettes and televisions blaring.

Billie switched on Johnny Carson. Still time on the cable for the monologue.

We heard some very interesting giggling coming from the parking lot.

I thought there might be a party going on in the Jacuzzi. This was no time to go to bed. I walked outside, but saw nobody in the hot tub, which, with the pool, was sunken below the parking lot.

Two women came out of nowhere.

"Got a corkscrew?"

The moon was up. I could see the hills beyond the town, heard the bubbles in the Jacuzzi. The trees smelled good. I looked at the two women.

One was plump and fresh-cheeked, more muscled than plump, actually, wearing a turquoise sweater and red cowboy boots; the other was taller, thinner, with streaked hair, sexier by my way of thinking. They held up an undistinguished bottle of Wente Grey Reisling.

"Cork screw?"

I took the bottle. The thing had a dead broken corkscrew already sticking out of the cork. I cut into it with my Swiss Army knife. Cut my bad hand.

"It just so happens," I said, all charming and insincere, "that I have a better bottle in the trunk."

I replaced the Wente with a bottle of Kenwood *sauvignon blanc*. Instant party.

Billie turned off Carson.

The women closed the door. The tall one pulled out a beautiful bud from her purse. Billie took a little pair of cuticle scissors from his shirt pocket and began to snip it up. We both took a pleasant toke. These trimmers worked for real people. The taller woman said she didn't smoke marijuana. Billie and I smiled. The plumper woman pulled out a wad of coke as big as the first joint on her little finger and lined it up on a cosmetic mirror. Okay. We did the coke. We did some more. Billie started signaling me with his eyebrows. He and I retreated to the bathroom.

Billie started the water running like our man in Havana.

"These women are hustling us," says Billie, his septum encrusted.

"So?"

"They don't want us."

Billie had already been around the block a couple of times in his short life. I'm so naive, as you know. Billie did not think the two women had any desires to motivate us outside to the hot tub. Billie thought something else was going on. Billie was right.

As it turned out, these two were cleaners up from Sacramento. They were sharing a suite down the corridor with two other women. One of the other women was the thin trimmer's stepmother. The stepmother was broke. Back in Sacramento the three younger women had talked it over. They felt sorry for the stepmother. She was much older, and she didn't do dope, but why not give her a chance to earn some good quick bucks? She needed them. So they had brought her with them on the long drive from Sacramento.

Stepmother lost no time.

Saturday night in Garberville. Stepmamma was only forty-seven. She went straight to the Blue Room, alkie headquarters, and picked up a twenty-year-old cowboy with red hair all over his body.

She brought the red-haired cowboy back to her suite and right in front of the three girls who had decided to help her out, who were trying to watch television, who had their hair up in curlers, who wanted to go to bed early so they could wake up and start cleaning and earn that $100 a pound and drive back to Sacramento, right there, stepmamma had proceeded to fuck the brains out of the red-haired cowboy, screaming and hollering and fogging up the mirrors, the daughters speechless. And when they were done, which wasn't that long, the red-haired cowboy had stood up on the pull-out bed, butt-red-fucking-butt naked, scanned the cowering crowd and called out, "Okay, who's going to be next, ladies?" his red dick still semi-hard.

He was serious.

Naturally, the trimmers ran from the room. Billie and I were the first people they had found. Any port in a storm.

Someone knocked on our door.

It was the third trimmer and her boyfriend. The boyfriend was real big and none too friendly. Billie checked him over for bulges as we passed around more blow. He was only packing a hunting knife.

Now there were six of us and the image of this red-hot stepmamma oohing and aahing in an already crowded room and hollering hi-de-ho like a juiced woodchuck seemed so funny that Billie and I *insisted* on a look.

We weren't afraid of twenty-year-old red-haired cowboys.

Another knock at the door.

This time it was the manager, a sixty-year-old retired type who, I'm sure, had no idea what he was getting into when he bought a plush motel in the redwoods and moved out of St. Louis.

"I'm afraid we can't have any partying," he said or something close to it.

He stood holding the door open. We could all hear music and shouts coming from ten different rooms around us.

"Hey," said Billie, "don't fucking worry about fucking us! We don't fucking party where we're not fucking wanted. No fucking way! We're fucking discreet."

We all left the manager and trundled down to the trimmers' suite.

The room looked as if the Go-Go's slept there. It was a mangle of bathrobes, dirty towels and hair curlers. The TV was wide-open, blasting. The big room had two beds plus the pull-out couch. The cowboy and the stepmother were still bedded down on the pull-out, just as we had been promised.

Neither was too happy to see the crowd back. But what could they do?

Stepmamma started talking in a raspy voice. She sounded as if she chewed cigarettes for breakfast. She clutched the sheet around her chest and one of her thin, quite nice, blood-yellow breasts fell out as she lit up a Camel.

"How y'all doin'?" she asked.

The red-haired cowboy locked his elbows behind his head on the pillow and checked us all out. He seemed disgusted. There was nobody else he could fuck.

The thin trimmer was embarrassed. It was her stepmother, after all. She walked over and turned up the TV.

Neil Diamond was singing.

I could see we were losing momentum.

Nobody said much. Maybe ninety seconds passed. Ninety seconds is perhaps the maximum time any decent American can suffer Neil Diamond.

Billie stood up and said, "I wish somebody would spray 2-4-D over Neil Diamond."

Nobody else except for me and the cowboy knew what 2-4-D was, the carcinogenic herbicide sprayed on Vietnam and the forests of California, Oregon and Washington. The trimmers were all from Sacramento, and Sacramento is a California agribusiness town where the restaurants serve herbicides in plastic bottles alongside the A-1 Sauce. Neil Diamond and Barry Manilow are respected in Sacramento.

Billie convinced the thin trimmer to turn down the TV. He switched on the cassette we had brought over. Black Uhuru "Chill Out."

Stepmamma shot straight up in bed and both her thin, yellow breasts swung out of the sheet. She tried drunkenly to put them back.

"GOD-AWFUL!" she rasped. "What is that GOD-AWFUL music? Don't you got no WILLIE NELSON?"

Billie stood up.

He was gentle, smooth.

"You don't mind if I dance, do you?" he said and looked at everybody.

He turned the reggae even louder.

Billie shivered and dipped. He shimmied his shoulders slowly and swung his knees to the floor and back up again.

"Louie, Louie," said Billie. "Louie, Louie," he sang softly. "We gotta go now."

The party of suburban trimmers was speechless in their nighties, towels and hair curlers.

All except for stepmamma. She pointed at Billie.

"I like that prick," she said, reaching for another cigarette. She sounded as rough as a Montana wheat field in October.

Billie and I left.

I didn't like the other trimmers. They were wimps, like Exene. But I liked stepmamma. She could have moved to Humboldt County.

The next day the manager taped a cardboard sign to the cash register in the lobby:

PLEASE, POSITIVELY, NO PARTIES!

The next morning Billie was gone for the winter.

16

LISA CASHES OUT:
  America's Most Grueling Athletic Event;
  Sober Joggers Are Sissies . . . No More Ca-
  sual Sex; Lisa Flunks a Wine-tasting; Carol's
  Question Resolved; John Hinckley and Ezra
  Pound Together at Last . . . Journalist/Gig-
  olo/Whore; Truth Time

One week later.

It's noon. I'm sore all over. I'm sitting at the Woodrose, the window table.

Yesterday, I competed in one of the signal events in marijuana country: the Annual Southern Humboldt 5 Beer/5 Bar/5 Kilometer Marathon. The Kona Ironman Triathalon is reputed to be tough, and I suppose it's possible to work up a sweat running the 26.5 miles of the Boston Marathon, but in comparison to the Southern Humboldt 5/5/5, these other races are for children, neurotic lawyers and psychiatrists wearing $100 running shoes and $20 satin shorts, their stomachs flat, sub humans, barely American.

The Southern Humboldt 5 Beer/5 Bar/5 Kilometer Marathon is for real Americans and only real Americans participated: paunchy, fat-calved barflies; the women with red noses and chunky butts, the men, worse, varicosed, betumored with beer bellies as big as small pickup trucks spilling over their street pants. Some of the Garberville contestants wore running shoes but most wore black Converse tennies laced with any bit of twine handy. One old man was even wearing hiking boots with rawhide laces.

No matter. The Garberville Triathalon is democratic.

We all lined up, 2,000 strong (or was it 200?) in the parking lot beside the Shelter Cove Grotto. There we were given our first beers. Some of the sissy Redwood Marathon types who had somehow gotten by the judges tried to pour their beers on the ground. I don't know what happened to these cheaters. I think they were taken into the woods and eviscerated. The point of the race, you understand, is to run and drink at the same time. This is not at all an easy thing to do. The effete digestive system of the average athlete would leave him puking beside the road.

We're off! Sprint the quarter-mile to the Brass Rail, pop your second brew (no spilling!), blast out to the highway (no monitors to clear the road, this is not Bay-to-Breakers, this is the real thing), up the intense two-mile gradient between Redway and Garberville. What a hill! Few four-wheel-drive Toyotas are able to negotiate the climb. Cougars and woodchucks sat and watched from the redwoods. Far below in the mighty Eel, the salmon thrust their fishy heads out of the rapids and gaped.

The smokers had the worst time of it. They kept wandering into the brush to light up Marlboros. The hacking and coughing woke the owls.

Over the final bridge into Garberville. Coming close now. First, to the left, the alchie cavern of the Blue Room. The Blue Room provided the largest mugs. Beer number three. Back out the door, round the block, a dangerous cul-de-sac, return, down the steep steps to the Cellar for the fourth brew, back up the steps to the Branding Iron and brewskie number five.

So, yes, I was sore. After all, I came in twenty-second. Mariel Hemingway was also in the race and she finished three-hundredth. . . .

The gentle lesbians at the Woodrose brought me fresh-squeezed orange juice, hash browns, whole wheat toast, bloody farm eggs and organic bacon. Halfway through the scrambled eggs, Lisa walked by outside. I waved her in with a fork.

Lisa had been up on The Land for a week, fasting and making resolutions.

Lisa is more principled than the rest of us. Her most principled resolution was: No More Casual Sex.

I could sympathize. Sex should always be formal, the way the Japanese do it, from behind with their robes still tied and their toes curling nicely at the Moment of Completion.

I suggested we amble down Garberville Avenue to the Humboldt Hot Springs Corporation. We'd keep to opposite sides of the tub, of course, but the visit could still be made worthwhile. It would ease my marathon muscles, and it would give Lisa her first chance to test out her resolution.

Neither of us got what we wanted from the Jacuzzi. Lisa broke her resolution, and my muscles did not mend.

By now it was already two o'clock. We had no choice but to keep going.

I happened to have a case of mixed *sauvignon blanc* in the trunk, twelve bottles from the better North Coast vineyards. Polite gifts for the growers in the hills, you understand. Just the way my father used to take a sack of apples and the morning paper out to ranchers in Montana when we went pheasant hunting. The growers always liked the wine. Everybody's a connoisseur up here. I was once invited to a Thanksgiving Day dinner in a converted bus. This grower lived in a rusty schoolbus on a ridge top, but he made sure to provide his guests with two cases of Baron de Rothschild champagne in an enormous wooden crate.

Like some other growers, Lisa is toying with the idea of putting in an acre or so of wine grapes as a hobby. Lisa feels she should test out possible varietal wines whenever possible. We rented a room at the Sherwood Forest and commenced testing.

The David Bruce 1980 was a tart little thing, tasty, but perhaps a little flinty for my palate. Sterling was good. Cakebread was excellent. But we settled on Kenwood 1980. Top-notch, almost edible, light, dry, molten and buttery as it went down. It went down.

Easy.

The Sherwood is a fun place. It pleases travelers yet it does not scare off the hill trade. We entered from Garberville Avenue under the big redwood arch. The rooms have new beds, tiled showers and pile carpets. Tacky but comfortable. An amusing outpost at the end of the Great Western Motel chain. There's the pool below the parking lot and the separate hot tub next to the pool. Lisa and I never made it out of the room. We lay there on the queen-sized bed, our backs against the headboard, naked with the heat turned on full, the rain smashing down on the roof, sampling the best California had to offer, and talked.

We talked over the harvest. We talked over the past. ("God grant me one thing," Lisa's mother would tell her and Sarah over and over, "may you both have children as wicked as you are.") We debated Carol's question concerning oral gender duty, and I think we resolved that one. Kissing is what counts in lovemaking. If you can sit in a motel room and kiss someone for hours, the rest does not matter. It's a sad truth, but not everyone is a good kisser. Lisa is.

And we talked about us. We each had a bottle of *sauvignon blanc* to ourselves by now. Mine was a Parducci 1981 (a very good year, considering the rest of Parducci). Hers was a Navarro (cold, frank and beautiful like the Mendocino coast).

"What are you going to do after the book's done?" asked Lisa.

"I don't know. Sleep. Head up to Montana."

"Why don't you stay here?"

"And do what?"

"Grow pot."

"Yeah?"

"And fall in love with me."

"I'm already in love with you."

"You're such a liar."

"I'm a slut."

"That's true."

"I've always been in love with everybody I've slept with."

"Fuck you," said Lisa.

Lisa didn't believe me. She may have been right. Women are realists in these matters. Men are the romantic sex. We engorge ourselves on endorphins and float like pink butterflies. I do. We believe our own bullshit. Lisa didn't believe me but she wanted to. She started drinking. She finished the Navarro. She was through talking. Three bottles is three bottles, be it Kenwood *sauvignon blanc* 1980, or Night Train.

Lisa slid off the bed. She crawled across the pile carpet to the bathroom. I watched her blond breasts swing. I figured we wouldn't get out of the Sherwood Forest for a day or two now.

Lisa stayed in the bathroom a long time. I didn't hear a thing. She wasn't throwing up. Ten minutes went by and I cracked open another bottle. The national news was coming on. They were keeping John Hinckley in St. Lukes, the same plush mental hospital that they put Ezra Pound. Hinckley was no more sorry than Pound. Fifteen minutes seemed like a long time to sit on the potty. Lisa doesn't use makeup so it couldn't be that.

I opened the bathroom door.

Lisa hadn't made it far enough. She was zoned out before the toilet, hands outstretched, head on forearms, legs under ass and ass on thighs. She looked as if she were praying to the toilet. Her ass! It was a cherry heart, with one cute dimple on the right side. I don't know why there isn't a dimple on the left. But she looked so cold lying on the concrete floor.

Oh, God, Lisa's OD'ed.

That's what I thought. Lisa has her private side. She likes black opium. All that wine. What had she taken before?

"Lisa!"

Lisa moved her head. She did not open her eyes.

"What?"

"Are you all right?"

"No."

"You didn't take anything did you?"

"I'm sick."

"You look good down there."

"Fuck you."

"Want a blanket?"

"No."

I brought Lisa a blanket and covered her with it.

Lisa put her head back on her knees. I tried to pull her up with my good arm.

"Come on, Lisa. I can't pull you up with only one hand."

Lisa did not move her head. Her arm dropped to the floor.

"I know," she said.

I left the bathroom and caught the tail end of the news. I felt bad but what was there to do? White wine is a powerful drug and it can do horrible things to some people.

No, the real problem is this. I like sleeping with Lisa. Lisa likes sleeping with me. She likes to talk. She likes to talk in bed. She likes to chew it all over good. On the other hand, most of the boys up here like to get in the crop, come home, do a little beer and plow the sheets. Guys who grow marijuana—I hope I haven't given you the wrong impression—aren't so different from guys who crop corn or mill soybeans . . . all right, maybe a little different. They think more about their lives; they can make the change, take the risk and run the adventure. They don't get bogged down in silly religions. But even the most adventuresome pirate rarely talks about the ins and outs of oral sex and the meaning of body hair. Even though these are vital topics to thinking Americans everywhere. The problem is: Men are men. Americans are Americans. So Lisa appreciates the occasional writer.

Lisa understands that I'm here to do the story. I've met her along the way. She's Sarah's sister. Lisa understands that. She's no fool. She knows that, crass as it may be, I need her for business reasons. Maybe I need her on top of that. Maybe I don't . . . That's one reason she's back in the bathroom shitfaced.

Commercialize your own love and you've laid a curse on yourself. A journalist who writes about his love is selling himself, no? Journalist/Gigolo/Whore. I've always hated journalism. Imagine, if you will, attending the funerals of people you don't even know, like Kathy Davis, just to write about it.

What if Lisa comes out of the cold bathroom a resolved woman? So drunk she hates me more than she hates herself. What should I do? Talk her down so that the story may go on? So that she'll keep traveling with me and showing me things?

Truth Time . . .

But Lisa's not in love with me, either. In love enough to get pissed on wine and pass out naked. Not in love enough to kiss me good-bye. Lisa's a slut, too, like me, and nothing wrong with that.

Eat life or life will eat you, as Maxwell says.

The next day she went back to The Land. The day after she took the Greyhound to San Francisco and Air New Zealand to Papeete, French Polynesia.

17

MAXWELL PREPARES FOR SOUTH AMERICA: Brazil! Blowguns! Muddy Rivers!...American Women; The Clap; Clitorectomies

Love doesn't come easily to Maxwell. Lust does.

Tomorrow Maxwell's heading for Brazil. Brazil! Rio! Blowguns! Muddy rivers! Tawny-thighed Amazons in native bikinis! Tawny-thighed Amazons wading muddy rivers in native bikinis holding blowguns in their salty mouths. Maxwell lays out the fantasy to anyone who will listen. The women he's going to meet will have such fierce lips they'll be able to send *curare* darts through solid oak doors without hardly sucking wind. Oh, yes. Max likes foreign women better than American women. American women lack passion, violence and insanity. There's something gray and dull about America's Anglo-Teutonic heritage. That's Maxwell's opinion.

Maxwell's bitter. Maxwell has the clap. That's why he didn't leave yesterday.

At least he thinks he does. He might. He could. He's not sure.

A woman in New York told him that he was infected. Max had gone East to check on the Preferred Customer. It would have been a good trip otherwise, because Maxwell decided the Preferred Customer had not ripped him off. The problem had occurred closer to home. Maxwell thought that over for a while. Billie? Carol? Max is very basic. He didn't think motivation. He thought opportunity. Neither Billie nor Carol, nor anyone else in his California operation, had had the chance. It could not have been them. Maxwell came to the conclusion it really was the clerk at Emory Air Freight in San Francisco. Never trust a five-dollar-an-hour clerk who is wearing a thousand dollars' worth of New Mexican turquoise. But, hell, thought Maxwell, the woman was working for a major corporation. Just what is this country coming to? No good. This country is coming to no good when trust has broken down in commercial transactions.

The clap? God, life's little responsibilities. Max is thankful it isn't AIDS.

Maxwell called two urologists in Ukiah and explained his suspicions. The doctors were disdainful. They suggested the county health office. He called county health. They were only open one day a week, Thursday, from eight to ten in the morning. Today was Friday.

Maxwell concluded that Mendocino wanted venereal disease. For their own strange, sordid, mysterious reasons, they welcomed the clap.

Finally, he reached a woman G.P. who consented to see him and everyone Maxwell has been sleeping with: Carol, Sally and Angela. Who are Sally and Angela? They are two women who are very reluctant to be taken to a doctor and shot up with penicillin. But Maxwell has insisted. Social responsibility.

Nobody's very happy. It's the first time the three women have met.

"How long is this going to take?" Maxwell asked the receptionist.

The receptionist looked at Maxwell.

"For you, we can make it quick. We'll chop it off. For the women, longer, unless we do clitorectomies."

Whoah! Big Tuna Smile from Maxwell. Laughs from everybody in the room. This woman's funny.

"Say," asked Carol a few minutes later, and I knew she would, "can you get a social disease from oral genital contact?"

Doctor's visit was turning into a trimmer's party at the hideaway.

The verdict was good. The New Yorker was lying. No clap. A couple of cases of bad vaginitis, however, so the whole crew, Maxwell, too, was put on Flagyl and told not to drink. For the first time, Maxwell will spend an entire season sober.

Max loved the shy, meticulous doctor. She told him she needed to take a smear from the end of his penis. So Maxwell dropped his pants and began to jerk himself up and down with his fist like a monkey.

"No, no, you don't have to do that. Please," said the doctor.

Maxwell looked at the doctor. He realized the doctor thought he was behaving strangely.

"That's how we did it in the Army, ma'am," said Maxwell.

Tomorrow, Rio.

18

SARAH AND WYATT IN TEXAS, FIREMAN AND LANNIE OFF THE LAND:
Dead Mice; Ralph Nader

It was snowing on The Land. I woke up inside Sarah's trailer. There was frost on my mustache. I ate the leftovers from a Eureka restaurant, spaghetti and garlic bread on a paper plate. The pasta crunched. The sauce was frozen.

Sarah and Wyatt had gone to Texas, where Wyatt's people are from. They loaded up all their manicured bud, packed it in buckets with plastic tops, put the buckets in the back of Sarah's ancient Dodge van, tossed a blanket over the pot and drove four days to Houston. The doors on the van don't even lock.

The goal was to trade pot for coke, bring the coke back to California and sell it at a much higher price than the pot would have brought. They plan to bring back good coke. Sarah hates it when people cut cocaine with Italian baby laxative, the most popular thinner. "Just hearing the word 'cocaine' is enough to send me to the bathroom."

All alone on The Land. Fireman hired on to guard a shipment to Phoenix. Lannie took the kids back to Boston for a visit.

Sleet is slicing down. Sitting in the front of the trailer is like riding an airplane. The storms break twenty miles away. They come for you, cover you in snow and twist off to the next ridge. I could watch winter for the rest of my life . . . if snow was hot like beach sand and you could walk through it barefoot wearing a Hawaiian shirt with fish printed across the fabric, ahi, ono, wahoo, aku, aluua, tuna, barracuda, marlin.

After an hour I ran for the whiz hole. In September, when I arrived this year, the hole had been twelve feet deep. Now it was nearly full with ice water. A dead mouse floated on top. The water was so cold the mouse was perfectly preserved, its grey hair, even its eyes. Next to the mouse was a page from a newspaper. A picture of Ralph Nader beside a story with the headline: REAGAN'S RULING CLASS. I aimed straight for Ralph's head, although I do like Ralph Nader.

Sarah and Wyatt would return in a month, Fireman and Lannie, in three weeks.

19

POLITICIANS AND RETAILERS MUST CELEBRATE, TOO:

The Elections; The Cruel Wits of Garberville; 15–1; Blowing Smoke; Hand in Hand; Red Skelton; If Marijuana Were Outlawed, the County Would Die; Goosen with Two "O's"; Scott Fitzgerald's Peasants; Choice Meats, Pit Bulls, Dobermans and Shepherds; Souls

Two weeks ago Fireman watched the November elections. The Fireman is a news freak. This is not an easy thing to be when you live in a trailer twelve miles from the nearest electrical outlet.

For the elections Fireman bought a little black-and-white television that runs on a twelve-volt battery. He drove his old pickup truck to the picture window and plugged the cord into the cigarette lighter. He ran the cord inside the trailer, placed the television squarely in the center of the dining room table and told the kids to shut up.

The picture was all snow. Fireman marched outside, reparked the truck as close as possible to the window and balanced the television on top of the cab. Perfect. We were ready to watch the elections through a window. The sound wasn't too good, however.

"Shut up!" Fireman kept shouting at the kids. "I said shut up! This is the elections. You want to go to bed?"

The local elections have been over for months. Fireman was

pleased with them. His favorites won for sheriff and district attorney, the two public offices that most directly influence his life. The other big office he's worried about is governor. Fireman is what you might call a single-issue voter when it comes to his choice for governor. To him the contest is between a candidate who so far seems neutral on marijuana cultivation, Tom Bradley, the black Democratic mayor of Los Angeles, vs. George ("Duke") Deukmejian, the former Republican attorney general, a wild, frothing, committed, no-holds-barred narcoraider.

But first the lesser issues.

Congressman Don Clausen has been knocked out of the box. Clausen was the old gumball-faced Republican hack who could do nothing about mass unemployment in the North Country except dump on the new alternative to logging and ranching: marijuana. He told the local papers that growers had better start looking for new lifestyles. Clausen had also shown rabid support for the MX missile, and Humboldt County, along with Fireman and the rest of California, was voting heavy for the nuclear freeze.

The other lesser issue was gun control. No ambiguity here. California went 2–1 against the gun control initiative, and Humboldt County voted it down 3–1. And of every four growers I talked to, none could imagine who the one "pro" voter was. They say that when guns are outlawed, only outlaws will have guns, but in northern California, none of the outlaws were taking any chances.

It was a boring election, even with the charm of watching precinct totals through a window while rain fell on the television set. David Brinkley and Howard K. Smith looked bored. (We could pick up only one channel.)

Then they announced that the Duke was going to win.

"Oh, fuck!" is all Fireman said. He walked outside in the rain and snapped off the set.

I don't know why Fireman was so upset. Marijuana growers helped to elect the Duke, too, even though the Duke is hardly pro pot.

Maxwell told me about a friend of his. Max asked him if he was going to vote for the Duke or for Bradley.

"I ain't going to vote for no nigger," said Maxwell's grower friend, and that is exactly why Duke Deukmejian is now governor of our largest state.

Still, I think the Duke is a man of unintentional irony.

When the Duke landed in Willits in his helicopter to bust the pot-growing grandmother, he stood before the television cameras of all three networks and said: "It is regrettable to come into an area so peaceful, calm and beautiful and find evidence of this kind of cultivation."

Three years later, a week before the election, he stood in the yard of a beautiful home high on a ridge in Mendocino. The sun was setting. The sky flushed as golden as the embroidery on the little forbidden marijuana leaf the raiders wore on their caps.

"California used to be the hope—the place where if you were willing to work hard and get your education anything was possible," the Duke told the L.A. *Times*. California was "always the model" for people living elsewhere, the place where they could come and prosper.

Except for the part about getting your education, the new governor could have been talking about Lisa, Sarah, Fireman and Maxwell. They had worked hard in California, and California had worked out well for them in return.

If Fireman was split on the elections, encouraged by the new power of marijuana growers like himself on the local and congressional level and discouraged by the hatred of the new governor and the president, Bernard DePaoli was unequivocal.

Bernard DePaoli was the Republican district attorney in Humboldt who lost bad. Mr. DePaoli, the first public official to arrive at Kathy Davis's house, does not play life close to the chest. He was raised in the interior of Nevada, the real West, and he says what he thinks. He's bitter. "Bitter and naive."

Mr. DePaoli has a perfectly round head. Not a hair is left from eyebrows to back of crown, and the DA has a very large forehead. He looks like a puckish Yul Brynner. The cruel wits of Garberville have said that if one were to stick a thumb in his mouth and a finger in each eye, a strike would result every time his head was rolled down the alley at the (old) Pyramid Lanes. Black-eyed, close-cropped, disciplined, yet given to western exaggeration, he is a handsome man actually, if an intense one, intense in the way that the blast desert around Battle Mountain, Nevada, is intense.

"If marijuana were completely eradicated or legalized, the economy of this county would be set back five years—at least. There are 108,000 people here. I would say 50 percent are dependent on marijuana for their livelihood, one way or the other."

DePaoli takes a fat swig from his fourth predinner Heineken and purses his lips so tightly his mouth becomes a short, straight slit.

DePaoli blames his loss in the elections to the clout of marijuana growers. He says that a prominent car dealer came up to him after the election and told him that he couldn't afford to vote for him. If DePaoli were ever to be successful in the war on drugs, said this nameless car dealer, he (the dealer) would have to lay off five salesmen.

Mr. DePaoli has told the media (and he tells me) that the vote in southern Humboldt—Garberville, Island Mountain, Honeydew and everywhere Commander Mouriski's raiders landed their helicopter—went fifteen to one against him. Fifteen to one. Not a good showing.

"I came out for confiscation of grower land by the Justice Department and the IRS. My opponent came out against confiscation. I was the establishment candidate. We had the newspaper and a committee of the thirty most prominent citizens. We were floored at our defeat, absolutely astounded."

Terry Farmer rocks back in his chair. Terry Farmer is the new DA. He's warmed this office chair for three weeks. He was not astounded at his election.

"DePaoli had a hang-'em-high attitude. I'm for confiscation but only after the grower has been convicted. Otherwise it's a violation of due process."

Terry Farmer, thin, bespectacled, confident before the camera of Eureka's single television station, plans to bust marijuana growers because "the fact of the matter is it's against the law."

He's just not going to blather about it before elections.

"DePaoli is blowing smoke!" seethes the new sheriff, Tom Rennert. Mr. Rennert can barely stay seated, he's so mad. "I busted my ass on that election. We worked our butts off!"

The police chief of Eureka, county seat and largest town, ran against Rennert. The police chief is a friend of Bernie DePaoli, and the chief, Ray Shipley, went public with the discreet statement that if elected, he would CALL IN THE MARINES AND MARCH THEM FROM ONE END OF HUMBOLDT COUNTY TO THE OTHER! That was the way to get rid of the marijuana problem.

The chief lost big, too.

"Sure the dopers and Indians voted for me!" shouts Tom Rennert, a big sack-of-potatoes man, the near legendary lieutenant of the Hoopa subdistrict who once had the windshield of his patrol car blasted out by a shotgun while he was behind the wheel. "They know I'll give them a fair shake! But DePaoli and Shipley needed an excuse for losing two to one and the marijuana growers are it!"

Rennert pulls out a sheaf of precinct reports and shows me that DePaoli did not lose fifteen to one in southern Humboldt at all. DePaoli lost by only two to one there, and his showing there in the prime growing area was better than anywhere else in the county.

There's no question that the losers are blowing smoke the way the good sheriff says. But Mr. Rennert is puffing a little smoke, too. Like Terry Farmer, he strove mightily to present himself as, at worst, the lesser of two evils. But now he's all for clamping down on marijuana, too.

"Go after the violent and commercial growers." This is what Rennert tells Pete Mouriski when the BNE pays a formal visit after the raids and the elections are both over.

This is not what he tells the media.

Along with Terry Farmer, the fence-sitting district attorney, Sheriff Rennert is mighty reluctant to admit that Humboldt's deputies participated in the big helicopter raids. In the press reports, "sources" will deny that Humboldt was even informed beforehand. Two rather different sources had little difficulty remembering the truth: Pete Mouriski of the Bureau of Narcotics Enforcement, and George and Trudy Ralph.

The awful fact is, marijuana growers exercise their democratic right in Humboldt County. They vote.

Many of these outlaws had never voted in Babylon before in their lives. In the election that swept in Farmer and Rennert, says Sarah, a cultivator set up a pup tent beside the locked gate to The Land for ten days and ten nights. He registered every American of age who passed through.

Humboldt County has been called a marijuana county, and this may be true, as true as it is of certain counties in Georgia, Missouri (hold the dioxin, please), Arkansas, Kentucky, New Mexico, Oregon and Hawaii.

Just what is a marijuana county? Well, a marijuana county is full of marijuana growers, of course, but at the same time it has a number of astute merchants, quite normal in their own lives, who realize who their customers truly are.

Bob Dias, for example. Mr. Dias understands his clientele. Dias owns the Toyota dealership in Eureka. Last year he sold 161 trucks. A four-wheel-drive Toyota pickup costs a little over $10,000.

"I don't even smoke cigarettes," says Mr. Dias. "What I know about marijuana you could put on the head of a thimble."

Mr. Dias ran full-page ads in the Humboldt papers last October. He advertised a "Harvest Special" on all new vehicles and featured the used cars as "Sharecropper's Delights."

The ads were funny. Growers laughed and bought. The county establishment groaned.

Mr. Dias is fifty-five years old. Pleasant, plump, red-faced, he flashes smiles like new quarters. He's making money and he thinks Humboldt County is a beautiful place to sell cars. He's only been here a couple of years. He used to sell cars in Oakland, a violent place which lacked redwoods.

An oil painting of a Red Skelton bum reading the *Wall Street Journal* hangs behind his desk.

"Face it," says Bob Dias, the Toyota dealer, "if the marijuana money were taken out of Humboldt, the county would die."

Pierson's is the largest building supply store in northern California. The young manager of the plumbing department says that fertilizer, chicken wire and plastic grow pipe are the big three purchases.

Pierson's sold six to eight semitruck loads of grow pipe last year. That's a lot of plastic pipe. Volume has tripled in the last several years, and since vinyl pipe doesn't wear out for eight to ten years, the manager assumes the buyers are all first-timers, or else they're expanding.

"No big deal," says the manager, who wears round John Lennon glasses. "It's a standing joke here in the plumbing department. You going to use my name?"

I'm expecting him to tell me not to.

"If you do," he says, "be sure to spell it right, my name. It's Goosen. That's Dutch. Thomas Goosen with two 'O's. I'm going to have a smoke on the way home myself."

I guess we are taking a walking tour of Humboldt County, stopping here and there at different unabashed establishments to show what long, obvious tentacles the dread weed marijuana has grown. Turning rural American businessmen into Omar Khayyám assassins, selling their souls to the hashish cultivators. What a strange country we live in.

Let's start in Garberville, that one-street western town which stretches past Pyramid Pins to become a narrow two-lane highway that jags and jiggles through the sharp mountain valleys to the Pacific.

Steve Helsley, head of the California Bureau of Narcotics Enforcement, the man who believes sinsemilla is so dangerously potent, two tokes and you're a communist, claims that the growers all put their money into numbered Swiss bank accounts like the coke smugglers in southern Florida.

The local savings-and-loan man, two blocks from Pyramid Pins, almost across the street from the Sherwood Forest Motel where Billie and I and the Sacramento trimmers stayed, agrees. "Sure they launder their money," he says. "Two years ago, in January, a grower came out of the hills with a trash bag. He walked into the coin-operated laundry down the street, tossed the bag in the dryer and went out to get a donut. When he came back, hundred-dollar bills were floating all over the washers. He had forgotten to latch the door. Sure they launder their money. Paper bills can get moldy if the Ziploc bag breaks in the ground."

On a side street near the Laundromat is a spiffy new deli that serves exotic teas, eclairs and fresh-roasted coffees from around the world, not the sort of place frequented by sheep ranchers. A new friend of mine is sitting at a window table watching the drizzle in comfort. The friend is an ex-writer from Chicago. He takes me around the corner to the bookstore, a large and well-stocked establishment. The gray-bearded owner admits his store could not exist in a town this size outside of marijuana country. The old pig farmers just wouldn't buy twenty copies of *Diet for a Small Planet* each month.

The ex-writer pulls *The Great Gatsby* off the shelf. "'Americans, while occasionally willing to be serfs, have always been obstinate about being peasantry.' Fitzgerald never made it up here," says this friend of Sarah's. "These people are peasants. They hate the government and taxes. They love the land. They live in shacks without running water and drive junk cars. They use their money to buy more land. Anything extra, they bury or blow on coke."

Up the street at Firestone tire headquarters the manager says he has heard there's still a recession going on in America. "But business couldn't be better here." And then it's back to tires.

At the liquor store a traveling salesman tells me he has just sold seventy cases of Mumm's champagne and forty cases of Blue Nun. "That's $12,000 wholesale," he says. How many cases would he sell in a nongrowing town this time of year? "Five . . . maybe five."

The biggest store in the Garberville area is Murrish's, grocery and hardware emporium. Murrish's features bulk flour, granola, beans and nuts, "choice meats," Champion juicers, kerosene lamps and heaters, and, of course, specials on heavy-gauge Ziploc bags, black plastic tarps and Weiss clippers. The store exhibits the nifty Weiss clipper (everybody pronounces them "Wiss" clippers) in bushel baskets by the checkout stands. Mike Murrish says they sell thousands every harvest season at $3.95 a pair.

"Lots of growers buy a dozen at a time. They're too lazy to clean the resin off the blades with alcohol," explains Murrish.

The Weiss clipper is advertised as a thread snipper. I wonder if the Weiss people in North Carolina really believe that some 6,000 ladies in Garberville, California, pick the month of October to start their new winter quilts. ("I could see how the Weiss clipper would work well for marijuana," James Godwin, vice president for sales, tells me on the telephone. "It's a good little snipper. But I had no idea. Shall we say it's a market we haven't discovered?")

Murrish's is one of those stores that has everything. When Mike Murrish and his Uncle Harold took the store over in 1977, they decided to orient the country supermarket to the local clientele. The local clientele grew marijuana, by and large. The store went from a $1.5 million gross to $4 million in five years.

Mike Murrish is a young, personable man with a wispy patch of beard at the bottom of his chin. The Murrishes are almost original settlers in Humboldt. They come from Dutch and Italian stock. Mike decided to leave Uncle Harold's store in Garberville and set up his own store in Hydesville, midway between Garberville and Eureka. Sixty miles seems to make a big difference culturally. All the difference in the world. A few years ago Hydesville was strictly logging country.

"In Garberville–Redway," says Mike, "shoppers were into organic food and gourmet wines—and they grew marijuana for a living. Big, big difference in Hydesville. Here the loggers are into Budweiser and chew—and they grow marijuana for a living."

Mike's a funny guy. His hobby is collecting antiques. One time he was visiting the old house of a rancher turned grower. The rancher owned a pit bull, the fierce little dog General George Patton used to affect, and had neglected to chain the dog for Mike's visit. The dog bit him in the upper-right thigh.

"We almost lost the next generation of Humboldt County retailers," Mike comments.

Uncle Harold preferred Doberman pinschers to pit bulls. He left his Doberman inside the Garberville store at night. One morning it got out and ran into the parking lot.

"Some grower's German shepherd ate it for breakfast," says Mike.

Uncle Harold owns an AK-47 Chinese machine gun, according to his nephew.

"I asked Uncle Harold why he wanted such a weapon. Uncle Harold was surprised at the question. 'Why Mike, in case more than one person comes for me at the same time.'"

The last stop on our walking tour should be the county agricultural agent. Someone like Ted Erikson in Mendocino, one county to the south, who will say that marijuana is the leading agricultural product, $90 million a year. Such a person does not exist in Humboldt.

And so our last stop must be a favorite haunt of mine, Brown's Sporting Goods. I've sat around the back of Brown's for an hour at a time with Darryl Brown discussing the certain subtleties of steelhead fishing, or the different gradations in quality rain gear. Today there is an argument at the gun counter. All dialogue is guaranteed verbatim.

> CLERK (speaking to a young minister): We can't get enough of these Colt AR-15s (which retail for over $500). They're the perfect weapon. Replicas of M-16s, so the vets love 'em. No kickback. They'll fire a clip as fast as you can pull the trigger, so women love 'em.
>
> YOUNG MINISTER: Why would you want a gun like that out here?
>
> CLERK: Why, for self-defense.
>
> YOUNG MINISTER: What's there to defend against?
>
> CLERK: You wouldn't ask that if you lived out in the hills and had a marijuana patch to defend.
>
> YOUNG MINISTER: I don't do that.
>
> CLERK: But if you did.

YOUNG MINISTER: In other words, you'd sell to anybody.

CLERK: Everybody needs a gun.

YOUNG MINISTER: You'd sell your soul for pure economics.

CLERK: I don't have a soul, sir.

20

HAWAIIAN GENESIS:
> The Morays Celebrate; The Polar Ice Caps
> Melt; Maxwell Almost Becomes the Perfect
> Smuggler; A Man As Big As a Small Cave;
> The Testicles Are Cut from an Associate of
> King Kamehameha I; Congregational Mis-
> sionaries from Yale Manage to Exhibit a
> Little Spirituality; Mango Maui; God Takes
> a Back Seat to the Green Harvest; Those
> Who Stick Out Their Tongues; Cap Wein-
> berger Tries to Lunge for That Button; Sus-
> picion

The sun is setting now beyond the balcony of the Rib Lanai at the Keauhou Beach Hotel. The air is not too bad. You can still see Japan, if you squint.

As I've told you, I have a job to do here at this open-air table set with silver and thick white linen. My job is to feed the moray eels. It's not particularly arduous. You stand up, take a piece of bread off the salad plate and fling it as far as you can into the lagoon twenty feet below. The eels do the rest, whipping about and snapping at each other and scaring away the yellow reef fish. They're nasty creatures, these six-foot morays. Teeth must be four inches long. It's a tough world we live in.

Like everybody else back Mainland way, I'm celebrating. Celebrating my escape from the rains of northern California. I read over breakfast that California may wash away this year. Rainfall has already exceeded all records since 1849 when records were first kept. The tall hills of Humboldt and Mendocino may be the last things left on the West Coast if the polar ice caps continue to melt. Northern California would become the New Hawaii then, an island in fact as well as in metaphor.

I know Maxwell would enjoy feeding the morays with me. The fresh mahi mahi tastes better here at the Keauhou than anywhere in the world, and the prime rib (captain's cut) is so rare that Maxwell wouldn't have to eat it raw.

But Maxwell's already been to the Keauhou and the big island too many times. He'd be afraid of being recognized.

In the 1970s Max made regular smuggling runs to Kailua-Kona. He never had to worry about customs. There were none. He was flying Mendocino pot into Hawaii. Nobody else had ever conceived of such an in-house trick. The markup was a quick 50 percent, and the risks, for a long time, were zero. The Mendocino marijuana would then be packaged by Hawaiian growers and shipped out to Los Angeles, New York and Houston, sold as pure Hawaiian at three times the price. Wow, man, Puna Butter/Kona Gold/Maui Wowie. Americans are stupid, explains Maxwell. They elected Ronald Reagan didn't they? They believe what they're told. Tell them it's from the Kilauea volcano above Kalapana, nurtured in lava soil with guava juice, perhaps show them the Hilo postmark, and they'll never imagine it was really grown in the red dirt of Mendocino County, California.

George White, the old rancher, had pulled off a similar trick years before when he sold twenty-seven "different" whiskeys from the same barrel.

This little scam went on for years, and Maxwell began to look forward to his Hawaiian vacations.

Then someone's brother moved from down Napoopoo to Santa Rosa, of all places, or maybe it was their auntie who moved, or perhaps Maxwell was bringing in so many suitcases, steamer trunks, even containerized cargo boxes, that he was cutting into someone else's legitimate Hawaiian scene. Maxwell never figured it out for sure.

The last night of his last trip, Max attended a party in a big house set among the macadamia and coffee groves overlooking Kealakekua Bay, where Captain Cook was murdered in 1779.

It was a good party. Good dope, friendly people. Lots of women. Maxwell always liked foreign women and Hawaiian women, while not exactly foreign since statehood in 1960, are a far cry from New York neurotics or western Mormons. Maxwell was doing a lot of dancing, a lot of drinking and after a while he checked out to the bathroom. He went in and he sat down. The house was ownerbuilt. There was a big window and he could see the moon over the surf. His pants were down.

Suddenly the door opened. A man as big as a small cave, according to Maxwell, stepped in. The man looked down at Maxwell's pants. Maxwell's pants were around his knees. He began frantically to pull them up. The man who looked like a dark cave hauled back and knocked Maxwell out with one punch. Maxwell came to a few seconds later. His pants were still down. He was in the living room. People were kicking him, three or four guys, including Mr. Cave. A Chinese man, older than the rest, stood a few feet away with his hands in his pockets. The women were gone. He was being kicked all over. Max curled up to protect his balls and his head. This time he passed out for much longer than a few seconds.

He woke up higher on the mountain. This mountain begins 14,000 feet below the water, climbs out of the Pacific at Kealakekua Bay, and rises so gradually that few tourists ever understand that they are standing on the tallest mountain in the world, Mauna Kea. Hawaiians ski at the top. Mt. Everest is taller, but only if the part below sea level is not counted.

The men drove Maxwell a thousand feet up Mauna Kea. As the air cooled, he woke up. The men were talking in the cab of the pickup and he could make out some of what they were saying, although not enough.

They stopped.

"Out."

Maxwell climbed out of the truck bed. He was so beaten up he could not stand. He tumbled to the dirt volcano road.

"Oh, God, don't shoot me, please, you'll never see me again," Maxwell started pleading for his life since that was all he could do. The men did nothing. The older Chinese man wasn't with them. Maxwell kept begging for his life, keeping a careful line between pleading and whimpering, and as he talked he massaged his legs until he could crawl. He crawled and then he stood up and then he started running. He looked back once. The men were doing nothing. They were watching him run. One was smoking a cigarette. Maxwell did not stop. He ran as fast as he had ever run in his life, and the ground was not easy to run on—lava, saw grass and banana trees.

That was a long time ago. It could have been worse, Maxwell says now from the safety of the Mainland. Max tells a Hawaiian story. There was once a rival for King Kamehameha's throne. Kamehameha I was the Peter the Great of the Hawaiian Islands. He unified the archipelago and then modernized as the British and Americans began to arrive in the early 1800s. One of King Kamehameha's rivals was so frightened that Kamehameha would have him killed, he decided to prove that he was no threat. He emasculated himself. Kamehameha's court was shocked. Kamehameha may have been shocked, too, although he was not easily bothered. He was said to have been able to break a man's back with his hands, and he was said to have been given to melancholy, too. Kamehameha did not accept his rival's condition. After a few months he put him to death.

I suppose Hawaii might be imagined by those Americans who live on the East Coast as a land 2,000 miles more mellow than California. This is not so, a short distance back from the luxury hotels that crowd the white sand beaches.

Not so, t'all bruddah . . . You want fuck with us, fuk wit you, yeah? Time you be leavin', Haole, yeah? Laters.

Certain people command respect merely by their physical presence. They don't require Colonel Colt's equalizer, especially if there's five of them and two of you. You've got on L. L. Bean hiking shoes and a seventy-pound pack. They're holding machetes. You thought Volcanoes National Park might be a pretty isolated place to take your fiancée. Only you and the geckos and the sound of the steam vents. Big mistake, bro. Big, big, mistake . . .

In 1983 Hawaii had the lowest unemployment rate of any state in the Union. Many millions of Mainlanders, Canadians, Japanese and Germans visit the islands each year. Honolulu is the head-quarters for the Pacific fleet. Guess what the state's leading industry is? It's not tourism, and it's not the military.

In many ways, the story of American marijuana begins in Hawaii. Hawaiian Genesis. Until northern California hit the media, Hawaiian bud was always considered the best, and to many who enjoy marijuana the way they enjoy sex or good prime rib, Hawaiian dope is still the best. I like Hawaiian. It is a more intellectual high, crisper, perhaps longer-lasting. It's that leggy

Sativa influence, the kind of plant Sarah grows, less of a kick-ass *Indica* bar stone. There's a spirituality to Hawaiian marijuana. It reflects the ocean and the black rock, the mountain, *mauka.* Perhaps this spirituality is what the maniacal Congregationals from Yale were searching for when they sailed into the middle of the Pacific. . . .

Hawaiian Genesis. Maxwell once had a friend who used to live on Maui, the valley isle, which lies north, between the big island and Oahu, where Honolulu is. The friend was quite a bit older than Maxwell, and he was a horticulturist, a pacifist. He did not grow marijuana for the thrill and the money, but for the perfection and the art alone. Although he did not grow poor.

Maxwell's mentor planted marijuana at the base of mango trees. As the plants grew, he would twist them around the trunks of the mangoes. The main stem would stay fairly horizontal while the buds reached straight for the sun. Each plant produced a dozen, sometimes three and four dozen, enormous buds. They tasted exquisite. They tasted sweet, like mangoes themselves. His crop was named "Mango Maui," and connoisseurs in many places recognized what they were smoking.

Maxwell's friend later pioneered greenhouse techniques. He fooled the plants with an elaborate series of shades. Over time, he gave them less and less light, until they thought autumn was upon them and they would put out to their limits. The man was able to grow four crops a year.

His largest greenhouse held 120 plants in different stages of growth. The plants sat on a long U-shaped runway. Each day he would move the entire line along. At the beginning he would add another fresh seedling, and at the end he would take down a mature plant and kill it. That's how he saw it, like killing a beautiful game bird whose time had come. He killed one plant a day, trimmed and packaged it. Each day, seven days a week, he made $450, which was a lot of money then.

Then he decided to give the indoor plants a taste of their own like the Mango Maui outside. He planted a strawberry at the roots of the indoor plants. The strawberries grew right along with the marijuana in the grow bags, and they were something special, too. Each strawberry was three and sometimes four inches across. Giant strawberries. Some of these plants tasted like jam.

The man's dead now, says Maxwell. Murdered. He got involved with some big people who had never thought of making marijuana plants taste like mangoes or strawberries. That was not exactly why they were involved in the trade.

Maxwell's friend was found one day at the end of a county beach on the big island with his hands tied behind his back, a single bullet hole in the side of his head, $40,000 in his pockets.

The big island. *Havai'i.* Be sure to lock your rent-a-car. . . .

Hawaii is a folksy place. It can be very raw or very folksy, depending on who you are and what you want. A two-inch article in the local paper, West Hawaii *Today,* informs that a man who last year had been designated federal Farmer of the Year on Maui (papaya, guava, mango, orchids—a lot of things grow well in Hawaii) has been arrested with 410 pounds of pot. Months later charges are dropped because another farmer confesses the plants were really his. Four hundred and ten pounds is a lot of pot, and the Hawaiian police, coming from an agricultural background themselves, count the weight more honestly than their Mainland counterparts.

The judge threw the book at the guilty farmer. After all, the man had stood by while a fellow American was almost convicted, wrongly. One thousand dollars fine and sixty hours of community service.

Sixty *hours.*

If this farmer had been caught in, say, Texas, he would have been drawn, quartered, exhumed, salt rubbed into his wounds, hanged, what was left of his ugly body burned and the ashes scattered over the carcinogenic tar pits of Port Arthur. (Which is as it should be.)

Sixty hours and a $1,000 fine.

Hawaii is a funny place. I once asked Guy Paul, chief of police on the big island, what penalty a first-time commercial grower might expect, a woman caught with twenty pounds or so. Chief Paul is not the mythical rural sheriff. He's soft-spoken, laconic in his sense of humor and sophisticated. He's wearing a faded but pressed red aloha shirt and blue cop pants. His family came over from Portugal to work the cane fields. He paused and looked stern. "Such a person could expect a strict judiciary. Thirty days in jail."

But while the court penalties are often slight in Hawaii, the threat of crop confiscation is possibly greater, and certainly more dramatic than anywhere else in America.

In Hawaii they have what is called the Green Harvest.

Four or five times a year, the helicopters descend and pinpoint the crop. "It used to be like picking cherries. Now plants are hidden and dispersed. But the basic truth is you get in a helicopter and fly anywhere at all and you'll find marijuana in five minutes," says Paul. The copters fly 500 feet above the ground and often much lower. These are search-and-destroy missions. No warrants are necessary in Mr. Paul's view, since a live marijuana plant is considered to be a felony in progress. When the pilot or narcotics officers locate a patch, they radio ground forces who hurry in on four-wheel-drive vehicles and saw down the plants.

Some nights I drink Myer's dark with a friend named Lonnie. Lonnie lives so close to the lava flow from Kilauea that one night we went out behind his house and pissed on the crusty *a'-a'*. Up and down the flow, which is only as wide as a county road, although about ten feet thick, strange, pale yellow, almost colorless, flames flickered from holes in the crust. Wherever we pissed, steam shot up. I couldn't stop laughing. Pissing on hot lava, you understand.

Lonnie's from Newport News, Virginia. He used to work in a shipyard there until he got laid off a few years ago. A lot of people got laid off the time he did, and some of them, or some others, weren't too nice about it.

One night he was home watching TV with his wife. Two men came through the door. They had guns.

"Hell, I only got but the television," Lonnie told them.

They took the television.

Lonnie decided that Hawaii might be a nicer place to sit out the Reagan years than Virginia.

It was and it wasn't.

A neighbor honked his horn and walked up to Lonnie's shack long before Lonnie heard the *WHOOPA WHOOPA WHOOPA!* Lonnie took the wife and they adjourned to Black Sands Beach further down the Puna coast. Black Sands is one of the most beautiful places in the world. The tourists buy post cards of Black Sands and send them home to Minneapolis. Lonnie went body-surfing and his wife swam. They watched the purple colors come up after the sunset and then they went home.

Lonnie's sixty plants were gone.

Lonnie is a good-looking guy, tall, wiry, with short curly hair. I've never seen him with a shirt on.

He smiles. Drawls. All his people are still back in the South.

"I guess I wasn't meant to have money in my pocket. I cried about it for a week. Now I'm back doing honest work. It's better that way, maybe."

Honest work in Puna, the Big Island, Hawaii, is clearing land, lifting volcanic rock and sawing down Cook pine in the southernmost tip of the United States. Very honest work. Six dollars an hour.

"Way I look at it," says Lonnie, "living rock-bottom in Hawaii is one damn sight better than living rock-bottom anywhere else."

He slings a bare arm around his wife's waist. (I once asked if she had a younger sister.) "Besides, I'm in love."

Green Harvest helicopters are National Guard helicopters. These wild machines dictate bust strategy.

"The way Operation Green Harvest is structured," says Guy Paul, "we've got to go for plants. We lose air hours when we stop and arrest people."

That's why during the Green Harvest two years ago only eighteen people were arrested, and why many more were arrested the rest of the year, outside of the raids. The police expect the people like Lonnie to be gone when they get there.

Green Harvest always seems ritualistic. It reminds me of the nearly symbolic fighting among the Maoris of the South Pacific. The Maoris bulged out their eyes and stuck out their tongues to ward off enemies. Sometimes they came in for the kill and bashed each other's brains out like Christians vs. Communists, but often the wild lizard look was enough to settle the contest.

Although they arrest almost nobody, these ritualistic search-and-destroy missions by the county police took off twenty-eight tons last year. Fifty-six thousand pounds. That is more than half a pound for every man, woman and child on the island. In the past five years Chief Paul's men have taken 108 tons of marijuana.

The Big Island is the main marijuana-growing island in the state of Hawaii, but it is only one of five large islands in the chain. Few people on the Mainland have ever heard of the place. Yet more dope is confiscated on the Big Island each year than is busted in all of northern California, perhaps more than in the entire state of California.

Sitting here, cutting prime rib, feeding the eels at the Keauhou, I am within miles of one of the primo dope-growing centers of the

United States, and in terms of quality, the marijuana *Chez Panise* of the marijuana world.

The island price is about $1,000 a pound (slightly more if you buy a finger from the boys on the Kailua dock or along Alii Drive), $2,000 to $2,500 a pound on the West Coast, $3,000 or more, sometimes much more, in New York. It's probably worth it, all things considered. No telling when old Cap Weinberger will step out of Grace Cathedral high atop Nob Hill in San Francisco, weary from the frustration of it all, convincing Americans that hate and hard work are what is needed to rid the world of atheists and pleasure-lovers, fly nonstop to Cheyenne Mountain and press The Button. Who will care then if six-year-olds should mainline marijuana with rusty hypodermics they've stolen from drunken pediatricians? Not even me. (I have often wondered: What does this Button really look like? It is red, isn't it? It can't possibly be a discreet black or brown sort of thing, a silver solenoid switch like they have on the new stereo receivers. This would seem to understate the situation. It must be a BIG *RED* button, red like an armchair in a state college student center, tall and erotic like a seventeen-year-old's nipples. Although I *hope* it isn't. Nothing too tempting must sit across the desk from the lined faces of Old Cap or Mr. Reagan. Thank you.)

The *Annual Report* issued from Police Chief Guy Paul of the Big Island reads a little like text from the war on those Lesser Communists, the misguided of Central America. Perhaps the chief's report is a little more truthful than a White Paper:

> Our eradication efforts make only a small dent, perhaps 10 to 15 percent, in the marijuana cultivation industry on the Big Island. We are having some impact. But the battle is a long, never-ending one. Our mission is to persevere.

Chief Paul estimates that 10 to 30 percent of the Big Island's work force grows marijuana or is dependent on it for a living. What is puzzling about Hawaii is that growers seldom use their power. They are not political the way growers are in northern California. Most do not bother to vote.

"A lot of jeeps are purchased for cash," says Andrew Levin, the state representative from South Kona. "It is clear to many businessmen that their livelihood is dependent on dope growers, but there is no political pressure from either growers or those they buy from."

Still, not all residents of the Big Island are willing to persevere in the never-ending battle.

At Green Harvest time the letters-to-the-editor column of West Hawaii *Today* fills with protest. The headline of one letter is: EVEN GOD TAKES BACK SEAT TO GREEN HARVEST. The helicopters, it seems, woke this Christian up too early on Sunday morning. Another headline reads: ERADICATE RATS, NOT PAKALOLO. The rat/pakalolo letter is quite reasonable for several paragraphs. Then it takes a distinctly racist plunge:

Let every law enforcement officer of Irish descent remember that even the blessed shamrock was at one time forbidden by the British to be grown on Irish soil. According to legend pakalolo is a holy herb and first sprouted from King Solomon's grave! So don't let the bastards wear you down. Happy planting, happy harvesting.

The letter is signed "Veteran Grower." And this in one of the most conservative newspaper chains in the United States. "Happy planting. Happy harvesting . . . King Solomon's grave!" Good, gosh, a-mazy, it's enough to make one want to vacation in Kansas! (Where's Toto?)

But my favorite letter in a Hawaiian paper (and I always love letters) is entitled, GREEN HARVEST VS. BIG RED. Why brilliant letter-writers like the following are not congressmen, senators and even presidents, is a fault of our plutocracy.

Editor:

I get one problem maybe you can solve. My problem his name Big Red. Big Red he one champion fighting chicken. He won five fights in three months and he never get beat. All other roosters fear him like plump tourist fears "Jaws." His last opponent so scared he try fly home to Maui, but if Alenuihaha (the ocean current) didn't get him Big Red would. Some difference.

"So what's the problem?" you ask. Last week Green Harvest come above my house. One helicopter come very close over chicken coop but he no find nothing. But he make Big Red to panic. Poor rooster he run and squawk everywhere to hide but no can find. Did you ever see a chicken cry? Pitiful. Rooster tears very bitter, I telling you. His lips they quivered like laundry flapping in a stiff wind. Finally he seek refuge in Tutu's bloomers (I think you call them). But wait, there's more.

I called Green Harvest police to complain but they only say he sick from Tutu's bloomers. Imagine! And now Tutu angry, too.

No, I say. That helicopter stole my rooster's fighting spirit and left me with one very nervous inferiority complex with feathers. I never can fight him now. At this moment he content to sit one egg.

Green Harvest owes me income now. Maybe they give me one job. I like be Green Harvest policeman. Easy, heh, and I sure to get very rich fast.

What you think?

Yours,
Mario

(True Hawaiian Pidgin will never be spoken on "Magnum, P.I.")

This suspicion on the part of many Americans close to the dope trade that the law enforcement agents appointed to protect them might be confiscating illegal drugs only to sell it themselves is an interesting and persistent charge throughout America in the 1980s. People in Hawaii, California and much of the South seem to think the French Connection pertains to them.

The flaw in the accusation is not lack of greed on the part of law enforcement. Too often it seems, only Baretta and Kojak would refuse a quick and easy turnaround. (After all, the man profiled in the next chapter, director of the war on drugs for the current administration, once helped to indict fifty-two of seventy narcotics officers working for the nation's largest city.) The flaw, as Maxwell pondered in analyzing who ripped off his first shipment of the year, is not one of motive but one of opportunity. Certainly, many raiders have the opportunity. One story rampant in Sonoma County, California, has it that two uniformed sheriffs once pulled up to a grower's home in a marked sheriff's car during business hours. The two deputies, allegedly, were so rude that they did not bother to step out of the patrol car. They opened the trunk with a switch under the dash, and commanded the bearded grower: "Fill it." Max said he knew a friend of the aggrieved grower. The grower was frightened like a fox. He went out to his patch—it was early in the year—and returned with enough short, male, pot that was as far from resinous sinsemilla as the bleachers in Shea Stadium are from the dugouts, and filled the corrupt sheriffs' trunk.

The real problem with such citizen paranoia is this: How do narcotics agents sell the marijuana they have ripped off? It is easier to understand how officers in Chicago and Manhattan might sell their heroin and cocaine. They are busting distributors, wholesalers and retailers, not dirt-clod farmers in Thailand, Turkey and Colombia. But those officers who bust marijuana farmers are busting Americans. These Americans speak the same language. Their kids go to the same schools as the children of the narcos, except for the federal and some of the state raiders. How do the officers develop clean and secret connections?

A small place like Hawaii is full of a thousand stories. Hawaii is an ingrown community, especially the outer islands. Large families, close-knit families, families without Mainland greed, but families that want to get ahead. It doesn't take too much confiscated bud to buy a solar-powered refrigerator; it doesn't take much more to cover the payments on a marlin boat. A lot of policemen come from large families without a lot of greed, but maybe just a little, yeah?

All anecdotes, of course—nothing firm, naturally.

Nothing sordid like what happens in places like New York City where the arresting officers don't even smoke or snort the drugs they steal and sell.

POLITICS

21

DRUG WAR, WASHINGTON, D.C.:
Bums; Rudolpho J. Giuliani, Nancy Reagan, Gary Coleman, Ed Meese, The President, George Bush, Attorney General French Smith; Moral Fiber; Just What Drugs Constitute a Drug Scandal? . . . Prohibition? . . . Bam, Bam, Bam; Articulate Woodchucks; The Solution to Youthful Drug Abuse and the Condition of Youth as Well; Simple Pleasures; Ovaltine and the Inverted Crow; Good Men

Long way from Keauhou Beach to the Justice Department in Washington, D.C. Late February. Time to abandon the aloha shirts with marlin on the back. It snowed eleven inches the day after I arrived in Washington. The airport will be closed tomorrow. But today I am amazed. Americans are conked out on the front lawn at the Justice Department. They're sleeping. I guess you could call these people bums. I've never seen bums in Hawaii or northern California. I don't have a blanket to give these guys. I've only got a borrowed parka. If I gave them that, I'd freeze myself, and you can't interview attorney generals when your lips are frozen. What do these chilled Americans dream about? Lithe exercise instructors kicking out the line at the morning aerobics session on the lawn next to the Keauhou? Doubtful . . .
Inside the Justice Department, a smooth, granite building

presumably broken apart by day laborers in Vermont decades ago, is Rudolpho J. Giuliani, operations manager for what must be called The Opposition.

Ronald Reagan has gone on record saying he will do whatever is necessary to end the drug menace and cripple organized crime. Nancy Reagan has teamed up with Gary Coleman, the strange dwarf on the television show "Diff'rent Strokes," to tell pre-teens of a sixth-grade marijuana addict who murdered his older sister when she wouldn't slip him the change to cover his habit. Ed Meese, president behind the president, has devised the most comprehensive drug policy since the British fought the Opium Wars for the commercial right to addict Asians to uncooked heroin base. Vice President George Bush is heading up the new federal strike forces, and Attorney General French Smith has been sighted on "60 Minutes," wandering about Pakistan in search of hashish factories.

But the brains behind the Reagan drug war belong to Rudolpho J. Giuliani, associate attorney general, a man (as they say in politics) who is strangely suited to his job.

Mr. Giuliani has spent some years litigating for the Rockefeller Foundation and the *Wall Street Journal* while in the employ of Patterson, Belnap, Webb and Tyler in New York City, but his spurs were won in narcotics. Always a dirty business. It turns good men into bad. Giuliani cleaned house on the special investigating unit of the New York Police Department, whose detectives were known as the "princes of the city," because they were the best, the brightest and the toughest officers and they were free to investigate narcotics violations up and down Manhattan without having to clock in like brogan-shod patrolmen. The trouble was, unlike Sarah or Maxwell, they lacked moral fiber, that sense of identity and purpose which comes, perhaps, from working in the open air close to the soil. When the detectives busted coke and smack dealers, they tended to keep any found cash for themselves. They found a lot. Sometimes they kept the heroin itself and sold it back on the street. Between 1968 and 1971, fifty-two of seventy were indicted for various transgressions while most of the rest served as the pardoned witnesses. Giuliani was a key prosecutor in the U. S. attorney's office, and the successful prosecution of the scandal along with the successful book and movie brought him to Washington.

Washington is currently reeling under another drug scandal, involving the Environmental Protection Agency. The Reagan appointees have been looking the other way while cancer-causing chemicals have been dumped from Los Angeles to New Jersey. Carcinogens have a way of killing voters (although slowly). The gofers in the section of the Justice Department where Giuliani works are running back and forth today crisis-managing the mini-debacle.

Still, there's plenty of time to discuss traditionally illegal pollutants.

"If we can reduce the drug problem 20–25 percent, we'll have a corresponding decrease in crime," says Giuliani.

"Marijuana is not a prohibition situation. The pressure to do away with the Prohibition amendment was much greater. Since 1979 there have been no reductions of penalties for marijuana in any state whatsoever.

"I have trouble separating marijuana at one end from heroin at the other. If we liberalize our position vis à vis marijuana, we erode the position vis à vis heroin. Legalization would massively increase use. As time goes by, what would that do for cocaine and heroin use? They would increase and then we would be dealing with a terrible, terrible problem.

"What we've done with alcohol is not a good example of what we should do with marijuana. It's a stupid kind of consistency to take one dangerous substance and make it as available as the first."

Bam, Bam, Bam.

Giuliani speaks with a slight whistle. The flaw becomes appealing after a while. He is a tall, bulky, earnest man. He reminds me of a sincere and articulate woodchuck. For punctuation at the end of his sentences, his eyeballs roll toward the ceiling until the whites show.

Somehow this big carpeted law office inside the Justice Department seems to be a long, long way from the mountains above the Eel River. Somehow I just can't imagine Mr. Giuliani walking the ridge line above Lisa's cabin in his Florsheim wingtips, the fog swimming up the valleys under the full moon and the crusty owls hooting at the tops of the redwoods like a bunch of snoring coots in an old folks' home. We're talking drugs here, and drugs are, *a priori*, from the git-go, make no bones about it, unAmerican. Mr. Giuliani and the others seem to have missed out on the logic of home-grown. While they've been scouring Pakistan, interdicting Cessna's over the Guijara Peninsula and poisoning Belize with paraquat, the gentle herb has taken root in American soil,

Kentucky and California. And the boys and girls at the drive-in and the bowling alley (nine out of ten of them adults, thank you) seem to like it right well.

Which makes it no less *evil*, you understand.

Mr. Giuliani is not bothered that 4.5 million Americans have become convicted felons through their affection for this "dangerous" substance. He agrees that 4.5 million Americans is a lot of Americans, but in the war on drugs, Operation Hot Pursuit, it is only "a matter of inefficiency." No matter that 20,000 persons are now in prison for marijuana crimes, that it costs $25,000 to prosecute each one, that $400 million more must be spent each year to keep them behind bars, that 400,000 marijuana cases cram the clogged justice system each year, that several billion dollars is spent annually in a clumsy war to interdict pot imports. So much marijuana is being smuggled in that wags at the *Wall Street Journal* have calculated America would be a net *importer* of agricultural products if anyone counted the national affection for *Cannabis*. Our marijuana jones may be the second-leading cause for this country's balance of trade deficit, according to the *Journal*. The first is oil. . . . Home-grown may save the economy long before coal and oil shale.

Of course, legalization would mean Gary Coleman and every other twelve-year-old would spend his life stoned. As George Farnham wrote in a marvelous tongue-in-cheek editorial in the Washington *Post* which favored the legalizing and taxing of marijuana, "It is no more in the national interest that every twelve-year-old spend his or her day smoking tobacco or sipping bourbon. It is equally unlikely."

Strip the "forbidden fruit" mystique from pot-smoking and fewer teen tykes will toke marijuana than sip beer now.

Of course, drug use among youth masks a far larger problem: these youth themselves. Sauntering around the downtown areas of our cities with ghetto blasters perched on their shoulders and surly smirks lazed across their mouths where polite smiles should be. Acting tough and insipid and ambiguous, eating bad food, sprouting unsightly pimples, turning their caps around backwards, asking too many questions about everything, hopping their cars, swimming in public areas without their trunks, chewing gum, always acting much too earnest, speaking even when not spoken to. What right do these whelps have, disobeying adult America? None. None whatsoever. They should all be rounded up with helicopters and nets and locked someplace far away where they won't bother decent folk. Perhaps Long Island. Nothing interesting has ever happened on Long Island. The place is worthless. Let us simply invoke eminent domain, help the current residents to start worthwhile lives in Texas or Minnesota and move this nation's teens east of Elmont. There they can drink Dr Pepper and smoke dope and diddle each other to their heart's content. Those lucky enough to live to age twenty can be welcomed back to civilized society with a *bris,* or something. That's the solution to the drug problem.

As for adults, the vast majority of marijuana smokers, who cares? If people want to toke up before they slide between the sheets, why not let 'em?

The problem to my way of thinking is not drugs but lack of discipline. People just refuse to turn off "Days of Our Lives" and finish the New York *Times* crossword puzzle the way they should. They suffer a little pain in the *cabeza* and they insist that Doctor Welby prescribe some worthless balm like codeine Tylenol. They make more money than their husbands and they grope for the valium. Entire movies starring Jill Clayburgh are made about these whiners. And the junkies! Look, if a person wants to kill himself, that's his God-given right. The government should issue these people shovels so they can go out to Nevada and dig their own graves next to an MX missile site. That'd be a whole lot cheaper than methadone.

I'm afraid I don't understand our species. We can't seem to enjoy the simple pleasures. I never drank a beer until I was twenty-one. I promised my father back in Montana.* I never touched the dreaded weed until I was eighteen when a naked woman dared me to. Really, a warm glass of milk and a long night in front of the TV are where I'm at. I can't understand what's the matter with the rest of you.

Well, perhaps, a little Ovaltine in the milk once in a while, and maybe somebody to French kiss with during the reruns of the "Rockford Files". . . .

Well, maybe after sign-off, we could stumble out to the Jacuzzi and, you know, you could slip on that camisole . . . and while you're up would you mind fixing me a Myer's and lime over?

Oh, God, don't stop that toe-sucking!

I do like variety.

---

*This is the truth.

Perhaps, after we get out of the tub maybe the Inverted Crow and then, I don't know, what say? Kung Pao chicken?

The simple pleasures. We Americans deserve something, don't you think? We work so hard to make the world a better place. . . .

Marijuana. You can listen to a hundred wimpy Ph.D.s bubble forth on "Good Morning America" about the dangers of abuse. You can read a thousand law enforcement manuals or sociological puff–papers without understanding why 30 million American citizens smoke marijuana. Here's why: Marijuana makes fucking even more fun. It relaxes the frenetic and it makes the shy giddy. It relieves boredom and it turns the sunsets a deeper orange. Any cheap, relatively safe drug that does all this cannot be easily stamped out.

SPRINGTIME

22

MAXWELL AND BILLIE

The last time I saw Maxwell, we were sitting in the cab of the big papa pickup in the parking lot of a cheap, but quiet, little motel on the south edge of Ukiah.

Max was driving to the San Francisco airport, then flying to South America. It was going to be a long trip. Max was rolling a few numbers for the road. He'd taken a small baggie of bud from his shirt pocket, the famed "polio," Maxwell's preferred personal smoke this season. He was clipping the bud with a little pair of cuticle scissors that he always carries and the clippings were piling up sweetly on a *Time* magazine he was using as a platform.

Suddenly, a bunch of kids piled out of one of the motel rooms. They were little kids, five or six years old, a girl and a boy, and I think another girl. One of the little girls was riding one of those unbreakable tricycles with the big yellow wheels.

She rode right over to the pickup and shouted up at Maxwell in a voice that was as cute and firm as her big wheeler.

"You been here long?"

"Why, no, I just got here."

Max is rolling away, clipping and piling and licking.

"Well, I been here longer than you have," says the little girl who's wearing some kind of pink T-shirt with an apple on the front and old jeans. Cute as a button.

"Longer than I have? Whoah! No shit?" says Maxwell. "That's impressive."

He brings one of the cigarettes to his lips and seals it.

The minute Max started talking the rest of the kids trotted over to the truck. Here was some action. Since the pickup is four-wheel

241

drive and elevated and the kids were small, they couldn't see what
Maxwell was doing in the driver's seat.

Without stopping his hands, Max leaned out the window and
looked the little crew over.

He growled.

"Do you know who I am?"

There's two twinkles in Max's eyes and one goofy smile on his
lips and the growl is as deep as a wolf's.

"No! Who?"

"I'm the *monster!*"

Maxwell's really growling bad. Of course, he's smiling at the
same time, and all the while he's tapping and rolling below the
window.

"Yes, I am. Yes, I am!"

Grrrrhh.

The little kids really eat this up. They're giggling almost out of
control, laughing and pulling at their clothes. The little girl in the
apple T-shirt jumps up and down in her little sneakers. She's got
her hands held straight and tight to her sides. She loves this game.

"You're not really a monster," she says.

Maxwell did not answer. He stared her straight in the face with
his dark eyes and huge bald head. He stared her down for ten
seconds.

"Okay," says the girl finally, "if you're the monster, what do
you do?"

"Why, I take little children and sell them to the gypsies."

The little boy speaks up. He's the youngest.

"Who are the gypsies?"

"Oh," says Max, the growl all gone, "you don't know who the
gypsies are? Well, if you're a gypsy, you have to travel all around
and do illegal things and wear funny clothes, too."

The little girl puts her hands deep in her pockets and just
squishes back and forth on her heels. She's beaming.

"You like that part about wearing the funny clothes, don't
you?" asks Maxwell.

"Yes, I do."

Max's eyes went up and he nodded his head with the biggest
Tuna Smile ever. He loved her answer: "Yes, I do."

A pink door opened behind the kids. An older man stepped out
of the motel room wearing white sox and no shoes, his shirt
hanging out. He looked about sixty and was probably their
grandpa.

"Jeannie," says gramps to the little girl in the apple T-shirt.

"How ya doin'? How ya doin'?" says Maxwell to gramps.

"Hey, not bad," says grandpa. "Nice day, isn't it?"

"Sure is," says Maxwell. "Yes, it certainly is."

Six weeks later I got a call from Maxwell, and he was talking a mile a minute. Maxwell never made it to Brazil. He got as far as Mexico, a little hotel in San Blas that he likes. Then he got a phone call. His father had died. He had been killed in a car crash the week before. The funeral was already over. The family had tried to locate Max, but how could they?

Max flew first to Texas where his father's big Lincoln had gone off the road. His father had been driving. He was alone in the car. Nobody knew what his father had been doing on a back road north of Odessa at five in the morning. The car had tumbled into a shallow canyon and burned, and then exploded. The shell of the Lincoln was still there. Max paid a farmer to take him to the site. The coroner and the local sheriff had already gone through the wreck, of course, but Maxwell spent the entire afternoon resifting it all. He found part of a gold wristwatch with half the band missing, and a few yards off in the dirt, he found two vertebrae and a section of his father's skull as big, says Maxwell, as a coffee cup. He put the bones and the watch in a box and drove north to Durango to the family ranch. He got there so late that the lights were out and everybody looked asleep. He drove on high into the mountains, the San Juans, to a little lake where he and his father used to go fishing for rainbow trout. At the far end of the lake, beside the inlet, Max buried what was left of his dad.

Maxwell hadn't slept for two days now. He hiked out of the lake and drove back to the ranch house. It was noon and it was hot even though there were strips of gray snow in the ditches beside the road.

The entire family was there: his brother, his three sisters, his mother, uncles and aunts.

They told Max about the will. Max didn't get a slice of the ranch. He didn't get a piece of the house in town, or any stocks, and no cash, either.

His mother took him into her bedroom.

"You don't get anything, Max, because Daddy said, 'You're a drug dealer.'"

Maxwell wanted to break his mother's face.

He walked across the kitchen where everybody was sitting. He knew they knew what he'd just been told.

He marched out to his rented car, and he opened the trunk to get his bag. The Colt was in the bag.

Max didn't have his parka on. He hadn't brought a coat to Mexico, naturally, and he'd come straight from San Blas.

He looked down at the canvas bag. He looked back at the ranch house. The blue mountains in the distance still held snow most of the way up.

Maxwell shut the trunk. He wasn't going to kill anybody for his inheritance. That would be stupid. Satisfying and fun . . . but stupid.

Maxwell got back into the car and drove to Denver.

He didn't much feel like going on vacation now. For some reason he wanted to go back to the hideaway. He wanted to walk the perimeter, and sit on the porch awhile alone, and maybe then head down to Brazil.

The minute he hit the airport, he started drinking. Fuck the Flagyl. He didn't understand why you couldn't drink with that medicine anyway, and he decided to stop using it. He hadn't taken a drink in months, since the night they thought they had killed the man in the blue sports jacket. Maxwell started drinking now. Bourbon doubles. He had so many so quickly that the bartender in the airport lounge suggested he might miss his plane. Maxwell wanted to throw the jigger glass in the man's face. He wanted to break the bartender's back across the bar.

Somehow he got on the plane for California.

He kept drinking on the plane. He sat down next to the best-looking woman on the airplane. Halfway to San Francisco she got up and changed her seat.

Maxwell was not sure why he had been cut out of the will. He was not even sure it was his father's doing. His father had fought in the Italian campaign and he had made some money importing German motorcycles, smuggling them on U. S. combat airplanes. He'd always gotten along with his father. The money wasn't the point. The last thing he needed was money. The point was something different.

Maxwell was not sober when he got off the plane. At the rent-a-car booth, he dropped his wallet. The clerk, a man, laughed. Maxwell reached across the counter and decked him.

He took a cab to San Francisco, rented a car downtown and drove north. He stopped in Sonoma and bought more Jack

Daniels. He rammed the rented sedan up the fire road. Nobody was home at the hideaway. Billie was supposed to be back by now. Max had to park the car at the top of the hill and walk down. He waited for Ginger to bark. Ginger was not there. Billie was supposed to have freed Ginger from the kennel as soon as he returned. Max didn't like cooping up Ginger. Ginger was a stupid dog, all mouth, but she was Max's dog and Max was running short on family. He opened the door and switched on the light.

The floor was littered with motorcycle parts. Billie had disassembled an entire BMW motorcycle inside the hideaway. There was a bucket of grease in the sink and an oil smudge on the carpet. Maxwell inspected the place. The stovepipe had pulled away from the ceiling and water had begun to drip in from the rains and Billie had not bothered to patch the hole. He was fixing his motorcycle.

Maxwell hit the Jack Daniels. Billie did not return. Finally, Maxwell climbed up to the loft and crashed.

He heard somebody coming in around three in the morning. He slipped on his jeans.

"Billie?"

"Yeah?"

Max climbed down and threw open the door. He started to yell and then he forced his voice down.

"Don't come in! Go away, Billie. Come back tomorrow and pick up your stuff. We're through."

Maxwell shut the door. He waited. Nothing. He started upstairs again.

Ten minutes later he heard Billie at the door again. Billie, he imagined later, probably only wanted to talk things over.

Maxwell jumped out of the bed and slid down the stairs. Billie was standing in the doorway, the moon behind him, peering inside.

Max grabbed him from the side, and in one motion drew the sheath knife out of his pants and put the blade tight to Billie's throat.

"I'm going to kill you, Billie! I'm going to kill you!"

Billie's eyes went white.

"I never would have killed him," says Maxwell over the phone.

Max let him go and Billie ran up the canyon.

23

FIREMAN AND LANNIE

I met Fireman on The Land in February. The rains were still on and the land would drip like a fern sponge until June, but this night was clear. I arrived late. Fireman met me at the door of his trailer.

"Can you help me with my dad?"

Lannie and the kids were in the front room where we had watched the elections. Something was wrong. I didn't even know Fireman's father was alive.

He was an older man in his mid-sixties. He had wanted to see the new baby and the stepkids, too. He came back from Boston with Lannie. But he wasn't well and the rains did not help. The weather kept him cooped inside the trailer. Going out was a big affair anyway since he used a walker.

He'd caught a cold, and then he'd gotten worse until at night he couldn't control his bladder. Fireman woke up and waited in the dark whenever his father went to the bathroom. The last time he heard a noise and he rushed in. His father fell into his arms.

For over an hour the old man refused to be taken to Garberville to see the doctor. Finally, Fireman drove twenty miles to the pay phone and alerted the clinic. He was going to take his pop whether he wanted to go or not. That's exactly when I had arrived.

We helped his father into his clothes and Fireman tried to get him on his feet. Fireman and his father have a funny relationship.

"Come on, you old fart. You're not going to go out on me now."

"I need you like a hole—" his father started to say, but he lacked the wind.

They were both smiling

We put the old boy in the passenger seat of the car so that we could recline him. It was a brand-new car, I noticed, the first brand-new car Fireman had ever owned in his life.

Fireman had gone on an adventure or two since I'd been out in Hawaii. He talked as nonstop as Maxwell had.

Fireman had guarded a run to Phoenix. He drove, the boss worried and the dope sat in the trunk, $50,000 worth. Coming into San Bernardino, at the top of a hill, Fireman was surrounded by three Highway Patrol cars. One slipped in front of him, one fell behind, the third cruised beside. Fireman was sure they had been set up. It turned out to be nothing more than a speed trap. And the CHP had gotten the wrong man in their radar anyway, since the Fireman had set the cruise control exactly at 56 mph.

They got to Phoenix. Fireman had never been to the Southwest. It was raining there, too. On the outskirts near the zoo, they pulled off the exit. The exits are marked by flashing lights and somehow, the two cars in front smashed into each other. Fireman slammed on his brakes. The two cars in back of him piled into each other. There wasn't a scratch on Fireman's car. Fireman took a deep breath and drove away.

He and the boss walked into the buyer's house with the dope. The buyer and his people put their guns on the table. The boss pulled his pistol and laid it on the table. Fireman had been paid to guard and drive, not to negotiate. He walked back to the car. The boss got back into the car with the money and started to count it. Fireman got paid, but the boss had been shorted $5,600.

A gurgling sound comes from Fireman's dad.

"Pop, you all right?"

His father is trying to say something.

It's a winding road north to Garberville. Even so, Fireman bent his head to hear what his father was trying to say.

"I'm just laughing," said the old man. "Just laughing."

They put Fireman's dad on oxygen when we got to the clinic.

Fireman was worried about his father but he felt good otherwise. The forty acres were his now, his and Lannie's. They'd made enough money in the fall of their first year to buy out Sarah. That was better, he felt. Sarah had her trip and he and Lannie had theirs, and they were not the same.

Fireman feels he finally got lucky in his life. He took some risks and things turned out all right. He's not so sure about next year. He thinks he might quit growing. The safety of the children worries him. And he's afraid of going to jail. What if something should go real wrong? What if he should end up in jail? He doesn't know if he could handle that.

24

SARAH AND WYATT

Sarah moved south of Garberville to Wyatt's place. Wyatt owned a little cottage on the Eel. He bought it cheap. The previous owner had been flooded out three times. Wyatt doesn't believe the floods will ever get him. He's a lucky guy, and Sarah's even luckier. Lucky people don't drown in cold, muddy water.

Sarah waited almost too long to have her abortion. But she had it. Wyatt went to Mendocino with her. She thinks the next kid, number four, will be with Wyatt.

"I hated all the rain but we didn't notice it because we were so in love," she says, standing on the porch now in the spring rain, inspecting her cardboard boxes full of seedlings. It's a light rain that's falling but it's still rain.

Wyatt comes into the kitchen and Sarah walks back inside to meet him. It's past noon but everybody's just getting up.

The two of them start arguing.

Sarah wants to go to San Francisco for the weekend to see Joan Rivers and the Smothers Brothers who are all on the same bill. Wyatt doesn't want to go. If it's raining here, it'll be raining there and he would rather sleep anyway. He's come up with the cock 'n' bull idea that the advertisement is a hoax. The ad says, "Joan Rivers and The Smother Brothers," no "s" on "Smother." Obviously, it's a misprint, but Wyatt is maintaining that the show is a trick. Joan Rivers may be there but Tom and Dickie *Smothers* will not. Some imposters will, some phony *Smother* brothers. Wyatt insists the whole thing is a cheap trick, the way when you go to see those old black groups like the Coasters or the Drifters, most of the guys are not the originals, but stand-ins working under the old name.

The whole discussion is absurd.

"You haven't given me a kiss this morning," Sarah says to him.

"Ah, you don't want me to kiss you," says Wyatt.

"Give me a kiss."

He kisses her on the forehead.

"No, a real kiss, on the mouth."

He kisses her on the mouth.

"No, a real kiss, with your tongue. Put your tongue in there."

He leans over and they get down to business, and here we haven't eaten breakfast yet, and it's still raining.

After breakfast, I say I really do have to get going.

Wyatt's in the other room looking for something. He doesn't want me to leave. He wants us all to play hearts for the afternoon. He's already hunted for and found the fall *Life* magazine with his picture around the pond at Kathy Davis's funeral. He's rummaging all over the living room for something else.

"Ah, come on and stay. We'll play hearts and then we'll eat some of that good smoked salmon. Me and Sarah are just simple peasants, aren't we, Sarah?"

Sarah rolls her eyes at me here in the kitchen.

"God damn it, Sarah! Where did I put that cocaine?"

Even Sarah is a little worried about the new violence. Some of the biggest commercial growers are changing the strange frontier utopia that she and others built without half trying. She thinks the solution is not to change yourself. Stay on the edges. Don't get greedy. Know what makes you happy.

Some people are happy, says Sarah. Some people are not.

25

LISA AND OTHERS

Lisa came back from French Polynesia. She called me once from a pay phone in Garberville. I love the pay phones up there. Nobody has a phone or a phone company calling card, so they stand in line with rolls of quarters waiting to make their long-distance calls.

Lisa was drunk but fast. An old boyfriend had moved into the barn on top of the ridge.

Humboldt County's too far north for me anyway. Too much rain. Too far away from Music Television.

Which isn't to say the country living bug hasn't bit me. I just don't want to grow pot. Forget marijuana. There's not enough money in it. I'm not like Sarah. I have expensive needs: vibro-beds, hotel rooms on the beach, '53 Buick Roadmasters.

I'm thinking frogs! Bullfrogs. Big money in bullfrogs. Big, big money.

Think for a second. What type of food hasn't been franchised yet? Not roast beef (Arbie's), not chicken (Kentucky Fried), not hamburgers (McDonald's et al.). Not even catfish. But there are no multimillion-dollar bullfrog chains yet.

Mine will be the first.

I'll call my original ranch "Casa Bullfrog-1." Casa Bullfrog has a nice ring to it.

There'll be the usual problems, but what were Americans born to do, if not to lick problems?

Poachers might be a threat, for instance, but the solution is simple. I'll build the ranch headquarters on an island. There'll be a

251

big deep moat all around the island, and, naturally, the bullfrogs will live in the moat.

Bullfrog meat tastes so criminally good, the legs especially, that I might have to worry about the law. But I'll hire the most expensive lobbyists, the way the tobacco industry does, and I'll hire them early on, before some ambitious bureaucrat like Harry Anslinger of the original Bureau of Narcotics and Dangerous Drugs can think to have frog meat outlawed. And if any wild senator persists, like that old bourbon-swilling, morphine-shooting, "Tail Gunner" Joe McCarthy from Wisconsin, I'll buy him off quick. My people will deliver frog legs to his table every night at six o'clock for the rest of his life or until he gets defeated at the ballot box, whichever comes first. And I won't let the Casa Bullfrog image be tarnished, either. No black saxophone players or Mexican-American fieldworkers will be allowed to eat frog legs from Casa Bullfrog. At least not on television. The TV ads will show Prince Charles and Princess Diana splitting bullfrog thigh-bones. England always needs the money. And the juice will drip down on the head of little Prince William.

No, Law Enforcement won't be a problem.

The problem will be the noise. Can you imagine the noise from 200,000 croaking bullfrogs? It would be deafening. Even the earmuffs Killer Jack wore would not be adequate.

I've got a solution to this, too. I'll hire deaf mutes. What do deaf mutes care how loud the frogs croak? And they'd be cheap, too, the deaf-mutes. Not that I wouldn't pay them top dollar because that's the kind of guy I am, but because the government would provide a handsome subsidy. I'm sure. Hire the handicapped.

For a sideline I'll raise escargot. The snails that turn out a bit on the thin side will be . . . yes, fed to the bullfrogs. It's ecologically sound.

You have to know how to do business in America if you want to get rich. Forget marijuana. Who needs the worries? Be practical.

Home delivery from Pocket Books

Here's your opportunity to have fabulous bestsellers delivered right to you. Our free catalog is filled to the brim with the newest titles plus the finest in mysteries, science fiction, westerns, cookbooks, romances, biographies, health, psychology, humor—every subject under the sun. Order this today and a world of pleasure will arrive at your door.

POCKET BOOKS, Department ORD
1230 Avenue of the Americas, New York, N.Y. 10020

Please send me a free Pocket Books catalog for home delivery

NAME _____

ADDRESS _____

CITY _____ STATE/ZIP _____

If you have friends who would like to order books at home, we'll send them a catalog too—

NAME _____

ADDRESS _____

CITY _____ STATE/ZIP _____

NAME _____

ADDRESS _____

CITY _____ STATE/ZIP _____